David Swing

A memorial volume
Ten sermons, selected and prepared for publication by himself

ISBN/EAN: 9783337266318

Printed in Europe, USA, Canada, Australia, Japan

Cover: Foto ©Lupo / pixelio.de

More available books at **www.hansebooks.com**

A Memorial Volume.

TEN SERMONS,
SELECTED AND PREPARED FOR PUBLICATION BY HIMSELF;

TOGETHER WITH A BIOGRAPHICAL SKETCH, TRIBUTES CALLED OUT BY HIS DEATH, THE LAST SERMON HE EVER PREACHED, AND HIS UNFINISHED SERMON; ALSO, A BRIEF HISTORY OF THE CENTRAL CHURCH, THE EVENTS WHICH LED TO ITS ORGANIZATION, AND THE FIRST SERMON PREACHED BEFORE THAT CONGREGATION.

COMPILED BY HIS DAUGHTER,
HELEN SWING STARRING

F. TENNYSON NEELY,
PUBLISHER. CHICAGO.
MDCCCXCIV. NEW YORK.

David Swing.

Born, Cincinnati, Ohio,
August 23, 1830.

Instructor in Greek and Latin
at Miami University, Oxford, Ohio,
1853 to 1866.

Pastor of Westminster, North Presbyterian, and
Fourth Presbyterian Churches,
Chicago,
1866 to 1875.

Pastor of the Central Church,
Chicago,
1875 to 1894.

Died, Chicago, October 3, 1894.

Dedication.

In Loving Remembrance of My Father,

David Swing,

I Dedicate this Book

to

All who Knew and Loved Him.

His Daughter,

Helen.

Of the One Thousand Copies of this Book
Issued to Subscribers this is

CONTENTS.

POEM — Consider B. Carter,	10
PREFACE,	11
BIOGRAPHICAL SKETCH — Frank Gilbert,	13
HISTORY OF THE CENTRAL CHURCH — Thomas S. Chard,	23

TEN SERMONS —

The Simpler and Greater Religion,	29
The Modern Christian Faith,	48
Phillips Brooks,	68
New Times Make New Men,	88
Things and Men,	108
Immorality,	127
Devotion and Work,	147
Radicalism — Root and Branch,	167
The Gentleman of the New School — Rutherford B. Hayes,	185
Our New Era,	205

TRIBUTES —

Poem — Dr. Frank W. Gunsaulus,	225
Funeral Sermon — Dr. Barrows,	228
The Poet Preacher — Sermon by Dr. Emil G. Hirsch,	247
Sermon — Dr. Frank W. Gunsaulus,	278
Sermon — Dr. Thomas Hall,	304
Sermon — Dr. H. W. Thomas,	310
Sermon — Dr. F. A. Noble,	325
Extract from Sermon — Bishop Fallows,	355
Extract from Sermon — Rev. H. A. Delano,	358
Extract from Sermon — Rev. J. P. Brushingham,	361
Extract from Sermon — Rev. T. W. Handford,	366
RESOLUTIONS OF FOURTH PRESBYTERIAN CHURCH,	368
REASONS FOR WITHDRAWAL FROM FOURTH PRESBYTERIAN CHURCH,	370
REASONS FOR A CENTRAL CHURCH,	373
LAST SERMON DELIVERED BY DAVID SWING,	391
UNFINISHED SERMON,	412

David Swing.

His noble soul passed with the fading year—
When all the flowers he loved, with drooping heads,
Had laid them down to sleep in winter beds,
The poet fell asleep upon his bier.
Oh, steadfast friends, with grieving hearts draw near,
And bear all gently to his dreamless sleep
The faithful pastor, minister and seer,
While men of all religions pray and weep.
Large was his faith and hope — his very name
A synonym for pure and noble deeds;
The passion of his theme a kindling flame,
His Christian spirit greater than all creeds —
Thus, loving men of every clime and name,
He fell asleep in death and rose to fame.

Consider B. Carter.

Preface.

The great Chicago fire of 1871 destroyed every sermon which David Swing had written up to that date. He always insisted that he was glad to have them put forever beyond the reach of publication. To his thinking, a sermon was manna for a day, or, at least, a sermon might be excellent in itself, yet unsuited for publication in book form. For a long time he positively refused to have his sermons published in book form except as essays; but, fortunately, in the spring of '94, he consented to prepare a volume of sermons for publication. Those sermons, ten in number, form the main feature of the volume herewith presented to the public. As Moses gave many laws and precepts, but put upon a plane apart from all others the Ten Commandments, so these ten sermons stand quite apart from all the rest. They were selected from many hundreds which had been published entire in newspapers. The original intention was to publish these sermons alone; but the death of the great preacher has made desirable a few additions: a brief sketch of

his life, a short history of the Central Church, the last sermon which the great preacher delivered, the one which he was writing when the Angel of Death bade him shake from his wings the dust of his body, his farewell to the Fourth Presbyterian Church of Chicago, his first address to the Central Church, and selections from the tributes paid to his worth and genius by his fellow clergymen of Chicago. With the exception of these added features, and the portrait, this volume is precisely as it was prepared by Professor Swing himself.

Biographical Sketch.

By Frank Gilbert.

DAVID SWING was of German ancestry, but, by a long line of descent, an American. The first of the name sought and found personal liberty on this side of the Atlantic before the name of the United States had ever been spoken. The best characteristics of the land of Goethe and Kant, blended with those of the land of Franklin and Emerson, found pre-eminent embodiment in the great preacher, whose prose was poetry, whose reflections were philosophy, and whose teachings were philosophy and religion applied to the conduct of life.

David Swing was born in Cincinnati, August 23, 1830. The father, whose baptismal name he bore, was in the steamboat business on the Ohio River, then one of the great highways of the nation.

The senior David Swing fell a victim to the cholera of 1832. This proved a turning point in the life of his son. Instead of spending his boyhood in what was then the metropolis of the

West, he was destined to nourish a youth sublime in the comparative solitude of a farm in a thoroughly rural district; for, when he was five years old, his mother married again and became a farmer's wife. This was the only notable change in the general atmosphere of his boyhood. The father, although a truly Christian citizen, was not a member of any church, while the stepfather was of the strictest sect, a Presbyterian.

There was nothing in the boy life of the great preacher which was especially noteworthy. He attended the public schools of his neighborhood, acquiring the rudiments of education, and showing no unusual taste for reading. It was not until he was fourteen years of age that the flower of his genius began to blossom. The State of Ohio was dotted over with small colleges, the policy of the early settlers being to distribute institutions of higher learning, instead of attempting to build up a great university. Still more numerous were the academies. As a consequence of that policy, almost any lad of that period and State, who was really eager for knowledge, could acquire a liberal education. The remarkably long roll of Ohioans who have risen

to distinction attests the wisdom of that policy. It is Miami University, at Oxford, which can claim David Swing as one of its graduates, President Harrison being a classmate. From college he went direct to the city of his birth, and, under the especial theological guidance of Dr. N. L. Rice, then one of the most eminent preachers and theologians of the more conservative branch of the Presbyterian Church, he studied for the ministry; but his thoughts turned to his college home. The life at Oxford, with its opportunities for enjoying the society of the high thinkers who made Greek and Latin literature so rich, and, to David Swing, so delightful, had special attraction for him. For twelve years he was instructor of Greek and Latin at Miami University, preaching in the meanwhile in some neighboring church. Those were the great years of his preparation for what was to prove his lifework. He settled to his duties at Oxford, expecting to remain there permanently. He had gone there a farmer lad, a stranger, and alone. He married Elizabeth Porter, daughter of the leading physician of the town, and it was there that his two daughters who survive him were born. Mrs.

Swing, it may be added in this connection, died August 2, 1879. The husband never married again. During those years at Oxford he enjoyed an enviable reputation as a preacher, but, when called to Chicago to accept a pastorate, he declined it, distrusting his ability to permanently interest a city audience. He had no conception of his own genius. But, finally, after repeated urgings, he accepted the pastorate of the Westminster Presbyterian Church of Chicago, and left the home of his youth and early manhood.

The success of David Swing was marked from the first. He always retained the title of Professor, a fit recognition of his classic culture. Soon after his removal to Chicago came the union of the old and new school branches of the Presbyterian Church. Out of the incidents of that union came the consolidation of the Westminster with the North Presbyterian Church, under the new name of the Fourth Presbyterian Church, Professor Swing being the pastor of the two made one.

The great Chicago fire of October 9, 1871, destroyed the Fourth Church edifice and all the homes of all the parish, including the pastor's.

In common with nearly the entire North Division of Chicago, the Swing family were obliged to flee for their lives, taking almost nothing with them. Professor Swing was accustomed to say that there was one comforting reflection, his old sermons were burnt up and could never tempt him to draw on his barrel instead of his brain. As an illustration of his genial wit and unfailing hopefulness, I give the following extract from a letter:

"On Monday morning of the big fire of '71 I overtook Professor Swing, his wife and two daughters, going up Clark Street ahead of the fire, and took him to my room in the school on North Halsted Street. Professor Swing had the baby's hand in his left, and with his right hand pulled the child's express wagon with a few pieces of table silver. 'Hello! Donald,' he said, 'these are all I have left. Gold' (pointing to his wife and children), 'silver and hope.' This hope never left David Swing, for the last words he ever wrote were: 'We must all hope much from the gradual progress of brotherly love.'"

At that time the most available audience room not in regular use upon the Sabbath was Standard Hall, in what was then the best residence portion

of the South Division, and there Professor Swing resumed his preaching. Many of his flock gathered about him, and others, who had never attended his services, were attracted by his depth of thought, beauty of diction, and unique eloquence. Soon the Standard was too small to hold the audience, and when McVicker's Theater was rebuilt—and it was one of the first large structures in the burnt district—Professor Swing preached there regularly every Sunday morning. Here also the house was too small to hold the people who wished to hear him. During that brief period between the destruction and reconstruction of the Fourth Church, rebuilt, as it was, on its old site, David Swing gained general recognition throughout the three divisions of Chicago as a pulpit genius, and began to be recognized throughout the country at large.

Putting aside all inducements to continue his services in the center of the city beyond the time necessary for his old parish to restore itself after the dispersion of that night of burning, Professor Swing resumed the regular pastorate as soon as practicable. Everything was moving smoothly, until April 13, 1874, when Professor Francis L.

Patton, of the McCormick Theological Seminary, and subsequently President of Princeton University, arraigned him for heresy. It is unnecessary to dwell upon that trial. No man was ever less inclined to spend his strength in controversy than David Swing. It was abhorrent to his whole nature. But, being forced to defend himself, he did it in a masterly manner, and was acquitted. His church, and the community generally, rejoiced exceedingly that the modern Daniel had come out of the lion's den unharmed. But Professor Patton had no thought of stopping. The case could be appealed to the Synod, and from the Synod to the General Assembly, and then, perhaps, be remanded to the Presbytery, the court of original jurisdiction, for a second trial, with a second series of appeals. The prospect of wasting so much of his life in the mere defense of his personal orthodoxy was so unbearable that David Swing quietly severed his connection with the Fourth Church and the Presbyterian denomination. There were no sensational features. His withdrawal was devoid of everything, so far as possible, that would savor of notoriety. But so large a place had Professor Swing already come to

occupy in the religious world, that his loss to the Presbyterian ministry occasioned a great deal of public discussion and contributed perceptibly to the liberal tendency of the period.

There eagerly rallied around Professor Swing at this period of his life a large constituency, drawn from all parts of the city, rejoicing in the opportunity of resuming, on a more suitable basis, the down-town services begun in McVicker's Theater. Central Music Hall was built for that purpose, and there, until his death, the beloved pastor of Central Church continued to discuss the high themes of religion and ethics. There, also, at stated intervals, the pastor administered the Sacrament of the Lord's Supper, to which all were bidden who were in sympathy with the service. The customary mid-week evening service was maintained in Apollo Hall, the small upper chamber of Central Music Hall.

The Central Church organized and sustained for many years a Mission School — Sabbath and Industrial — in the northwestern part of the city, besides taking a large part in the general charitable and humane work of Chicago. Personally, Professor Swing was specially interested in the

work of the Humane Society, to the efficiency of which he very largely contributed.

With the opening of the pulpit year of 1879, Professor Swing began his largest pastorate. From that time until his death, his sermons were regularly published each Monday morning precisely as delivered. For fourteen years he occupied that press pulpit. There was not a State or a Territory where his voice was not heard. Even Alaska contributed to that vast audience. Nor was that all. Many newspapers throughout the country frequently made liberal extracts from those sermons. Thus the power and influence of David Swing became a distinct and important factor in the higher life of a multitude which no man could number. When, at last, with only a few days' warning, the end came, not only did Chicago mourn the truly irreparable loss, but that larger congregation shared keenly in the sorrow.

Without lingering by the deathbed of this second Erasmus, nor yet trenching at all upon the ground so well covered by the tributes herewith published, this sketch can not better close than by reproducing the poem written by

David Swing in memory of Garfield, and the tribute verse from the pen of Frances Cole:

> Now all ye flowers make room,
> Hither we come in gloom,
> To make a mighty tomb,
>   Sighing and weeping.
> Grand was the life he led,
> Wise was each word he said;
> But with the noble dead
>   We leave him sleeping.
>
> Soft may his body rest,
> As on his mother's breast,
> Whose love stands all confessed,
>   Mid blinding tears.
> But may his soul so white,
> Rise in triumphant flight,
> And in God's land of light
>   Spend endless years.—DAVID SWING.

When some beloved guest takes scrip and staff
For further journeying, or our heart's son,
Conscious of pleasant days of childhood done,
Girds up the loins of manhood with a laugh
And goes forth full of courage; then we pace
A little way with each the upward slope
Till the hill's brow hides him, and we trace
Our way alone back to our lonely place.
So now, benignant teacher! that the cloud
Hath hid thee closely from our straining eyes,
This planet's air grows chill; our hearts are bowed
With sense of evening shadows in the skies;
In unknown tongues the page of life seems writ,—
Our friend is gone who should interpret it.
—FRANCES COLE.

History of the Central Church.

By Thomas S. Chard.

[This paper was read to the Central Church on the first Sunday after the funeral of the beloved pastor, together with the unfinished sermon, which is also given in this volume.]

In the year 1866, Professor David Swing, then hardly known beyond the confines of his own native State, was called from the Miami University, of Oxford, Ohio, to the pastorate of the Westminster Presbyterian Church of Chicago, which then occupied a small wooden structure in the North Division of the city. Accepting the call, Professor Swing began his pastoral work, and, by the breadth and originality of his views and the beauty of his literary style, soon drew a large following of those who loved liberal thought, when held in balance by spirituality and reason. In those far-away years his brilliancy of mind was astonishing. One expression I recall, among the many like thoughts which

adorned his discourses: "How precious in God's sight must be this star, for out of its very dust he made a man." Search where we will in literature, such gems are found elsewhere only in Shakespeare, and they were sown thick in every sermon he delivered. The congregation soon grew too large for its small building, and united, under Professor Swing, with the North Church, occupying the more commodious edifice. The great fire of 1871 swept away this church, with all others in that part of the city, and scattered the homeless congregation. It reassembled at Standard Hall, and, later, re-enforced by a multitude of persons of all shades of religious belief, bound together by a common love for their leader, met for a while in McVicker's Theater. On the completion of the present Fourth Presbyterian Church, Professor Swing occupied its pulpit as pastor. Here, as elsewhere, David Swing was a lover, follower, and teacher of the truth as God gave him to see it. With that happy commingling of profound philosophy, delicate poetic sentiment and large humanity, enlivened by a wit which left no bitterness, he charmed and convinced men, and held within the influence of the

church many of our ablest thinkers, who, but for him, would not have enjoyed the gentle ministrations of the sanctuary.

Of the heresy trial I need hardly speak. It removed David Swing from the Presbyterian Church and gave him to humanity.

In November, 1875, Professor David Swing, enjoying the confidence and affectionate regard of the Chicago Presbytery, and beloved by his own congregation, resigned his pastorate of the Fourth Church. Immediate arrangements were made to organize a new church society, with Professor Swing as pastor. An agreement was executed as follows:

"We, the undersigned, believing it to be desirable that David Swing shall remain in the city of Chicago and continue his public teachings in some central and commodious place, and having been informed that the annual expense of such arrangement can be brought within the sum of $15,000, including an acceptable salary to Professor Swing, do hereby severally agree to pay the deficit, if any there shall be, arising from the conduct of such services, to the amount above named, for the term of two years."

To this agreement fifty names were signed, each subscribing $1,000. These names are as follows:

J. D. Webster,	Leonard Swett,	Wirt Dexter,
N. K. Fairbank,	Franklin Mac-	Alfred Cowles,
John S. Hunter,	Veagh,	A. M. Pence.
William Bross,	Walter L. Peck,	A. N. Kellogg,
W. W. Kimball,	O. F. Fuller,	R. N. Isham,
Samuel Bliss,	A. L. Chetlain,	Ferd. W. Peck,
C. I. Peck,	A. T. Andrews,	J. H. McVicker,
H. A. Johnson,	H. I. Sheldon,	John B. Drake,
E. L. Sheldon,	V. C. Turner,	W. R. Page,
C. A. Spring, Jr.,	Frank M. Blair,	Henry Potwin,
W. S. Henderson,	O. W. Potter,	Edmund Burke,
A. T. Hall,	P. C. Maynard,	F. M. Corby,
G. B. Carpenter,	W. E. Doggett,	J. V. LeMoyne,
Perry H. Smith,	C. B. Holmes,	Murry Nelson,
J. G. Shortall,	Chas. H. Lane,	George Sturges,
Robert Harris,	Enos Johnson,	H. M. Wilmarth,
Eugene S. Pike,	Jos. Medill,	J. C. Dunlevy.

The guarantors of this fund were not called upon, as seats were rented for a sum amounting to about $15,000 annually.

The creed adopted by the church was short, simple and evangelical. Without raising nice metaphysical distinctions, it dealt mainly with the practical side of Christian life.

From McVicker's Theater, where the society was first called together, the congregation removed to Central Music Hall, January 1, 1880, and has continued to occupy this hall until the present day.

The history and noble work of Central Church since that time are well known. Its Sunday sermons have been read each week, from the Pacific to the Atlantic Ocean, in numberless Christian homes, and they have most powerfully contributed to mold, sweeten, liberalize and elevate the religious thought of the day.

David Swing died Wednesday evening, October 3, and his funeral services were held in Central Music Hall on the following Sunday. Here, where his eloquence so often inspired your nobler thoughts, you covered that which was mortal with the flowers he had loved so well, and gave to him the tribute of your tears. He has left you, as a father leaves his children—not forever, for "beyond the smiling and the weeping" we shall meet him again.

He once repeated some beautiful lines, with that tenderness of feeling which so characterized him, and you may wish to listen to them now:

Life! we've been long together
Through pleasant and through cloudy weather;
'Tis hard to part when friends are dear;
Perhaps 'twill cost a sigh—a tear;
   Then steal away, give little warning;
Choose thine own time;
Say not "Good night," but in some brighter clime
   Bid me " Good morning."

Ten Sermons

The Simpler and Greater Religion.

I fear lest your minds be corrupted from the simplicity and purity that is toward Christ. II Corinthians, xi. 3.

Many who live and think in our age are longing for a simpler religion. This desire is heard in sermons, in common conversation, and is seen in the volumes and essays of public men. It may well be a matter of wonder what is meant by a simpler religion. It may be these longing minds are thinking of a more rational Christianity—a form in which reason is more visible than miracle. It may be they are thinking of a life as distinguished from a belief. It would seem a good time for making a morning study out of this oft recurring public desire. If we are at some time to have a simpler form of Christianity, or are to work for such a result, we ought to map out our wish and study it, that we may know when it is gratified. Perhaps such a religion has already come. We have all heard of the "simplicity of Christ." What is it? What was it? Will it have any merit and beauty when it shall appear?

Events are defining for us this new term. Each year is pointing out to us that the past

Christianity was too complex. It was easily put out of working order. Often machines are made which involve so many movements, so many changes of the direction of power, that it is almost impossible for the instrument to do a continuous work for a single day.

Genius has labored long to make a type-setting machine, but the task to be done has been so complex, so full of motions and choices, that the wish of the publishing men has not yet been fully gratified. It was for a long time difficult to make a good watch which, besides keeping time perfectly, should strike the hour and minute and should continue to work only in one hour until another hour had come. The old tall eight-day clock had less difficulty in finding its field of service. A pendulum, a couple of weights, and a few wheels, and all was ready for a performance of duty for a hundred years without any stop for repairs.

In the material pursuits of man it is often necessary to have complex machines, the demand being imperative, but in his spiritual kingdom there is no such inexorable demand. Complexness is never unavoidable. Indeed it is purely gratuitous. There is no more demand for a com-

plex religion than there was for the literary style of the poet Browning. It would have been quite an increase of fame and fortune to that talented man had he possessed a style as clear as that of Shakespeare or Lord Byron. He had noble purposes and great power, but his words always became entangled like a skein of fine silk.

His thoughts were indeed silk, but it was difficult to pull quickly out of the tangle a long needleful of good thread. The greatest of all thoughts can be best expressed in the utmost simplicity, because the idea, like a mountain, must stand forth all alone that it may be the better seen. But when a mountain is mingled with a long group and is modified by foothills which reach away in all directions for a half hundred miles, there is the most sublime Alp or Apennine injured by a complexity. Christianity is much like an author or a piece of art: it can rise up in its own grandeur and express its divineness, or it can be almost hidden and ruined by surroundings in which there are no traces of greatness.

When Pascal lived and created such a sensation in the Romish Church of the seventeenth century, his power lay in his ability to raise a

laugh over the obscure metaphysical inquiries so dear to that period. Born a geometer and a mathematician, his reason could strip all ideas of their false side, and could detect instantly a piece of bad logic. He loved to ridicule the absurdities of the middle ages and to plead for the simple gospel of the first four centuries. His influence came chiefly from his power to lift up a great idea until by its altitude it made all other ideas contemptible. He turned the morals of the Jesuits into contempt and the name of God into sublimity.

One of the last lessons learned by mankind is this: that simplicity may be power; that it is nearly always the most powerful element in thought and art. The most intricate and senseless of all philosophies are those of the earliest and most ignorant races. The religions of India are unreadable in our age. No modern mind could find the courage to work its way through such wonderful admixtures of fact and invention. Many of the absurd inquiries which attracted the school men and held them captive up to the sixteenth century came into Christianity from the old East. Nearly all of those questions about the

size of a spirit, about its ability to travel fast from star to star, its ability to dance on a needle's point came into the Christian period from the heathen world which had flourished long before the birth of Christ. All semi-barbarian races have loved a pomposity of speech and style. As some of the African women in the interior of the Dark Continent wear 100 pounds of iron rings on arms and ankles, assuming that, if a ring be an ornament, then, the more rings, the more beautiful the girl who wears them, so, in the old theologies, the more abundant the notions, the richer the creed. So rich was the Hindoo philosophy at last that it would have filled volumes, had the conglomeration ever been fully expressed in writing.

This fondness for entanglement we see in its better days in the Apocalypse of Saint John. There is no doubt John was one of the most beautiful characters of all who have lived, but this moral beauty did not save him from being led away by the prevailing charm of excessive figure and of wide labyrinths of thought. In the first chapter of his gospel he exults in the enigma of the Word; and in the Revelation he hands his

mind and soul over to the cause of a bottomless mystery, and no doubt drank in much sweetness from thoughts which are bitterness to this century. John had in his heart some great poem to be inscribed to Christ, the church and heaven, but the past ages had shaped for him his form of expression, and the result was a poem which, instead of standing sublime and simple, like the words of Jesus, lies before the modern world like the wreck of some royal galleon, all marked from sails to anchor with the splendors of the kings of Spain. Over such an ornamental ship the ocean sighs and the suns of summer shine, but the beautiful boat will never sail the sea. So the Apocalypse is a gorgeous barge that will never be under full sail again.

Should any one, curious over the past and fond of comparisons, wish to compare the Jesus and the disciple he loved, he will find much of that difference contained in the mental simplicity of the Master. With Jesus, the greater the truth, the simpler its expression. As his ideas grew in vastness, they diminished in number. As our earth has many little lakes but only a few oceans, because there is no room for many, so Christ

offered only a few truths, because each truth had to be thousands of miles in length and breadth. What Christ said is as clear, as rich, as divine to-day as it was eighteen hundred years ago, whereas much which John wrote is now as faded as the flowers which bloomed around him at Patmos. We see in those two faces the Master and the gentle disciple. John was all the more beloved because he was only the companion planet of the flaming sun. The central sun did not need help; it needed only a companion in the realms of space. St. John was this companion, and Christ and he will journey onward forever, hand in hand, the greater and the less.

The many shades of Christianity having reached this period of reason are compelled to halt for a time. All these modern churches have come through many a tribulation, but, above all, they have come through one long jungle which had thickened ever since the times of the old Aryan tongues. They all halt now because our period asks them what all their enigmas are worth? The age does not seek the money value but the moral value of their stuffs. A priest in a large city is having hymns printed in English, to

be sung by all his congregation, as hymns are sung here, for, he says, if the English language can speak our wisdom, our wit, our love, our friendship, can it not utter the emotions of our religion? What a sad blunder of society if Cardinal Newman can compose such a hymn as "Lead, Kindly Light," and then must have a little choir sing some Latin words for his congregation, whose hearts and tears are, in his English, living thoughts! Often highly educated persons are able to lend their soul to two or three different tongues; but, with the millions on millions of people, there is only one language in and around their spirit. It is the arms, the feet, wings, and senses of their mind. In it is light; out of it all is midnight. In that one language the people live and move and have their being. Coming up to the English tongue the church must throw away its Latin, and talk and sing and pray along with the living heart.

We must throw aside childish affectations and live real lives in a real world. When a Christian church crosses the line and enters Germany it must use the language of Goethe and Schiller; in France it must use the language of Paris; in

America it must use the language of Webster and Clay. To use the Latin tongue is only an affectation like that of many of our youth who love nothing unless it lies over the sea. What a wretched blunder had Schiller attempted to write in French, and Ernest Renan attempted to compose his books in German! Dante began his poem in the Latin tongue, but it was too dead a speech for the living Florence. Thus the Latin of the church is only a colossal act in the long history of affectation.

But what the Romanists are guilty of in language the Protestants have been guilty of in their relations to doctrine, for they are attempting to carry onward a bundle of ideas which are fully as dead as the kings who built the Pyramids. Even were they not dead, they are only expressions which pleased generations which are no longer here. There is no public here which cares to discuss the natural inability of the sinner, or the totalness of an infant's guilt, or the inability of a saint to lose his piety, or the worthlessness of morality, or the efforts of Christ in behalf of a few, or that a general and endless punishment of mankind is for the glory of God. There must

be a half hundred of ideas which once possessed the power to thrill the public heart, but which now lie dead and friendless. The fashion of this world passeth away. The love of doctrine has declined.

There used to be recognized several kinds of faith. There was a faith in miracles, a faith in the divinity of Christ, a faith which even devils might cherish, and last and best of all came a saving faith. This kind would come only by the intervention of miraculous power. What kind of faith an inquiring soul might have found or might find was exceedingly uncertain. The soul might be mistaken and be like the men, who, in digging a well on their farms, have come upon iron pyrites and have held a feast and invited in all the neighbors to rejoice with them over the discovery of a fabulous vein of gold. It is within living memory that many a young person has longed to have a saving faith, but has been uncertain whether what he had was the purest of gold or only the cheap sulphide of iron. All these old shadings of faith have melted into one—a faith in Jesus Christ as man's beloved friend. If we had asked the poet Cowper whether he had faith in his

mother, and whether it was a faith in miracles or in testimony, or a faith which a devil might possess, he would have scorned all our theological chemistry and have said: "I shall love my mother forever." Behold in Cowper's reply the coming simplicity of Christianity! It will rear at last a sentiment which will make earth beautiful and heaven near.

The old theologies were a kind of exhaustive chemical analysis of man as a religious creature; they were a physiology of the religious nerves and tissues, a microscopic study of the cellular structure as affected by the religious emotions. Among its conclusions one will find the deduction that if a babe should die unbaptized it would be punished in perdition forever by a God of infinite love. Many centuries were thus dominated by a scientific Christianity. Repentance was analyzed and quite an assortment of repentances were found. There was a repentance without sorrow and one with sorrow; one without reform and one with reform; and then came the chase after that kind which itself needed to be repented of; and then came the search for that sin over which repentance was utterly useless.

Equipped with such a scientific religion, the many churches did their work for many centuries. Under it wars, murders, persecutions and tortures were most common. The spirit of Christ had little to do with the case, because that spirit was not an easy victim to such a theological laboratory. When our vivisectionists cut to pieces a living dog or a living horse, they report on the creature's bones and sinews; they never report on the animal's friendship for man.

The vivisectionist sustains no relations to mercy or goodness or justice; his world is made up of weights and measures and times, causes and effects. In Africa, a negro chief, having been presented with a rifle by Captain Speke, and seeing no bird or animal upon which to try the instrument, fired at a slave who was at work in a field. The chief went to his palace proud of his gun. What a marvelous combination of lock, stock and barrel! How bright the iron and steel! how polished and how carved the wood! As for the slave, he lay dying in agony. Such is the science of vivisection—a science of knives and saws, with the human soul and the animal soul left out. It is the African rifle, with the dying slave omitted.

Thus has theology been too scientific. A year or two ago a railway car was thrown over, and a priest who was not hurt in the least, but who was compelled to wade out of deep water and mud, came up the bank swearing in an anger and with oaths which consigned to future pain all the railway men who had ever lived in any land. And yet the theology of that priest was a most complete science of salvation. It contained all the dogmas of the church as discovered between St. Augustine and Cardinal Richelieu. Nothing was absent from the theology except religion.

From this elaborate science our age desires to break away and to enjoy more of religion itself. We all perceive that the millions of people do not need the theories of Dr. Briggs or of those who opposed that theologian— they need a great, deep friendship with the man of Galilee, who held in his soul all that is great in human practice or belief. Having had eighteen centuries of analysis of religion, how ready the world is for a taste of the good analyzed so long! Newman and Fenelon possessed it; so Calvin and John Knox carried it in their hearts; Paul and Apollos were full of it when the world was young; it

sprang up in the soul of John Wesley and came to Whitefield; it inflamed the bosom of Mme. Guion, and away it went to live with the missionaries who traversed these snows in winters long since melted into summers, which also are gone. But if minds so scattered through two thousand years met in one Christianity, then there must be a religion which lies apart from the hundreds of doctrines and which cares for none of them any more than the sea cares for the artists who sit on the sand and attempt to paint its picture. We can imagine the ocean saying to the artist: "Are you trying to make a picture of me? Me! Why, I am ten thousand miles wide, and am not even in your sight! Paint me! Why, I am not here for you to paint. I am washing the shores of England, America, Spain and France!"

To John Calvin we can imagine Christianity saying: "What! are you delineating me? How can you paint me when I am not in Geneva alone? I was with Magdalen when she prayed; I was with Joseph who asked to furnish the tomb for my crucified Christ; I was with the mother of Augustine more years than I was with Augustine himself; I was with all the little children whom

Christ held in his arms; I was with John when he was preaching in the wilderness; I was with the five thousand once and gave them all the bread of two worlds; I was with the disciples when they sang a hymn, and I was with all the martyrs when they died. Oh, thou citizen of Geneva, thou canst not express me in articles, for I am measureless; I am not a science of plants —not a botany. I am the blossoms themselves— the color and the perfume!"

The Christian religion often seems like that vast structure in Rome to which many architects carried their deepest and most serious genius. Bramante came first. He died, and the great Raphael took his place among the arches and columns. The grave soon called Raphael. Then came Perruzi to stay by the stones for a half of a life-time. Angelo then came and gave the great sanctuary twenty-two of his precious circles of the sun. Genius followed genius for one hundred and twenty years.

In that long procession of Italian summer times these great architects hated each other and quarreled, each with his neighbor. Castelar says that Bramante and Angelo, separated by the things

of earth, are now united in immortality. While
the builders were often enemies, the temple grew
in its grandeur, because its arches and columns
and dome could take no part in the quarrels of
daily human life. The great basilica arose each
year toward the sky, and each year left further
below, down among the marble chips, the
many quarrels of the workmen. It absorbed
from the architects their love and their genius,
and left all else behind. Thus Christianity can
make use of the hearts and powers of genius,
but it remands back to oblivion all the discords
of fretful minds. It can extract something from
a Cardinal Newman, something from John Wesley,
something from each cathedral and each
little chapel in town or field, but in its vast life
which is to follow the human race forever it will
work its way up toward its God long after we
shall have gone away from our quarrelings among
the useless chips around the base. It will rise a
single shaft, sublime but simple.

Christ was so essentially a life that His religion
must follow closely the plan of its Founder.
There are many intellectual inquiries upon which
the church does not know what was or would

have been the Nazarene's opinion, but the life of Christ admits of no doubt. The demand of the whole earth is expressed in a few words—a life like that of Jesus. With such a piety before man and in man, his present and his eternity will be one wide field of blessedness.

It must be remembered that a simple Christianity does not mean an unadorned religion. Mount Blanc is simple, but it is wondrously adorned. Coleridge saw it rising majestically "forth from a sea of pines;" he saw on its sides "motionless torrents" and "silent cataracts;" he saw "flowers skirting the edge of eternal frost;" he heard there "a thousand voices praising God." Rising up thus in all the matchless beauty which eternal winter could heap upon its summit and which eternal spring could weave around its base, yet is that gigantic pile impressive in its central simplicity. It holds no enigmas. It appeals to all the human family and speaks in a language all minds can interpret. So, by a simple Christianity one must not mean a desert. Around a simple creed may be grouped the rich details so much loved by the human heart.

In the simple religion there is a greatness which only the greatest music and eloquence can express. The grander the doctrines of the church, the more impressive may be the beauty which they may wear. It was often the misfortune of Europe that it had to place a royal crown upon the forehead of some young idiotic king, or of a royal leader in only the infernal realm of vice. Happy Europe could it have placed its crown jewels upon only those foreheads which were broad with wisdom and power and white in purity!

Thus has the church often attempted to attach its gorgeous service to a little and false thought. It has waved its silken banners at the burning of a heretic, or has compelled its organ and choir to chant a "Te Deum" over fields soaked with innocent blood. When a simple greatness shall come into the creed, then can a new beauty come into the service of God's house; for, since all the arts are only so many languages of the soul, they will rise in impressiveness when at last the soul shall have great truths to follow and express.

Man does not live in a desert. It pleased the Creator to make wondrously beautiful the world

of His children. All that these children make and have shall catch something of ornament from the very planet on which they dwell.

When Christianity shall teach its simplest forms of doctrine, it will still be in the world of music and color, and all sweet and rich beauty. It will ask ten thousand voices to join in its song; it may ask all instruments to accompany the multitude in their hymn; it may invite more flowers to its altars, and then to the material emblems of what the heart loves the simplified church will add a pulpit which can have no themes but great ones, and which can easily find that eloquence which, as aroma lies hidden in sandal, wood, lies high and deep in the being of God, in the life and deeds of Christ's, in the relation of man to man, and in the mysterious flow of our race toward death and the scenes beyond.

The Modern Christian Faith.

These all died in faith.—Hebrews xi. 13.

The term "faith" has resembled many persons and ideas in having alternately enjoyed and suffered an eventful history. It sounds always the same to the ear, but it has passed along among the nations and among men with many a change of signification. Often the term has stood for a deeply religious feeling which had God for its object, and often it has stood for the Christian's attachment to his Master, and often it has implied a mind's loyalty to the doctrines of a sect or a state.

When our Puritan colonies gave signs of withdrawing from England, there appeared at once two parties—the Royalists and the Whigs. The former clung to royalty, the latter desired to found a republic. When in early times the Church of Palestine began to array itself against the other religions of the many races, faith was a political term and implied loyalty to a great political instrument. In all those latter centuries, in which the church and state were united, the faithful

man was simply a loyalist, while the man who opposed the religious state was an infidel — a Tory, a Whig, an incipient traitor. When the Mohammedans speak of the situation, they designate the Christians as "infidels." When the Christians carried on those amazing crusades, reaching from England to Palestine, their motive was to rescue the tomb of Christ from the dominion of the infidel.

There was a time in the history of the English establishment when Quakers and all independents were infidels, because, in differing with the state church in some one idea, these persons threatened the throne of the state. In Calvin's day "faith" was a matter which imperiled the state. If a party should spring up around a Servetus, it might so expand as to become a rival, not in piety or good works, but in politics. In these political surroundings and perils it was deemed best to put Servetus out of the world. He may have possessed the faith of Abraham or St. Paul, but such a condition of things would be of no value in that particular period. So Mary Stuart entered Scotland as Queen, but she carried with her the Roman Catholic faith, and,

however valuable it might be at the gates of heaven, it was not highly prized at Edinburgh, nor was it afterwards admired by Queen Elizabeth.

While our United States was fully bound by its constitution to protect the property called slaves, the abolitionists were all called infidels. Their faith was most useless because it did not include the idea of the subjection of Africans to the white race. In those long years the true, pure faith included the doctrine that the slaves must be obedient to their masters. In those days one of the most beautiful of all moral scenes was that of a "believing master." He sat in his pew in sweet accord with revelation; while afar north the infidel was hoping a great day of liberty might soon come.

Thus for many centuries was the word "faith" bent hither and thither by the political exigencies which lay around it. Those in power were the faithful, those out of power were the infidels. And after a time the many sects came to subject the word "faith" to further twisting and distortion. The Episcopal Church of England held the "faith;" the other sects had no religion. The

houses where they met were called meeting-houses. In Scotland the Presbyterians held the faith. It was not long before the Baptists got possession of it, and would not commune with the Church of England or the Church of Scotland. In this continent the same scene was enacted. It has been now just about forty years since a Presbyterian clergyman published a series of articles to prove that the Methodists did not hold the true faith, and could not hope for salvation. It is still quite common for some of the most proud and distinguished sects to confess that independents may be saved by some special mercy of God, but that there is no visible provision made for their comfort beyond the grave.

Whoever will now scan the horizon will not fail to note that the grand cardinal word in religion is making its escape from both the state and the sects, and is beginning to enjoy the liberty and the fullness of itself.

Epictetus was for twenty years a slave. He possessed a mind equal to that of Plato. He was learned, just, patient, deep-thinking, but he was for half a life-time the servant of some classic nabob. He had his leg broken by one master. At

last he gained his liberty, and at once began to receive the friendship of scholars and thinkers, and began to bless Rome with his morals and philosophy. Not otherwise, "Faith," a being of a divine genius and of a noble ancestry which ran back to Abraham, having a philosophy deeper than that of Greek or Roman, and being more poetic than many Homers, was long a slave, and was scourged with whips in many a land. At last this beautiful slave has found liberty, and hails now the new arena of labor and joy. For a long time she was a slave of the State, and was compelled to fill all mean and cruel offices. Then she was the slave of many sects, and was compelled to obey instantly the mandate of a hard master. At last this most noble slave has found liberty. It is not her first taste of freedom. She was free when Abraham was trusting in God, and when Christ was saying, "Our Father who art in Heaven."

In late months many distinguished persons have gone from the world, and "all these have died in the faith." Time was when we could not have enjoyed such a thought. Once Tennyson, Whittier, Mr. Hayes, Mr. Brooks, would have

been looked upon as living wholly outside the bounds of a saving belief. Tennyson's creed was exceedingly brief. To a life-long friend he said: "There is a power that watches over us, and our individuality endures. This is all my faith." He said: "My greatest wish is to have a clearer vision of God." In a moment of irony, not badly founded, he said: "The majority of Englishmen think of God as an 'immeasurable clergyman.'" The idea in religion which this poet loved with most passion was that of a life after death. Our age does not know in what details of religious thought any one of these men lived and died. A local high-churchman intimates that Phillips Brooks was a Unitarian. It is not generally known what was the religious creed of Mr. Hayes. It would thus seem that not only is the special creed not vital, but it has ceased to be a matter of common curiosity. The life of each one of these men was plainly seen, and the religious nature of each was plainly visible. In the faith they lived and died. In them we see a faith that was free—free not from its own intrinsic worth, but free from the chains of a slave.

What a misfortune should some potentate catch you and twist your thumbs or arms to make you a Catholic, or, if you were a good Catholic, to make you a Protestant! To what a blessed freedom has faith come! The emancipation of our slaves is a scene scarcely more impressive than this emancipation of faith. It will never return to the old bondage, because that advance of intelligence which gained this liberty will keep the prize it has won. The contest of the present is between faith and atheism. The sects were but little against each other, because all the phases of Christian faith are of one essence, the antagonist of which is atheism, or that other unbelief which abandons all inquiry as hopeless.

The modern faith stands forth a new creature. Like many other ideas, it has been deeply affected by the study of human rights. The knowledge of right no more comes to man without study than astronomy or geography comes to him without his research. Ignorance of rights is as natural as ignorance of mathematics or of languages. Olden times used to speak of the divine right of kings. The modern nations have taken away the divineness of that right and have placed a

king's right alongside that of a carpenter or a blacksmith—a right that depends upon the wish of the people.

Along with this divine right of kings came the divine right of a white man to enslave black men, and along with these moral notions came the divine right of a husband to whip his wife. In the old economy the wife and daughter were at the mercy of the great masculine head of the house. It has been fully two hundred years since civilization began in earnest the study of the rights of humanity; and the progress mankind has made in inventions and discoveries is not greater than the advance it has made in unveiling the privileges of each soul. All human beings suddenly find themselves in a larger world. Each pursuit, each honor, each office, each pleasure is open to all. There are a few criminal laws which come between a bad man and his fellow creatures, but the forbidden field is small compared with the field of personal liberty. Men like Tennyson and Whittier have lived a long life in the world without being aware of any limitation of their freedom. The only compulsion from which they suffered was from the world outside

of man. Death came and commanded them to go away from earth. They obeyed in sweet submission; but as for this world, it overflowed with the full tide of emancipation.

This deep study and love of privileges have affected religious faith, because, in confessing the liberties of the individual, society has taken away the right of society to touch a Quaker, or a Calvinist, or a Methodist, or a Baptist. In the name of all great principles, all are one, because these variations of thought and belief do not affect character or conduct. As soon as the highest forms of law began to tolerate all forms of religious opinion, then society began also to smile at those differences of views which once seemed so great. It was necessary for law to run on in advance of the church and announce the harmlessness and the right of opinion. The church had not the courage nor the motive that gave promise of a democracy. It desired to urge onward its peculiar form of thought. It was necessary for a heroic politics to come, and, after the State had made many names and many forms of thought all lawful in one republic, the church could not but follow and admit a large group of sects into one

religion. If a nation could contain many forms of politicians and join them all in the one name of patriot, so the church could follow such a path and designate as Christians the members of a hundred sects. Thus had liberty and politics soon created a liberty in religion.

As a republic assembles human beings in the name of all the wants that are general, assembles them in the name of those places where all the paths of action and being meet, so religion could not but imitate a republic, and make its "faith" expand so as to include many millions of minds which, differing in many lesser ideas, were all one in some great principles. Thus the power which shattered the thrones of the old kings shattered also the thrones of the Calvinist and the Catholic and permitted Faith to go free. Faith is free, because it is a time of wide emancipation.

To the influence of republicanism must be added the power of increased reason. That was only a feeble intellect which could once assume that the infinite Deity would make a belief in a certain astronomy essential to the salvation of the soul. Yet when Galileo announced that the earth went around the sun, his soul was imperiled. The

modern reason can not suppose that a form of baptism plays any part in the future destiny of an adult or infant soul. The modern reason can not find this final salvation located in any one church, for as you would not require of a candidate for the Presidency that he should be born in a frame house, or a log house, or a brick house, so you can not possibly assume that a candidate for heaven must have been reared in the Episcopal or Methodist society.

It has been claimed by the Catholics and high churchmen that the soul could reach heaven only through their walls, but all the great Romanists, at least, have abandoned this thought, and the recent Popes and Cardinals claim only that their sanctuary is the best way to Paradise, but no longer the only road. All the old exclusiveness of the churches thus falls to the ground. Reason is a new earthquake under these old miraculous walls, and, while they are crumbling to the dust, human souls are flocking to heaven from the fireside of many a home and from those woods and fields which were so full of the presence of God. Modern intellects can no more connect the word "Salvation" with the word "Episcopacy," or

"Catholic," or "Calvinism," than they can make it depend upon Gothic churches or upon the presence of a great clock in the church tower. Church chimes are indeed beautiful to hear in a summer evening, but beautiful also is the sighing of the great boughs of the oaks and elms, and the Infinite cares not which sound the heart chooses for its vesper tone. Once, when a Greek village was burning, the farmer saw a philosopher passing out, but carrying nothing. He said to him, "Have you lost everything?" and he said: "I have lost nothing, for there was nothing of me except myself." Thus our age is rapidly hurrying to that point when religious persons can worship in any sanctuary or grove, because they are carrying their divine sentiment and obligation in their hearts. They carry nothing in their hands. They can place the left hand upon the bosom and say: "This is all there is of me." Such is the modern faith—free, great and loving.

Within the borders of Christianity its objects are God and Jesus Christ; in the rationalized religions its supreme object is God alone. In either field faith is adequate, for if, as we are taught by the present Christianity, God and Christ

are one, then the utterance of Jesus is doubly true, and they who have seen the Father have seen the Son. In this logic the Unitarian and the Jew can not escape the worship of the Trinity, because the Father and the Son and the Spirit are inseparable forever. Such ought to be the orthodox estimate of the objects of faith. It remains more real and true that either of these faiths is the glory and safety of man's being. If we claim that a personal faith in Christ is essential, we take away not only the piety and hope from the pagan lands, but we overthrow the worship of that vast Hebrew republic and empire which was as full of faith as our prairies in summer are full of flowers. And, furthermore, if looking to Christ is essential, then comes the inquiry: "Whither did Christ, himself, look?" Richter asks this delightful question: "Whither do those sunflowers point which grow upon the sun?" To whom did Jesus pray? Oh, ye Jews! Ye Unitarians! Ye devout ones in all the pagan lands! Hesitate not to pass in silence all the theological schools on the earth and pray to our Father in heaven! Jesus of Nazareth did not come to destroy such a worship, he came to make faith grow more powerful

in all the generations which should come after his appearing. He did not come to limit the beauty of earth or to make faith difficult, but rather he came to make an intelligent and simple trust in God the grandest sentiment in man's life. Had Christ been present when each martyr was bound to the stake for some deviation in the paths of theology, he would have unfastened every cord and have bidden each prisoner go free; had he been present in authority in the fourth century when the pagan Hypatia was lecturing on the gods and the high spirituality of Plato, he would have been a rapt listener to such a spotless life and to such a high eloquence; and the Christian Bishops would not have dared butcher such a worshiper and stain the streets of Alexandria with the blood of a bosom so religious, so learned, so white.

Our age having thus emancipated faith, it clothes it each year with new dignity. The age which simplifies it makes it more sublime. That power which detaches Christian belief from the Gothic windows, from the candles on the altar, and from the chimes in the towers, hands it over to society as a philosophy of the human

career. When an atheist utters his negatives and deduces all forms and all life from only dust, he has no outlook for himself, and can offer nothing to mankind. Not only does each individual life cease wholly at the grave, but it is without great impulse while it is passing its days in this world. Having come without a cause it wanders causelessly onward. It has no errand and needs no inspiration.

Contrasted with such a negative mind, faith comes to man as a philosophy. Faith in God, faith in the Son of Man as God in the flesh, rises up in all the dignity of a sublime science. Under the United States lies a group of great laws. They are gathered up into a constitution, and this day all the States which lie in such a large number between the two seas, and all the citizens in these States extract from those principles their progress and happiness. Faith in God is a similar constitution under the soul. It is a vast theory which permeates the bulk of man's years. It is with man wherever he goes. As each day he sees the sun forever coming back into his childhood, his youth, his middle life, his old age, the same sun sprinkling the fiftieth year as it sprinkled the

first, so each day man goes forth in this faith—a strange encompassment from which he can not escape. Often, indeed, is this faith clouded, and days come and go without the brilliancy of noon, but even then a diffused light filters down through the clouds, and the heart full of sadness carries still a blessed hope.

It is an error of many pulpits that they make faith only a means of saving the soul from God's wrath. There is in our East a preacher who declines the invitation to meet next summer in any congress of religions. He asks if he is expected to mingle his pious books and truths with those of Swedenborg and Mozoomdar and Channing? In his words one may note at once that he thinks of "faith" as a machine for performing a singular task. His machine is inseparable from robes, holy water and thirty-nine articles. Such a mind would be out of place indeed in a congress of religions; for such a congress would love to see faith, not as being a sectarian potency, but as being a philosophy which encompassed Jacob's pillow with a vision of angels thousands of years before the little candles were lighted by this eastern altar, and which made Christ look to God

and Heaven long before this modern priest made himself comely in vestments.

The congress of religions must be an effort to teach all clergymen and the thinking millions that there is a faith which has been and is and will be the philosophy of man's coming hither and of his going hence. As Bishop Keane, the Catholic, could leave his Roman College for a day to talk to the Unitarians on the being of God, as he possessed the intelligence which could think for an hour away from the ideas of transubstantiation and a Holy Father at Rome, so can all minds which possess any traces of greatness find in a religious congress some life-like portrait of religious faith. As a thousand voices can in music join in the "Hallelujah Chorus," and make the holy song beat upon the listener's heart as the sea smites its rocky shores, so can a thousand religions combine in eloquence which can make faith in God stand forth as the matchless philosophy of our race. Grand congress, to which each one coming will leave behind him his littleness, and journey, carrying with him only the greatest truth of his hours of worship—a congress which will ask from each man only those moments which are great!

What form of philosophy is this modern faith? Is it an entangled web of thought like that of Hegel? Is it a problem, an enigma, like the theories of Berkeley and Locke? It is nothing of such nature. It is something so simple that even optimism is a name too learned for its daily wear. The earliest youth casts its young heart into it; the missionaries have taught the Indians to sing its hymn. To teach simplicity, Isaac Newton became a child. To illustrate its simplicity, Christ used the humblest of all speech, and wore the simplest robe, and took little children up into his arms; and when lately our great men were dying, one of them said: "I shall soon be with my loved one;" the other said: "I am going home."

Let us, indeed, call this modern faith the optimism of our world—the most roseate optimism which has yet emerged from the heart of the common man or from the porch of philosophy. Strange to say, it issued from all human conditions at once. While the philosopher was framing its agreement, the negro and red man were chanting its psalm; and while the divine Jesus was preaching its hopes and promises,

a group of fishermen became inspired and a common womanhood baptized it with happy tears. It is the optimism of earth. It shakes the poison out of all our wild flowers. In eloquence, it surpasses all the orators; in poetry, it transcends all the poets; it is time's greatest music; it is man's greatest gallery of art. Happy the young persons who are just entering this arena of a free and vast faith. Happy fate, to live where many creeds mingle into one, and where many denominations meet in one love for mankind and God! The young heart which can appreciate such a simplicity of belief need not stand aloof from the organic churches; for a denomination is nothing but a brotherhood organized for both the duties and pleasures of religion. No soldier should love to march or battle alone. His heart wishes to hear the tramp of a regiment, and to see at times the flag of a great cause. Thus the religious heart should never attempt to march the way of salvation alone. It can, indeed, all alone, unbaptized, find piety and find heaven, but the highest usefulness and the highest happiness come, when hand is joined with hand, and when the heart feels the presence of a host of glori-

ous comrades, and when the ear catches the hymn of high worship sung by many voices. The fields and sky inspire, spring inspires, summer inspires; but man extracts most of his inspiration, not from skies and oceans, but from what is greater than all else—the mysterious God-like humanity.

Phillips Brooks.

Honor all men. Love the brotherhood. Fear God.—I Peter ii. 17.

It would be an act of ingratitude were this congregation to pass in silence the death of Phillips Brooks. Our church lay on the outer border of his bishopric. When, two or three years ago, in a loftiness of body which was only an emblem of a loftiness of mind, this preacher walked down this aisle to join you in worship, you all felt as though he were an elder brother in your religious family, and had come to visit his kin. Many of you, when spending a Sunday in the city where this modern apostle spoke, went joyfully to hear words which you knew would fall like manna from the sky. At last each of you seemed to hold some personal interest in Phillips Brooks; and now to-day we must all come up to his memory bringing our tears. Chosen Bishop in 1891, the new title could not make much headway against the name of Phillips. In instances not a few, when the title of "Bishop" is conferred upon a preacher, it does not take the previous name of the man more

than a few minutes to get out of the way. If large bodies move slowly, the converse ought to be true and tell us why, often, when a common preacher is made Bishop, his name as a human being instantly disappears. In the case of this great friend who has bidden us "good-by," the human being could not be easily displaced by any office in the gift of the church. As the names of Edmund Burke and William Pitt and Daniel Webster never needed any decoration from the catalogue of epithets, thus the name of Phillips Brooks did not take kindly to any form of prefix or supplement. If the peculiar duties of the office could have gone without carrying a title with them, the scene would have been happier; but to attempt to confer upon Phillips Brooks a title was too much like painting the pyramids.

William Pitt was called the "Great Commoner," not only because he was a member of the "House," but because he was by nature a dealer in the most universal of ideas—those ideas which were good not only for royal families but for all mankind. When the Colonies attempted to secure their right from the Crown, Mr. Pitt gave

his eloquence to the cause of the Colonies, because his mind could see the human race more easily than it could see the little group of grandees with the King at their head. Into the mind of Pitt all the human rights which had been detected and expressed between the Greek period and the time of the Earl of Chatham crowded to be reloved and respoken. As science deals in the universal truth about trees or stones or stars, so William Pitt dealt in the propositions which held true in all lands.

In the vast empire of religions Phillips Brooks was the "great commoner." Whether his mind passed through the pages of the gospel, or read as best it could the history of the primitive church, or read the confessions of Augustine and saw him pick up a psalter or heard him pray for the dead, or if he read all over the dogmas and practices of the Roman Catholic fathers, he always emerged from the study infatuated with only those truths and customs which seemed most needful to the character and salvation of the human multitude. He never possessed the power to turn a little incident into a great doctrine. He could not by any means mistake a piece of

the cross for a potency which could heal disease; nor was he able to look upon a lighted candle as playing any part in any form of natural or revealed religion. He stood at that point where all the Christian sects meet. No preacher could go to Christ without seeing this brother as being in the same path. All denominations walked with him and enjoyed a conversation which made their hearts burn on the way. He was like that lofty arch in Paris toward which all the great streets seem to run. When we think of the discords which are now sounding all through the field of both the Catholic and Protestant denominations, we must recall Phillips Brooks as the reconciliation of the nineteenth century.

But no one who loves war can fill the office of such a "great commoner." That fame must rest on an intellect which is wreathed with the garlands of peace. This man did not fight the ritualists or the Romanists; he came forward with the large and positive truths of religion and permitted all that was false or little to die of neglect. His pulpit was so full of light that his people forgot to bring candles to the chancel; the fragrance of the gospel was so exceeding

sweet that no acolytes were needed to swing smoking censers in front of the holy altar. We have all sat before him when the light was all in his forehead and the incense all in his heart.

In the late generations the Episcopal Church has been producing some great men. When the clergy of that denomination in England had become remarkable for the absence of learning and piety, and remarkable for the presence of ignorance, indolence and vice; when few who wore the name of clergyman possessed education enough to compose a sermon, and had not piety enough to care for the parish whose taxes they consumed, the Wesleyan reform sprang up. That effort was wholly a contempt for a dead sanctuary and an ardent longing for a religion like that of the Savior of men. It was a new effort to rescue the tomb of Christ from the hand of the new infidels. Jonathan Swift and Laurence Sterne had divided their time between the writings for the pulpit and writings for the promotion of depravity.

Sterne published a few sermons, but his literary books were so disreputable that the sermons were soon forgotten in the pleasure which the vulgarity of "Tristram Shandy" gave to that age.

It was the prevalence of such churchmen that compelled Wesley to rise up in behalf of a Christian life that bade fair to be forgotten. Wesleyism did not contemplate a new church; it was an uprising against ecclesiastical infamy. Awakened by Wesleyism, the National Episcopacy underwent a great reform and ran boldly forward.

A pulpit paid by national taxes easily falls from virtue, and, as often there were parochial schools where the teacher regularly drew a salary from the state but had an empty school-house, so there were pulpits which gave a living to some man in holy orders, who seldom read a service and still less frequently wearied himself or an audience with a discourse. It is now about fifty years since there came to the English Episcopal Church a second great impulse. It was not wholly a reform, but it poured into that old sanctuary so much new piety and enthusiasm that it can not but be called a marked part of a forward movement. It passes now in history under any one of several names: the "tractarian movement," or the "high-church movement," or the "ritualistic movement," or "Puseyism." A few minds, deeply religious,—men who in the seventeenth

century would have been the companions of Fenelon—began to study the far-off church of the fathers. They longed to rebuild their plundered and razed Jerusalem. In the long reign of vice and neglect even the beautiful buildings of God had become battered ruins. The house was as fallen as the heart.

These men, sons of Oxford, went back in history to find that day of splendor at which the worship of God began to sink. They shoveled away the earth from their buried Pompeii and soon found the rich old colors upon the long hidden walls. It was a most valuable labor of history and love, for out of it came the rebuilding and repairing of the churches and chapels of England; and came also a living religion which joined a pure belief to a holy life. Hundreds of millions of dollars soon went into the rebuilding of the houses of religion; but there is no money which can express the new Christianity which began at once to re-adorn the soul.

The men who came back from that historic study, and who joined in this pious renaissance, soon divided into two classes, the high church and low church, the former comprising those men

who brought back all the rites and emblazonry of the earlier times, while the low church became eclectic, and, feeling that the present had outgrown the emblematic period, asked England to accept the simple religion of Jesus and his apostles. The high church became enamored of all they discovered and made valuable old attitudes, old positions, a facing the east, showy vestments, priestly offices, candles, incense, confessional, and many a genuflection.

These were the ritualists, with whom the sandal of a Christ was the essential part of the Savior of mankind. The low church became equally enamored only of that part of the New Testament which they found in the old lava beds, and, making of little moment the robes and motions and incense of the remote yesterday, they espoused Christianity which reached out a kind hand toward the sects which had filed down from Calvin and Wesley. The high church used its relics for building a wall around itself. And thus it stands to-day, walled in, and as exclusive as though it feared that its friendship might escape and be wasted upon a Presbyterian or a Wesleyan, and as though the love of God might escape and

invade some meeting-house which did not make the sign of the cross, or might escape and save some infant that was dying at midnight without being baptized.

It can not in reason be charged upon the ritualists that they make religion too ornate. Man has not lived in this world long enough to enable him to say that any part of life can hold too much of real beauty. The temperate zone from the Gulf to the St. Lawrence is beautiful in June, but it has never dared laugh at the more abundant blossomings of the tropics. Many of us have had happy moments in those sanctuaries where grand choral music has marched up and down and in and out.

There may be other minds which love to face the east, and other minds which love to see incense rising as though it were carrying heavenward the burden of human prayers. Persons of little or much culture must be eclectics in the realm of beauty for the church, or city, or the home. If the ritualists feel proud of a pictured religion, and ask that many texts of scripture be uttered in material emblems, and that the candles of Solomon's Temple reappear in the modern

house of God, they have a taste we are all bound to respect. We concede the same right to those Christians who love the rite of washing each other's feet. We confess the ritualism of the Salvation Army, which pictures Christ as the Captain of their host and which follows Paul in the dream of being a good soldier of the Lord. Let ritualism appear where it may, in the high church, or the Roman church, or in the Salvation Army, it must pass along as a lawful form and variation of human taste. Its harmfulness has of late years come from minds, which, instead of admiring and enjoying ritualism, have descended to the worship of it—the worship of such fugitive and unimportant accessories—which made it difficult for a Bishop's crown to reach a forehead which loved the sublime spirituality of Jesus more than it loved the fleeting pageantry of perfumes and colors, and which loved the face turned toward all the sects in their hour of prayer more than he loved a genuflection or a face turned toward the east.

In the east we see only the sun, but all around this man lay the hopes and griefs of the human soul, more tremendous than a thousand suns. If

any proof were wanting, to show that ritualism, when idolized, turns men who might have been scholars and thinkers and orators into half childish natures, busy in the ornaments of an altar, like children around the Christmas tree, that proof may be read in the difficulties which lay between Phillips Brooks and the high office for which he seemed to have been born. In itself, ritualism may be a lawful form of religion, but history shows that it may be cultivated until it excludes what it once ornamented, and ends by becoming only the tropical efflorescence of human vanity. A deep attachment to ritualism may be taken as a good-by bidden by the young preacher to the height and depth of thought which belongs to the pulpit in all the great period of church life. A high ritualism is a most perfect and most alluring means for keeping the mind of the clergyman within the limits of a perpetual childhood. A ritualist ought to admire his ceremony as a man loves flowers—happy when the blossoms are near, but happy also in the barren fields of winter or in Sahara's leafless sand.

If one thinks of the high churchmen and the low churchmen as visiting the old past to find

once again the lost church of the fathers, one must see the ritualist entering our age, not only bringing much of the apostolic doctrine, but also as having his arms full of candles, of priestly robes, of curtains fastened by "loops of blue each to its sister," and full of "badger-skins dyed red"; and the same spectator must see the low churchman coming from that act of exhuming, carrying in his hands the words and deeds and life of our Lord. You may all, if you wish, admire many a high churchman acting in his peculiar office, but for this absent Bishop you can not but cherish a greater admiration and a deeper love. He reached out his hand to all men, and so sincere was he that his hand always pointed out the path of his heart.

When the heart studies the bygone years, it ought to esteem great in the past that which it wishes to come true in the future. We ought to look deeply at the yesterday in order to catch the image of to-morrow. And, as the soul of Phillips Brooks longed to see a Christian unity and equality, longed to see a civilization which should resemble the life of the Son of Man, he gathered up from the fathers the doctrines which tended to

make noble men and to join them into a wide brotherhood. The ritualists seem, by some error of locality, to have exhumed the Mosaic age; the low-churchmen seemed to have laid open to view a more recent arena—that of Jesus.

In his wanderings in the old religious world, this lamented mortal recalls that Dante who, in his great dream, drew near a holy mountain, which lifted up its form not far from the paradise of his God. The devout wanderer did not see any candles or vestments or studied posturing; he saw no apostolic succession. The world around him was too great to be in harmony with the rites and emblems of some fleeting year. One by one the angels came over him, but each one was chanting some benediction which had once fallen from the lips of the Master. No sooner had the words sounded, "Blessed are the pure in heart," than on came some other winged choristers saying, "Blessed are the merciful." To the same Italian worshiper at last a great chorus chanted the Lord's Prayer, all amplified like a tune in music which breaks up into four parts:

"Oh Thou Almighty Father! Who dost make
The heavens Thy dwelling, not in bounds confined,
But that with love intenser there Thou viewest

> Thy primal effluence, hallowed be the name.
> Join each created being to extol
> Thy might, for worthy humblest thanks and praise
> Is Thy blessed Spirit. May the Kingdom's peace
> Come unto us, for we, unless it come,
> With all our striving thither tend in vain."

These are the words which our great American "commoner" heard chanted in the lofty cathedrals of the past, and these are the words he wished to hear sounding in the greater aisles and corridors of the future. He extracted greatness from the past because he wished history to be only another name for his soul's hope. His mind conceived of a service and an anthem too great to be read or sung by his limited sect. His ritual must include a hundred Books of Common Prayer; his vestments must include the robes of a Louis XIV, the habit of an exiled Quaker, and the seamless coat of Jesus. He found his universal and perpetual harmony in the words: "Blessed are the pure in heart."

If you would find a reason for the confessed eloquence of this eminent Christian, you must begin by studying the advantage found in a mind which loved the whole human family, and then loved all the great truths which hold the people's

happiness. Eloquence is the utterance of great truths in a manner worthy of the truths. But there can be no such utterance without passion. This man was capable of loving even the negro slave. When those old days of trial were brooding over the nation, Phillips Brooks flamed up on the slaves' side. After the slaves were free he traveled a thousand miles to plead in this city for the cause of the education and full citizenship of those homeless Africans. Only a little group of our citizens appeared in the large hall, for the orator was young in his fame and the city was young in its power to appreciate such an appeal from heart to heart. None the less did the speech run like molten iron from a furnace, thus teaching us who listened that oratory is great truth uttered with great passion. Gesture and tone are insignificant.

It is necessary for this truth and passion to enjoy the noble accessories of language and style. It is difficult for a great mind, great heart, great language, and good style, all to meet in one human being. The distance between orators is therefore very great. Only a few come to us each hundred years. In Bishop Brooks, all these ingredients

mingled. He had by nature and by study mastered the one language of his race. It became at last the hundred gates of his soul's Thebes. At these portals the riches of his age passed in and out. He used no dead words, no old, worn-out phrases, at which the brain of the listener sinks to sleep. His words were all alive, and they came singing like the string and arrows of the wonderful bow of Ulysses. His words came too rapidly indeed, but his ideas were instantly seen and instantly felt to be true. Each word was distinct, like a single note in some rapid melody, an inseparable part of a beautiful song.

What a simplicity there is in all such high speech! because the theme is so large and so absorbing that it shames away the most of artifice, and makes the little art of the piece wholly invisible. If those final words ascribed to the Bishop were indeed spoken, his mind was not greatly under a cloud, for the simple sentence whispered to a servant: "You need not care for me longer; I am going home," is made of the kind of words which earth needs when it is fading, and which the final home asks for when it is opening its gates to a noble spirit, once a pilgrim here. Death

always asks for simple language, because its mystery and sadness and hope are all the ornamentation the speaker or listener can bear. Ah! sad loss such a being to all the churches of our country! He was a man so symmetrical and so fitted to all the hours and need of our land that the office of bishop went to him, not to add anything to his fame or power, but to be itself honored and exalted. It was the office that went to be crowned. As an Episcopal bishop he was much less than as the great, free orator of the Christian philosophy. But the terms "bishop" and "commoner" are both made sacred now by the sudden advent of death.

It is certain that this name will long remain the center of a magic power. The Baptist, with his close communion, can not but be impressed with that scene of brotherhood which lies so outspread in this churchman's life; the Unitarians can also look towards Phillips Brooks, to know how rationalism of a high school may be joined to the most marked spirituality and piety; the restless and debating Presbyterians may study him, to learn what peace and usefulness they can find in a Christianity many times simpler than

their confession of faith; to him may the low-church look for perpetual vindication; and to him should all the young ritualistic clergy turn, not to abandon their pictured and highly colored worships, but to mark how the pulpit of a Christian teacher and thinker towers above the swinging of censers and the adjustment of robes and the graceful bowing of the body in its acts of devotion. He should warn them against the folly of a half wasted life.

While we are thus standing by such a grave, the inquiry comes from many whether ritualism and Romanism are to displace the simpler churches and come into almost despotic power. Of this result there seems little probability. The broad church is young, but ritualism is as old as the world. It ruled in the Mosaic age. It ruled in India, Egypt, and in all great nations before the Son of Man came, and then entering Christianity it filled with its pageant all temples up to the days of Luther.

The broad church has been in the world only half a century. In that brief period what master minds it has produced! It is nothing else than the old Christianity of rites and doctrines smitten

by the deeper thought of these later generations. That reason which has created the modern world will most surely drive religion toward a holy life, a simple piety and a wide brotherhood. Romanism will be smitten by the same hand, and one by one shall fall from it the follies and vices which that church gathered up by passing through the middle centuries of ignorance and sin. That new thought, which has transformed despotisms into republics and slaves into the citizens of England and France, will not spare the old life and ideas of the temple of prayer. The antiquity of Romanism and ritualism will not protect them. Many things thousands of years old have died in this century. It is the great graveyard of antiquity and the beautifully draped cradle of a new youth.

When it is said that reason will smite the old churches, it is not meant that any violence will come. Heaven keep violence far away from all those Roman and Protestant altars where our parents said their prayers! Reason will smite them only as it smote the valley of the Mississippi and covered it with civilization; smite them only as the sun smites the fields in April and

makes them bloom; smite them as reason touched Phillips Brooks when he was young and made his heart warm with love and his forehead white with pure truth.

New Times Make New Men.

And the child grew and became strong in spirit.—Luke i. 80.

We should all be glad at the return of those days which ask us to study the life of some great man. It is a maxim in the old books that youth is taught by nothing so much as by example. All the philosophies and theories of human life are dull reading when compared with a simple history of some actual heart. Some abstract writer, like Hegel or Herbert Spencer, might have told the world what a single human being might do were he left alone upon an island far from all the paths of the ships, but a simple story, like that of Selkirk, outweighs all the *a priori* reasoning that could be written. Should some professor offer to lecture to us upon the vocal cords, nerves, lungs and ribs that are used in producing the eight tones, very light would be our interest in the lecture should Parepa Rosa or Jenny Lind offer to us, instead of the learned paper, a great throat full of sweet song. Thus biography comes to us with an unequaled charm. It is not a talk about life; it is life itself. In the realm of the

abstract we are all half infidels. We do not believe half you say. When you come back from great scenes and attempt to tell us of the vale of Tempe, or of Yosemite, or of the canons of the West, the words fall dead in our ears.

A half day in a wonderful spot of mountain or sea, a half day where the pyramids stand silently, or where the Acropolis mourns over her scattered marbles, takes all unbelief out of the soul and lifts it far above all indifference. Thus great names like those of Washington, Hamilton, Jefferson, Madison, and Lincoln are the realities of the great scene, and while we are in their presence the theoretical has all stepped aside and we seem gazing at real faces and to hear real voices.

Mr. Emerson says that we all love to read history because we make it personal and are full of the feeling as to what we should have done had we been there. When we read of the dome of St. Peter's, we feel that it is the kind of a dome we should have thought of had we been in Rome at the time; and when we read the speech of Demosthenes on the Crown, we feel that, had we been in Athens on that day, we should have

been glad to utter similar sentiments. It is probable Emerson's thought is defective; for the great beauty of history comes from its power to lead the mind away from the abstract and over to the actual. Philosophy may describe a nightingale: history is the bird singing in the hedge of blossoming thorn. Each object, be it religion, or patriotism, or faithfulness, or love, is best seen in some human being; expressed in a life. The popularity of a novel comes chiefly from its being a book in which two or more human beings act out the poetry, joy and sadness of a great sentiment. A high novel is the biography of an attachment.

When, each winter, the day of George Washington comes back to us, it sends the mind off in contemplation of some part of the past landscape. In no one year can we study and enjoy all the picture. The birthday has passed by before we have feasted fully upon the foreground or background or central part of the impressive canvas. How can we exhaust in an hour a soul which it required centuries to create? How can we examine in a day a life that was in length sixty-seven years? Those years were all full of events of

great interest, for the latter days rolled back their splendor upon the early life and made the school-house, the surveyor's compass and chain, and the adventures among the Indians, all full and active partners of the times of battling for liberty, and of the times of peaceful sway over a happy republic. Should our children come once a year to the study of this birthday, there would be at the end of a long life fields of direct or cognate truth over which their traveled feet had not yet passed. After the childhood of Washington had been reviewed there would come the school-book scenes. Washington and his mother would be a theme. Washington and the army, Washington and England, Washington and France, Washington and victory, Washington and religion would be mighty subjects for reflection of our youth or old age. Sad thought that we shall all die without having seen in all lights our nation or those who laid its foundations!

Each age is always busy making men out of the material it may have on hand. The child must possess all these mental powers which can be taught and expressed. Given natural genius

and sensibility, the age then shapes the drift of all powers and gives color to thoughts and emotions. That must be by nature an extraordinary mind that can catch all the good of a period and can reject all its evil. As to a devotion to liberty and the power to express all the arguments in behalf of a republic, Thomas Paine equaled George Washington; but in picking up the qualities of the age Mr. Paine seized upon too much evil and omitted too much good. We must always be thankful to Thomas Paine for the great help he rendered the infant nation; but we can now see that he did not become a full utterance of the eighteenth century. He could not hold his own mind in a beautiful equipoise. He could not treat with respect men of all shades of religious opinion. He was restless, aimless, intemperate, more like the wild Rousseau of France than like the symmetrical man of Mt. Vernon. It was not to the injury of Mr. Paine that he was not orthodox in Christianity, for his deism abounded and took in many of those who were greatest in that day. He absorbed too many frailties and omitted too many of the great attributes of mankind.

When, long ago, the ax-men went into the woods to find among the trees one suitable to be shaped into a mast for a large clipper ship, thousands of trees had to be passed by with only a glance. One tree had been twisted by the wind; one had been creased by the lightning; one had, when young, been bent down by some playing bears; one had been too near to its neighbors, and had been dwarfed in the top; one had been too near a stream, and had had too much sun and air on the side next the water, its trunk had bent toward its greatest limb; one had in youth been scorched by the fire of a hunter. At last a tree is found from which all defects are wanting, and up, straight as a draftsman's rule, runs the wooden shaft for a hundred feet. The woodsmen all rejoice, for the mast is found. The tree is elected from amid its fellows, and soon, instead of wearing its verdure in the forest, it goes careening on the ocean, holding up white sails to the journeying wind. Not otherwise when some weak colonies need a chieftain for war and peace; they must pass by many a name great in fame before they find the citizen who holds all, the virtues they know and love. No one dare say that

Washington was the only man who could have performed the needed task. There may have been one other or many others who could have led the people to independence. The one man having been found, the people did not pursue longer the search. Such a search would be a foolish task for an historian. Having found the mast, the ax-men left the woods.

There are few scenes more attractive than the picture of a new age making new men. The eighteenth century was a new era. Its new life did not take the direction of railways and telegraphs, or of physical implements and machines; rather did it make a study of new principles in politics and religion. It was a logical storm, and the storm centers were monarchy and the Roman Catholic Church. England and France were storm-swept districts, England studying politics and deism, France studying both politics and religion. The thirteen colonies were upon the border of the disturbance, and, while men like Burke and Pitt inflamed their love of liberty, Bolingbroke, Hume, Gibbon and Voltaire undermined the Roman Church, and, under deism and republicanism, monarchy fell in France and freedom arose on both sides of the sea.

Hume's life-long home was Edinburgh. Thus the attack upon orthodoxy reached from Edinburgh to Paris, and was violent for nearly a hundred years. The political churches in England and Scotland were almost as deeply hated as the one in France, and at the close of the century there were few statesmen that paid any great deference to any orthodox form of Christianity. Deism and republicanism traveled together.

This was not a logical necessity; it followed from the fact that in both France and England the church and despotism had long been full partners. To fight against the miraculous claims of the church was to make a path for freedom. The history of the Church of England was the history of all forms of wrong; the Scotch Church had been less cruel because it had been less powerful; the Puritans in New England had shown terrific violence; the Roman Church had surpassed all because it had reached over more millions and over more centuries, and thus had trampled upon humanity with a malignant cruelty which now surpasses all modern powers of belief. Statesmen created in such a period had to become cold to orthodoxy when they became ardent for

liberty; and we can not wonder that when at last they drafted the fundamental law of the land they left all religion wholly outside of the constitution. Many of these framers of law carried in their hearts a simple Christianity, but they had seen enough of the union of church and state. They were men of a new era.

Society is not merely an eating, drinking, feasting throng—not merely a student, a worker, but it is also an assemblage of ideas. It is a common storehouse, to which the past wills its thought and to which the present adds its accretions. But society is made up of men and women. These persons, then, are the final massing of truth, and when we examine the close of the eighteenth century we find each being who was sensitive and who moved about in his time, laden with all the wisdom which lay exhumed between his birth and death.

Thus it comes to pass that Voltaire, Bolingbroke, Hume, Pitt, Burke, Franklin, Washington, Lafayette, Jefferson, Paine and Hamilton moved along in a wonderful unity of belief, both political and religious, each one wearing some little beauty or deformity of disposition, but all

marked by one religious rationalism and one love of a republic. They all had come up out of the destruction of a great past and were all carrying the weapons which had driven the church from crime and vice to virtue, and had driven kings to a hasty but deep study of human rights. It is a beautiful sight to see all those great foreheads and mark them grow radiant in the increasing day of the eighteenth century.

The kind hearts now living recall with regret that George Washington owned and used slaves. That fact can not be justified, but it can be partially explained. Sympathy with black slaves had not yet come in the days of our great chieftain. All eyes were turned toward the despotic church and the despotic throne. The eighteenth was the white man's century. White men had been worked, whipped, burned, murdered, exiled, tortured for many generations. On one occasion sixty thousand men and women had been murdered in a single night. All the pages of history were red with innocent blood. France was on the eve of the greatest revolution of all times, and the thirteen colonies were about to rebel against the most powerful kingdom on earth.

We must not rudely demand that the Washingtons thus watching the European sky should feel the wrongs of the negroes in Georgia or Virginia. The mind has always assailed evils one at a time. Washington all through his manhood carried enough of care and even acute pain. It was no light thing to sunder the ties which bound him to the mother country. His ancestors were over the sea. English rule had honored him. To rebel against country and church and help win and secure independence were subjects enough to fill up a mind and heart for a score of years.

When the great leader did touch upon African slavery, his words were in harmony with the great emancipation which came in the next period. The men around Washington did not reach the rights of women, because, noble as those men were, they could not be infinite. It seems enough that they created the greatest of all republics. They reaped the peculiar harvest of their period, and stored its yellow sheaves. Other ideas must wait for some other day to come.

The "other idea" did not delay long its coming. When the thrilling events in France, England and the colonies had become the prop-

erty of history, and all the men who made them had fallen into their graves, then in the nineteenth century came slowly the wave of a new sentiment. Early in the new era the Breckinridge family in Kentucky began to advocate the removal of the negroes to Africa. The colonization scheme was the first form of this sympathy. At times some master would break over all barriers, and remove all his slaves north and set them free. Many a group of slaves found themselves moving toward liberty, their master leading them towards the promised land. Abolitionism as an idea, as a political truth, and as an evident form of humanity, followed the colonization, and had all its orators in all the border slave States before the North had burst out into a flame. Memory can easily recall Cassius M. Clay and John G. Fee, who made the interior of Kentucky hear, from first to last, the pathetic story of the slave. Kentucky women shed tears over slavery before you were born.

As the years came the number of orators and essayists increased, and sermons, orations, novels, stories and poems began to fall like autumn leaves, only not in the world's autumn,

but in its spring. In 1833 England set free all her slaves; and by 1838 the song sung too soon by Cowper had become true in all the wide empire over which the girl-queen Victoria had just begun her sway. That noble girl of nineteen years, just crowned, might have chanted the words of Cowper, then just fulfilled:

"Slaves can not live in England; if their lungs
But breathe our air, that moment they are free;
They touch our country and their shackles fall."

If the eighteenth was the white man's century, the nineteenth was the century of mankind. Within its richer years a wider justice and a greater kindness were to come, and no color or sex, or youth or age, or wealth or poverty, were to affect the play of human rights. From 1820 to 1860 there was but one eloquence for the nation, and but one great song—the one theme was the release of the slave. There was no eloquence or song against the black man, for he who opposed liberty could not be eloquent, and the song which would uphold shackles could not be sung. An argument runs rapidly when it has but one side.

But who was present in those years when the young Queen Victoria was looking over a mighty empire which held no slave? What sensitive mind was studying and feeling all truths and sentiments in those days when the songs of freedom were rolling over this republic as rolls the melody of the song birds of spring? Who was living his early thoughtful years when all the great principles taught by Washington and Jefferson were blossoming into sentiment and filling the whole air with a new perfume? The Lincoln child was born in February, 1809, and thus all that life lay in those years which had dismissed France and Voltaire, Thomas Paine and the Church, England and Europe, that the American public might see in all its details the cloud of negro bondage. Going to New Orleans with his flatboat the young Lincoln saw the slave auction where mother and son were parted, and where a fair woman was sold like a dumb animal. His heart made a vow.

Thus each age creates a form of manhood, and, as a group of noble men came up out of the eighteenth century, so another group was created in the nineteenth; the former were mighty

in their battle for the white man, the latter, mighty in their battle for the race. O thou brief month in midwinter! For all thy days of physical sorrow, days of suffering poor, of dark storm and drifting snow, Nature has given thee compensation in thy perpetual nearness to two names, the greatest in human history! Thou dost not need leaves and blossoms for thy joy, for when thou wouldst think of things beautiful thou canst point to two men who are the eternal decorations of our fatherland!

That was a singular association of names made recently by Mr. Ingersoll. He linked together in greatness Abraham Lincoln and Charles Darwin. Never before did that orator utter such a strange sentiment unless it was when he said that Dante and Milton were not poets. Charles Darwin deduced all animals from a primitive cell, and offers us a theory not valuable but curious. His teachings sustain no relations to church or state. They are so unimportant that few care whether they are true or false. So a naturalist discovered that the swallow spends its winter in the bottom of marshes and ponds. But he and Darwin can never be named along with the men who have

made a free nation for many millions, and who are sweetening the hearts and intellects of millions of young men who are living their awakened life under freedom's flag. Darwin and the oyster! Lincoln and justice! The chief theme of these remarks is not Washington and Lincoln, but rather the spectacle of an age creating its master intellects. Each period loads its clouds until they move in a storm; it nourishes its blossom-buds until they burst. March, April, and May carry water and air and sunshine to the plant, until at last the passing school-girl shouts with joy, for the plant has bloomed. Later on the farmer lifts his eyes and says: My wheat has come! Thus we gaze at the ministry of the years and see the mind of the public yielding to the mighty powers of the air. When the school-girl plucks the wild-flower she is not a part of its cause. Nature would have made it had she never passed along that path; but when an age makes great characters, all youth, all girlhood, all womanhood, all manhood, are melted to compose the new compound of greatness. Washington was the utterance of many millions of souls. Each woman who is thinking and acting nobly, each man who

is discarding all the vices and exalting all the virtues, is helping compose the omnipotence of his century. One noble man utters us all. He is the speaker of the age.

The present Pope is perhaps the most wise and tolerant of all who have ever held the highest office of the Roman Church. Like Mr. Lincoln, he had to garner up the lessons of his time. Born in 1810, this Catholic lad, acute, sensitive, and moral, had to see all the followers and all the theories of myriads of Voltaires; his ears had to catch all that rationalism which issued from the French Revolution; he was in the midst of the political tumult which reached out twenty years from Mazzini of 1840 to Garibaldi of 1860; he saw the revolution of 1848; he lived on to see Victor Emanuel separate the old church from Italy; he saw stones and mud flung at the funeral cortege of Pius IX; he heard shouts of laughter rise above the solemn dirges chanted by the priests; he had long heard the eloquence of Cavour and Castelar, and had felt the breeze of liberty blowing from France, America, and England, and his heart must follow the law of nature and take the color of the adjacent world. His proud spirit

can not make a full surrender. It hates the new breadth of religion, but it flings out to science and to new customs many a kind word.

A new century leaves us children little option. Its arms are strong; if we will not walk forward it carries us. Pope and king and queen, student, toiler, man, woman, all are carried by the tide of years. Of which sublime movement the explanation is that God is dwelling among His children. The Pope, Leo XIII, shrinks from the world-wide friendship demanded among the disciples of piety, but the touch of that friendship has fallen upon his heart and will fall there while he shall live, not only in a new Italy, but in the world's new civilization.

In its power to make men, society can not go back and make again the shape of intellect it once fashioned for the public use. Neither the Romanism nor the Calvinism of the past can ever come back. Nothing that divides humanity into parcels, and which makes one group kill another group by God's altar can ever return. Exclusiveness has died; inclusiveness has come. The little Romanism, the little orthodoxy has been succeeded by humanity. An acorn may turn into

an oak, but the oak can never go back into the acorn.

Naturalists and poets used to ask us to note that the evening clouds never repeated their marshaling and colorings in the west. The winds, the vapors, the temperature, the atmosphere, the sunshine can not all meet twice in one power, one bulk, and one quality. Thus the elements which made the old church and the great men of the past can never meet again in Italy, or France, or America. But the moral scene excels that of the sunset clouds, for the moral changes are all made in more and more of beauty. Old Romanism and old orthodoxy must die to make way for some more divine assembling of religion's beauty on the morning and evening sky.

When one thinks of society as shaping a sensitive soul, one can not but pass from Leo XIII and Washington, and Lincoln, to him whom Palestine cradled and reared and crucified. According to the sacred biography he grew as a human youth grows, but he surpasses all the names in history, because he drank in the highest truth of all times and all races. He was more universal and perpetual than the great moderns whom we

love. His laws were for the great kingdom of which Italy and America are only small states. Washington and Lincoln absorbed and expressed man's love of rights and liberty, but the greater one of Palestine, after expressing the most sweeping and delicate justice, uttered the world's feelings of piety and its hopes of a second life. To the nations of man He added that vast Fatherland to which all earthly greatness moves with solemn steps. To him all the great statesmen and philanthropists look. He is the universal ideal and guide. These great names of February are the children of one continent, the leaders of one people, but the Nazarene surpasses them, for he leads all the multitudes of many periods, and was not the son of a nation, a state, but the Son of Man.

Things and Men.

What went ye out into the wilderness to see? A reed shaken of the wind? A man clothed in soft raiment?—Matthew xi. 8.

The Columbian Fair began in the contemplation of physical things. The growth of manufacture, art, and science had for a century been so prodigious in quantity and quality that it seemed best to sum up all the fairs of counties and states and nations in some display for the world. The people of this continent, as often as they contemplated the many shapes of its arts, inventions and products, felt disposed to thank Columbus for having been so kind as to discover such a valuable piece of idle ground. By slow degrees this gratitude to Columbus spread, and instead of saying as is customary, "Let us build a statue of that navigator," it said: "Let us hold a gigantic fair in his memory." This was the sentiment which at last prevailed, and each day that now passes brings us nearer the opening of the gates and doors of that unusual exhibition. The present year itself is, in this continent at least, to be made memorable by the event. Our

century has seen many great years, and this one, differing from all in its color and essence, will take its place in the group of those destined to be historic. It will not be associated with any fields of battle, nor with the sad questions of disunion and slavery; it will stand forth gay and brilliant, but valuable and impressive.

The conception of the work was large in the outset, but not many months of public discussion had passed by before all first thoughts became inadequate, and grounds, buildings, contents, beauty and cost doubled the size in which they were first seen. Like the **Fama** of Virgil, they gained forces by going. "*Viresque acquirit eundo.*"

In the very outset all was materialistic, but the country had not thought long before it began to say, "Let us have not only material things, but let us have also spiritual things. The age is not wholly composed of inventions and discoveries, of pictures, statues, architecture, railways and electric lights and powers; it is composed in part of mental phenomena. Let us add these things to the Columbian memory." This idea ran swiftly, and now when the year is just opening

we see a picture never offered the world before —a fair to be held in the name of both dust and spirit. If a flower or a tree or a ship or a car is organized dust, then education, politics, social philosophy and religion are organized soul. We may well all rejoice that jewels and machines and robes of silk and velvet are to be here next summer, but we may also be glad that the human soul is to be here—here in its science, its ethics, its eloquence, its education, its religion and philanthropy. All the material things will indeed be the work of the human mind. The steam engine, with its self-acting valves and with its enormous power, is only a form assumed by man's thought. Recently, when a ship-load of people found that in mid-ocean the shaft of the ship's great wheel had become shattered, they must have felt like children who had lost a father or a kind guardian. Out in the ocean in a floating palace! but in the palace lay this dead giant whose power, ten thousand times greater than that of Hercules, had been day and night on their side. Thus all instruments and machines are incarnations of man's mind; but, after these have all been seen and studied, there is much of mind

left, and man out of his machines is greater than man in them. Our age can construct a marvelous steam-engine of which Watt little dreamed, but the instrument would be of little value had not man possessed great errands over land and sea. The rail-car is great in itself, but it is often made greater by the souls of the travelers. Men going upon great errands of mercy or justice or goodness confer honor upon the ship that bears them from shore to shore. When Franklin stepped upon the shores of France; when Lafayette stepped upon the shores of America, each man would have been greater than his ship had its hull been made of plates of pure gold. Thus, after the mind has invented and made all the buildings and the objects that shall be within the buildings, it will still contain within itself a great residue of beauty and power.

One of the blessings of the year ought to be found in the fact that such a congress of nations ought to lead all minds to think the world's thoughts—thoughts good for the world and for all time. If literary men from all lands shall meet here, they ought to unite in demanding a universal purity of style and in making a cov-

enant to deal only in the most high and noble of truths. They should band together to make greater and greater the most powerful agent at work among men. All the arts are dwarfed by the power of literature. Each other art can express only some part of the mind—music a part, architecture a part, painting a part; but literature can express all the thoughts and emotions of the entire spirit. And this art one can carry with him when he travels, it can flourish in one little room, it depends not upon wealth or house or gallery, but where the mind has a common education, there this art can find its home. A poor girl's heart may be the gallery of this form of excellence. In one hand she may hold a volume which may contain more truth and beauty than can be found in any collection of art.

If she may hold only some of the immortal books of the world, she has near her heart something greater than all the canvases in the magnificent rooms of the Louvre. These books travel like wind and light. They do not wait for the poor boy to grow rich that he may make a long journey to them. They pity his poverty and go

to him. A few books went to the Lincoln lad in Kentucky and Indiana; a few volumes went to the young Henry Clay, a few to our Washington when he was a lad; but when these books went they carried the soul of the world, for literature means the mind and heart of our race. Humanity thinks all the time. Thoughts are as countless as the grains of sand upon the shores of all oceans; but as, of those sands, only some of the grains are gold or sapphire or pearl, so of all the thoughts of all time, only a part are rich in value and beauty. Literature is the final collection of these scattering jewels. Whether gathered by Plato or Cicero, or by the Man of Nazareth, or by John Milton, they stand for all that is great and good in mankind. It is one of the greatest attributes of our earth that it scatters its greatest works with the most generous hand, and enters the door of the cabin and offers to the boy without coat or shoes the use and joy of the highest of all the arts.

In the presence of such a full, powerful and wide-spread influence how can we avoid wishing that our coming congresses of scholars and students may vow to make literature cut loose from

vulgarity once and forever? What the students of the world did in the recent exposition in Paris has had a marked effect, for it is now confessed that France is rapidly moving toward a literature which appeals to only the highest taste of the enlightened world. It ought to be easy for our literary congress to lend a new impulse to a chariot which is already in motion.

The reform of literature would imply a reform of the drama, for when the public learns to love one pure art it will ask that all kindred manifestations of the intellect shall be high in their style. The low drama, for many of the dramas are still disgraceful to all concerned, will never lack for friends in a nation which could praise a poet whose vulgarity was simply infinite. We must appeal to the congress of nations to aid us in the suppression of immoral books and in building up a new world of letters into which slang and vulgarity can not enter. The gates of literature should be, like those of heaven, made of pearl. The world from Germany to America is growing ready for such reform. May all the scholars and students who ever assemble vow to magnify literature—that art of all arts!

Our fathers in the church erred by their efforts to expel the drama and opera from the face of the earth. The tendency of their practice was to make the world a desert. They were deep and wide in their hates. The fiddle itself came in for a large share of their displeasure. Nearly all games were suspected of wickedness. Assuming that the earth had been cursed by Adam, they were inclined to think that all the earth produced was full of depravity. Of course, the drama and opera, and the fiddle and the dance, were wicked, for otherwise the earth would not have produced them. All good came through the church; the earth was the kingdom of Satan. Such teachings were equivalent to a robbery, for thus was society to be robbed of many and beautiful goods. The old theory of total depravity has failed. The depravity was at least total in its failure. It remains now to assume that the earth is prolific in goodness and beauty, and that this beauty must be separated from deformity, just as literature must be rescued from the slums and the gutter. We do not wish to mow down the wide expanse of flowers under the pretense that they are weeds. The church said they are

all weeds and nettles. We have lived to know better. Our world is a rich valley, made by the Almighty to yield flowers, and we must help the Creator in his wish that the plant should blossom and the birds sing.

There is one "hobby" which no age has yet ridden. The Greeks and Latins rode upon Pegasus, others rode upon the war-horse, the church made a hobby of its creed, many different times have mounted many different things; but there is one idea to which society has never yet given its hand and heart, and that "hobby" is a beautiful decency. When language came to us from the sky, we were not satisfied till we had it filled with oaths and gibberish and slang; when art came, society said, "Let us make it indelicate;" when literature came, great minds said, "Let us write its pages that all who read will blush for shame;" when the drama offered us the sublime pictures of human life, the play-makers said, "Let us make our plays and scenes infamous;" when the drama came in the name of the greatest song, then our leaders again said, "Let us invent an absurd and silly ballet and hang it like a hundred mill-stones on the neck of a divine music."

Thus our world has never made a hobby of honor in literature or art. But we may be on the eve of a great change. We may infer from the unrest of civilization that it has grown weary of the past. It has become convinced that the world was made for greatness, beauty, and goodness.

In the moral department of the World's Fair the officers have invented the motto, "Not Things, but Men." This motto must have reference only to a division of labor-that some days will show us things, other days will show us men. The motto for the whole exposition may well be "Things and Men;" for we love to think of things as the products of man's genius and the servants of his wants. Nearly all things are the expression of man's power. The steamship is only a form assumed by Watt and Fulton. When the telegraph speaks to us, it is Morse that speaks. Thus, things are men. Now the argument is this—that if man can pour his power into a steamship which will carry a thousand persons over an ocean, so this man, this thinker, this creator, can pour a similar power into religion, or politics, or art, or life, and make them all the most faithful servants of the race. Can not the congresses of men help

lift up a suffering world? If the genius of man can make things, can it not make men? Sad day for us if we can build a beautiful house for men to live in, but can not fabricate a noble man! Shall we tear down the house? Oh, no! Let us rebuild the occupant. The genius that fabricates an exposition can fabricate a society.

It is confessed now that the architectural scene on the fair grounds is perhaps the greatest the world has ever seen. We can not go back to Babylon to see how it looked in the day of its hanging gardens, nor to Carthage to mark its wonders in the time of Hannibal, but, compared with all existing emblems of the builder's art, this new picture is most impressive. It was created not by one city, but by the whole age, for ideas are there from the Greek, the Roman, the Gothic, and the Oriental lands. In that piece of ground the great builders, dead and living, all meet. Rome is there with her arches, Greece with her columns. But the inquiry which that enchanted field raises is this: Can not such an age build a wide and pure civilization? Can not our times build up a richer spiritual realm? Can not the assembled men bear witness against the

disgraceful passion of war? Can they not make reason and justice seem grander than battlefields? Can they not cover with perpetual infamy the day when one Frenchman and one German exulted in the slaughter of half a million of their brothers? Can not the congress of moralists utter against the drinking habit some word which will encircle the world?

Shall such congresses of men leave to women alone the conflict with the greatest vice upon earth? The existing spectacle is singular at least—that of ten million women attempting to close the gates of death which ten million men help to keep open. The temperance reform may well remind us of that scene in the classic Inferno, where a man was doomed to make a rope of hay to reach to the outer world of light and liberty, but, while he was busy twisting his life-rope, a flock of wild asses stood behind a wall eating up the grassy string with a calm and perpetual delight. Thus womanhood twists her temperance rope in vain. She will never find the longed-for light and liberty. There is too much consuming ability at the other end of the rope. It is to be believed that our ethical congresses will take

some action that may make the war against distilled drinks the war of manhood and womanhood alike against a destructive vice. In the face of all the temperance work of the past few years Boston sent more rum to Africa in the past year than it has sent in any one season of recent times. With the Christians on the one side of Africa stealing men and women for slaves, and with Christians on the other side sending the negroes cargoes of rum, the scene is one worthy of the thought of a world's congress—worthy of its debate, its tears, its action.

It is now true that the continent of Africa is to lie for eight days before a Columbian assembly next summer. The fact was made the theme of a pamphlet in November last. The essay was written by Mr. F. P. Noble. of the Newberry Library of this city. In those eight days eminent men, from many parts of the world and from Africa itself, are to state all the sad and joyful facts in the great case, and are to outline some policy for civilization to adopt and pursue. Africa is three times as large as all of Europe, three times as large as our republic, it is one-fifth of all the land on the globe, and yet it has been the historic scene

of desolation, and the place whither the Christians have repaired when they wished to contradict every teaching of their Divine Master. It has sustained two hundred millions of blacks whose ignorance made a market for rum, and whose poverty and docility made them valuable as slaves. Mr. Noble estimates that only one in two hundred ever met a Christian teacher acting as such in the name of God's love, but it needs no mathematical figuring to teach us that few of those millions are strangers to the white man as a bloody warrior and as an unfeeling thief. The slave trade and the rum trade have made all Africa fully aware of the existence of a white man's world in the North. They know it by our depravity.

It is a blessed thought that this Africa is to lie in her mangled and bleeding form for eight days before the eyes of cultivated people convened from all parts of the enlightened land. There will be cheering facts to be set forth, facts which will kindle pity into hope; and there will be plenty of that wisdom which can come from men who have lived in the land of which they will speak. We all want music to sound all through those summer months, and machinery to speak,

and art to speak, but do we not also wish for an Africa to stand forth and plead her cause with an eloquence born out of her centuries of bitterness? Our rail-cars will seem greater if they are going to penetrate the Dark Continent, our telegraph will grow wonderful if it is thought of as holding Africa in its net-work and making noble words pass quickly to and fro in that area of prolific nature which reaches in length or breadth five thousand miles. And all music will sound nobler when it shall offer rest and peace to hearts that have been made tender by sympathy with the needs of our race.

"Men and Things" make the best motto, but with the men exalting the things and the things empowering the men.

The fine arts and music and literature, great as they are, are not the end and measure of human life. The fact that society lives by political truth, social truth, religious truth, and scientific truth, marks out for us the place for all the beautiful things. Were it not for music we should live a less happy life, but were it not for agriculture we should all die next summer. Painting is a delightful art, but were it not for political science

we should all be savages. Sometimes young people of an extreme style boast of taking no interest in the social sciences, they are so fond of music and society; but had not science come, their music would now be a tom-tom and their elite society a band of Digger Indians. It takes utility to make a world, and beauty to adorn it.

Neither is utility the aim and measure of human life. To live for politics or agriculture or social science alone is to commit a sin against nature. This is to use only one half of the soul. If we are to plow a furrow to grow bread, we ask to be permitted while we plow to hear the morning bird and to see the blossoming orchard. The plowman is to be greater than his furrow. As the girl must be greater than her music, so the farmer must be greater than his plow. The girl must reach up her hand and touch the realm of utility; and man must turn from his labor and visit the kingdom of beauty. To despise either social science or beautiful art is to pass through life with only one half of a soul. As the great Columbian buildings are made of iron and then adorned and shaped by art, they stand as the symbols of man's life, for it must possess both delicacy

and iron, plenty of high music and the iron of deep thought. As artists and art lovers the world's public may journey thither next summer; but the many ought to come hither as men, and be both the world's iron and the world's taste.

Here, where common sense is to deal with politics, with labor, with capital, with the pure in letters and art, it will make a review of religion. Would that such a congress could make religion simpler and ask the church to sum up Christianity in an imitation of Jesus Christ! The whole length and all the centuries of Christendom have been deeply injured by a religion of forms. The creed has always been greater than virtue. The Roman Catholic Church has groaned for centuries under a load of crime and vice; the Church of England was but little better. Dean Hole, of Rochester, England, wrote recently of days not far past when many an English rector lived far away from his parish and simply drew his living from the church rates paid by his neglected people; that one of those absent and fashionable pastors resolved at last to go and see his flock in some mild and gentle weather; but on the edge of the village he met a woman with a basket full

of such old, spoiled fish that the servant of God ordered his carriage to face about for home. In the meantime the Presbyterians drank heavily and waited for God to choose converts through the mysterious art of election. Such was the Christian church all through those years when a scheme of doctrine displaced a Christlike character. If a congress of religions can do anything in favor of a simple imitation of Christ, they will change the whole quality of the world. Bishop Ireland would evidently welcome some reform that would prevent his foolish people from watching for miracles on church windows, and should lead them to seek for pictures of Christ and angels in their hearts. The only miracle of any value to the church of to-morrow is a miracle of a righteous and benevolent life. Toward such a final miracle the Christian church is slowly turning. May the congresses about to convene make the movement universal and rapid.

Never before lay before our civilization questions so many and so great. It seems that many of the largest themes of reflection waited for this period to arrive. The themes of poverty and riches, woman's mission, universal education, com-

munion in its good sense, war or peace, pure or low art, temperance, government of cities, humane laws and religion, are all here waiting for a hearing in the high court. It is the greatness of the court that has evoked the high cases. This is the first century which has been bold enough and thoughtful enough to be worthy of presiding over debates which once would have been argued with blood and fire.

Let us all listen to all the pleadings which gifted counselors can make. That was a much smaller day when the two Greek orators debated about the price of honor—a golden crown—for then the city of Athens lay in doubt between two kings; but now the whole of Christendom lies in doubt between religions worthless or divine, between acts low or pure, society trifling or great, between awful wars or sweet peace.

What went ye out to the wilderness to see? A reed whistling in the wind? Ah, no! We went to see the holy face of a prophet and to hear the last years of the nineteenth century pour out its many-voiced eloquence.

Immorality.

My brethren, these things ought not so to be—James iii. 10.

We need not attempt to find the origin of the feeling of obligation. All agree with the far-off Saint James that there are many things that ought not to be so, and there are many things that ought to be so. The ancient moralists used to wonder whether this feeling of obligation came from the gods, or whether the gods were themselves bound by it. Differ, as many thinkers may, as to the origin and warrant of morality, morality itself is felt to be here and to be the hope and ornament of society. Cicero uttered regrets that morality could not assume a personal form, and be visible to the eye. In his essay on ethics, he exclaims: "What affection would virtue call forth could she only become a visible personage!" He was, perhaps, thinking of the Camillas and Dianas who had been seen in wheatfield or forest; he also remembered the Venus who had often been visible in some form more beautiful than life. He lamented that the idea of morality could not sweep along before society,

and take away from all hearts all doubt as to the matchless beauty of her form and soul. Plato preceded the Roman essayist in this wish, for he said: "Could this supreme wisdom be visible to the eye she would call forth a vehement affection by her charms."

The term "morals" must signify that form of conduct which most regards all rights, and which leads each and all to the highest welfare. Many definitions might be given, of which each might be good and all imperfect. A convenient definition may be this—that morals are the best moral ways to the best ends. It is declared by many that perfect morals might be found and followed in a nation where there was no religion, in a nation which might have rejected the idea of a God; but such a proposition is rendered purely theoretical by the fact that no nation has existed without a religion. In those countries which have produced a few atheists the civilization has been made by the overwhelming majority. We have never seen in any land a public virtue that had never been touched by a religion.

Men who may differ greatly over the tenets of Christianity and natural religion, all meet in

the department of morality. Morality is the hope of our race. To oppose virtue is to declare oneself a pirate, and is to merit a sentence of outlawry. Morality is a word that stands for the common weal. It surpasses in significance the word "art" or "beauty" or "culture," because society might do without those blessings, but it can not exist without morality.

An event occurred not long since which gave all local moralists a thrill of delight. Thoughtful men of name and fortune were asked to express their views as to the merit of a fashionable park at which horse-racing for money was an annual and fashionable pleasure. It was an inspiration to hear from great capitalists and public, fashionable citizens a plain condemnation of all such forms of sport and gain. They lamented that their beautiful piece of ground had become disgraced by the gambler's art; they had ceased to visit the once pleasant resort; they would delight in the death of a "club" whose happiness and gains must come from such a degraded and degrading source.

All these men had been in the world long enough to have their minds fully made up as to

what paths lead to the best ends. They had seen young men and young women, too, allured to ruin by the betting mania, and had reached the conclusion that a racing and betting park could not take any part in any of the games and pursuits of a decent civilization. That part of our public which wishes well to humanity had not for years heard words that surpassed in truth and goodness these few sentences from our public men.

Men, old and young, thrown into the betting-fever of this aristocratic race-course, soon went in their delirium to a field some miles away where a lot of innocent animals were whipped and spurred over frozen ground or through deep mud to gratify the passions of persons who had become at the same time insane and brutalized. When a Washington Park can live by gambling, it can count upon having plenty of more infamous parks as its degrading offspring.

If such race-tracks constitute an immorality, all newspapers are immoral, so far as they advertise the disgraceful events. Every newspaper ought to be a moralist. It need not be a preacher of some dogma that may save a soul, but it ought

to be a preacher of all that will save humanity. As society asks for a pure art and a pure drama and a pure literature, so it demands a pure newspaper. The men who are capable of writing editorials for great journals ought to be unwilling to join their essays to an advertisement for some coterie of infamous men and women. It ought to be unpleasant to a great writer when he has read over his own column on literature, or honor, or benevolence, or the progress of the age, to find some other column of his sheet all devoted to the advance of vice.

A newspaper can not be divided into two parts—an editorial part and a business section. The proprietors can not be half villain and half saint. If there is any virtue on the editorial page, it must color the business section. In the dissolute years of the church, archbishops made a distinction between their conduct when in their robes and their conduct when in citizens' garb; but the thinking world soon abolished this division of the high official, and the whisky section of the archbishop was at last suppressed. So the modern editor can not fashion himself into hemispheres—an editorial page that resembles

the essays of Addison, and the business page that delights the gambling and fighting fraternity. A newspaper possesses just as definite a personage as belongs to a president or a bishop. No soul can make a moral distinction between its literary hours and its business hours. As the English bishop or rector can no longer appear in two roles, those of the prayer-book and the bottle, so all editors and proprietors and all men must live and act in only one part, that of morality. Life means morality.

It should also be stated here that nothing immoral is business. Business implies an honorable industry or trade. We do not reckon footpads and burglars among our business men. The maxim, "Business is business," is very much of a falsehood as it is used, for it means this: that an archbishop is an archbishop, even if he is drunk. Such a use of language our world has outgrown. The men who once used it will soon all be dead.

If we interpret the word "immorality" as meaning that which always injures the body or the mind or both, then we have a field of thought quite distinct from that of orthodox Christianity,

and no one need fear that in giving his heart to morality he is supporting the church.

Not a few men are afraid to be moralists for fear they may be mistaken for clergymen. Not long since a clergyman attempted to reason on our streets with an inebriated man, but the staggering gentleman said to the preacher: "I am not one of your white cravat fellows. I take whisky when I please." He was only one among millions who connect morality with some church creed; whereas morality belongs to the profound study and welfare of society. England sells to China each year sixty millions of dollars worth of opium. Such a transaction is simply immoral. There is nothing of virtue or honor in such sale of goods. As a result China has millions of men who are mental and physical ruins; but the scene has nothing to do with church or creed; it is simply a scene in the history of the human race. The man who can not separate morals from the church has an intellect not calculated to excite envy. Religion ought to make its votary a more ardent student and lover of morals, but the welfare of man ought to make morality an aim of being.

If we examine those laws which the Christian Church calls the laws of God, and which it alleges were taught through inspired men, we find that they are taught also by human welfare. Thou shalt not kill, steal, lie, covet, are all laws of common human happiness. Thus when Christ says, "Blessed are the pure in heart; blessed the peacemakers," he is passing along among the people letting fall those benedictions which reason repeats in all her sober hours of reflection. Thus there is a morality upon which even the highest religion bases all its rules of conduct. Christ came not to invent or create a code of morals, but to teach and adorn the one universal and everlasting code. He said with others, but more eloquently than all others: "Oh, that virtue were a visible personage, that mankind might stand amazed and entranced at her beauty."

The unpopularity of the Sunday idea comes from the foolish sensibility of many about being imposed upon by the church. They fear it is the clergy that make whisky a forbidden drink. Thus many associate Sunday with the orthodox religion, while the real truth is, the abrogation of that day would be an act of immorality. And it

would be a more immoral act in our period than it was in past times, because our age is, beyond all ages, labor-ridden, care-ridden and gold-mad.

We are indeed so gold-mad and pleasure-mad that we are often stone-blind to virtues and vices. We have come to a time when, instead of having our work lessened by machinery and inventions, we perceive that it is doubled. All our leisure hours are gone. In an inventory of our minds and hearts it is uncertain whether we should all be classified as fools or slaves. Our names are hidden away somewhere in the neighborhood of these two terms. If there is anything we need it is a Sunday of rest and reflection. On all the Saturdays of summer all shops, stores, offices, and factories should be closed at noon, as a confession that machines have lessened labor and that our nation is inhabited by men of thought and kindness. On each Saturday afternoon all toilers should have the liberty of air and sunshine, play and beauty, and on Sunday they should taste again the sweetness of rest and peace.

We should all entertain a high regard for steam engines, telegraphs and electric railways, but we should not permit our souls to be swin-

dled by those elegant things. They must not come between us and our books, our churches, our homes, our benevolence, our friendships. If Sunday possesses a moral quality and contains something good for each soul upon earth, let us not sell out the day for so much gold. Let us turn Saturday into a holiday and keep Sunday for rest and peace. It is highly immoral to ask what gate-money a Sunday would bring.

Our city is not so glutted with goodness that it feels constrained to unload. Our nation at large has no ideas to sell. It would much better enter the market as a purchaser. And if what we want is gate-money, we would better buy all the Saturdays of next summer; for our Sunday of peace and rest may be more beautiful and more noble than the Columbian Exhibition itself. Among the articles of exhibition next summer we ought to point the world to a Western civilization. Our fame as a howling bedlam is complete. Our fame as a noble home for morality and culture is yet to be won. The opportunity is near. That fame might be secured in the space of one rich summer-time. Saturday is the day we want for the pleasure and profit of all the laboring

classes of the coming days. Let us even enter our sweat-shops and set free our slaves.

Let us return to the general study of immorality. A French thinker and writer has published a little volume upon a form of vice little discussed. Moses passed the vice by when he made the decalogue, and Plato and Cicero overlooked this shape of public injury. The name of this evil is luxury. The first Latin writer who made a paragraph out of this sin came in the last days of the empire, and said over a dead friend: "Thou wast never betrayed by that sweet curse called luxury. With a pleasing face that enemy surrounds body and mind with a cloud, and weakens man with drugs more powerful than the poison of Circe." It is singular that no one can define the term.

This Frenchman says: "Luxury is something that costs much and is of no value." "Man does not need it." But it is not necessary to define the word. The fact is here, that there is some power or passion sweeping over our country and touching millions who once lived in simplicity and under divine law. One of our states is attempting to pass an act to suppress the manu-

facture and use of a kind of poison smoked by young men. Not only does the article cost much and contain no value, but it carries an injury. But it would take many laws, indeed, were the State to attempt to turn the money of the workingmen and of the upper classes along channels of lasting value. Perhaps one-fourth of the earnings of the laboring man goes in the direction of some curse, as the Latin says, "some sweet curse." Many laborers confess that their drinks cost thirty cents a day, while many men of small salary and small means spend two hundred dollars a year on the luxury of smoke. Great sarcasm is hurled by the poor laborer at the rich man who buys a costly diamond for wife or daughter; but the poor laborer who is so sarcastic, instead of buying a diamond for ornament and investment, buys one hundred dollars' worth of beer each year, thus robbing self and wife and daughter; for beer is nothing but a dead loss to the consumer, even when it is not an injury.

When we pass from the malt to the distilled drinks, the havoc caused by luxury becomes immeasurable. All the folly of earth diminishes when compared to this attachment to drink. The

opium habit in China is a small local disease when compared with this epidemic. People are now wondering whether cholera will come next summer. Whisky has come. The cholera makes its call once in about eighteen years, and slays a multitude. Whisky comes every day in every year, and by its ravages makes the epidemic from Asia a mere weakling. Englishmen spend five hundred million dollars a year in drinks; Americans certainly not less. And yet the laboring men, who help make this evil, will complain at the human race for having diamonds and carriages. The cholera is a mystery of the air; drink is one of man's own home-made luxuries. The savages got along quite well when their luxuries were feathers, beads, paint, and great feasts of corn bread and venison, but when the white man's luxury came to them they staggered and fell. Wonderful invention of the white man—a drink that will quickly turn a statesman or an Indian into an idiot! These drinkers will laugh at the Roman Emperor who was so sensual as to make a dinner of birds' tongues, and will then draw a bottle from their pocket and take a drink. It need not require much reflection to decide whether the Roman or the modern were the greater fool.

Luxury as a general rule is the displacement of real life. It does not tell us where man and woman are, but rather it points out the place where they used to be; or it suggests by sorrowful contrast the moral beauty which they might have reached. As some of the savage tribes in Africa ornament their women with rings and accouterments until the decorated beings can not walk or even stand, thus in civilized lands luxury points out not life's triumph, but the place where it sunk. Luxury is not the throne of manhood or womanhood, but its grave. As men who are to run a race, or to engage in the physical arena, dare eat and drink only in simplicity, as the college athletic clubs must live near to nature's simplest lines, as great singers will not ruin their voices by gluttony, as orators must live simply when they are to make a great argument, thus all the forms and hours of human life must look to simplicity for its triumph and to luxury for its defeat. How often, in the street or in society, do we meet the early ruins of both forms of beauty, that of the body and that of the soul! They touched modern luxury and sank.

In the long history of man there have come at regular intervals tears of both religion and phi-

losophy over the ruins made by this immorality. Socrates in his simple garb was a protest against the age which at last put him to death. Christ is the most sublime and thrilling protest the earth ever had or saw. His gospel was that of a life, simple on its physical side, but on its mental side rich to a divine magnificence. At regular intervals society has become so besotted with its vices that loud and hot protests have come as though even the stones must speak.

It comes to memory now that an early Christian, Lactantius, published in the fourth century a letter which he pretended a Hebrew patriarch had written before the time of Moses. These are a few of its words: "I know, my children, that in the latter times you will forsake simplicity and will cleave unto money, and leaving innocence you will cleave unto guile. * * * I am one hundred and twenty years old, and have never drunk any wine, to be led astray thereby; I have never longed for anything that was my neighbor's. When men have wept, I have wept with them. I never have eaten alone. I have shared my bread with the poor. True simplicity broodeth not over gold; it defrauds not a neighbor; it does not long for

manifold dainties for the table; it does not delight in varied apparel." Thus runs this long letter, and whether it came down from the old Hebrews or was written by Lactantius, it points out fully one-half the wrongs and sorrows of our century.

Our times must face this old fact; give an age money and the age will sink in luxury. Such a charge should soon cease to be true. If intelligence and true taste are being amassed rapidly, these new giants ought to filter the immorality out of society and make all its pursuits noble and all its pleasures high and everlasting. Taste and money ought to border all our old race-tracks with a tropical wealth of trees and flowers. Make the boughs of trees meet over them. Make the noble animals march in a floral cavalcade, and charge us all for seeing such a splendor of nature. Let gambling die, let beauty live! Long, long ago all this weak immorality ought to have been in its grave, and true Beauty on her throne. Why do we so long and patiently labor to make our world too vile to be man's home? One sentence is distinctly audible: it is full time for immorality to cease its ravages. This sentence comes not from the church, but from the millions of human

hearts that ache and bleed. We put in the balances against all immoralities the hot tears of our race.

Such is that argument which society here in this world weaves against all harmful vice. But not even the deist or atheist ought to complain if the Christian adds to this argument drawn from society that additional influence or persuasion that comes from the teachings and sentiments of a high religion. It will not take away from the repulsiveness of immorality if, in addition to the hate cherished toward it by good men, it is thought that there is a God who hates it. It will not harm the law of simplicity and honor if besides issuing from the welfare of our race it comes also from God's central throne. Can it be blamed upon the religious man that he fights sin too earnestly? Is it a reproach to John the Baptist that he preached too loud against the Herods of his day? Is it a reproach to Jesus that he made his faith an inspiration against all wrong and a motive of goodness? Is it a reproach to Xavier that he sailed upon seas too rough and to help men too savage? Is it a reproach to Marquette that he taught men who were too red and

passed his winter in snows too deep?' The irreligious man who sees the awful depths of vice in city and town must look only in admiration upon those who make the belief in God and immortality an inspiration to labor and die in behalf of our race. The church admits that the laws of society are found in society itself, but it claims the right to think of God as the maker of society and as the Being, faith in whom will make social laws all shine as though written in letters of gold. The moral men of this world only ought to confess the assistance they receive from the minds that believe in a life to come. When the atheists of America perceive the vices which ought to be checked, and the millions of men who ought to be lifted to a higher character, they may well welcome the help of those who feel that humanity did not come from dust but from a God. Each moral atheist ought to welcome the assistance of a man who believes in heaven.

The more divine society is, the greater are the laws which encompass it. Honesty, simplicity, kindness are noble even if they sprang from the realm of only earth, air, water, and heat, but they are nobler if they be also the voice of a Supreme

Mind, just as the nightingale would sing more sweetly to us if we knew that God put the song in its heart.

It is not only true that the heavens declare the glory of God, but it is also true that God enhances the glory of the heavens. It is this dream of the worshiper that makes the distances of the stars so appalling and the whole mystery so profound. The star-depths speak out in sublime poetry when man makes them a part of a creator's empire. The stars sing to us:

"A million torches kindled by God's hand
   Wander unwearied through the blue abyss;
They own God's power, they move at His command,
   All gay with life and eloquent with bliss.
What shall we call them? Piles of crystal light?
   A glorious company of golden streams?
Lamps of celestial ether burning bright?
   Suns lighting systems with their happy beams?
But God to these is as the noon to night."

This Deity which so ennobles the heavens, ennobles also the moral laws which encompass mankind. They seem no longer the relations of dust to dust but the advice of an infinite friend, the conclusions reached by the Supreme Wisdom, the sweetly-rolling eloquence of the sky. An economist may teach us law, but Jesus Christ

makes the law beautiful. He loves it, he weeps over it, he dies for it. Reason can teach, but religion can inspire.

It is the new glory of the modern church that it has begun to assail immorality. It has grown weary of seeing a beautiful world trampled down by a degraded manhood; it beholds for the first time the length and depth of a needless desecration; it hears the Supreme Judge say to the Christian: "If you will make this world beautiful I will take care of your immortality." In a few years more the church will deeply love the laws of this terrestrial kingdom, and, dying in a redeemed and adorned earth, will be ready to pass with joy through the gates which open into a world free from all immorality and adorned by countless virtues.

Devotion and Work.

I must work the works of him that sent me.—John ix. 4.
I passed along and observed the objects of your worship.—Acts ii. 23.

Man is the only animal whose condition is dependent upon work. All creatures must indeed seek food, but we can not designate the lion or the bird or fish as a working animal. The relations of man to work are without any parallel. Man and work are inseparable. When an individual passes along from infancy without meeting anywhere a task to be performed, that individual dies young or makes a most wretched career for both his mind and his body.

When the Creator gave man a growing, infinite nature, He annexed to the gift an endless amount of industry, because this expansive mind could not reach any of its desires without working for them. If this gifted creature longed for music, it had to work for it, and the man who would be a musician had to work like a farmer or a carpenter. If the heart longed for skill in any language or art or science, it had to pass over the field of toil. The Latins discovered this pe-

culiarity of man's life and summed up the fact in their popular sentence that: No excellence is possible without labor. Plautus says: "Success is like the meat in a nut, surrounded by the hard shell of labor." Terence says: "Industry will give man what he seeks."

The vast number of things wanted by the world shows how universal and varied must be the public industry. As civilization grows, the human wants increase, and, therefore, there must be a growth of labor with each growth of the public culture. If the mind can secure some assistance from instruments and machines, it may do so, but there must always be a growing industry of the mind itself, which no machine can ever supplant. The inventions and discoveries made by Fulton and Morse did not leave those men idle afterward, nor generate leisure; they changed only some of the forms of work. The machines of England have not created any new leisure for either the statesman or the poet or the average citizen, for the civilization which brought the new machines brought a new activity of the mind and heart. The telegraph and railway have not made Mr. Gladstone a man of more leisure. Man

and work are inseparable, and the more he enlarges his world, the more quickly will he have to take steps in its confines. The only problem is to find exactly the quantity of work that shall be most in harmony with the perfect health of mind and body. Each art, each science, each emotion of benevolence, each new friendship means an addition to the work of the age.

When you hear that some man becomes attached to trees or dogs or flowers or music, you must give him credit for industry, for no lazy man ever formed an attachment. An indolent mind can not form a friendship for trees, plants, or music, or nature, because a friendship implies action. An attachment means work. It makes the work sweet, indeed; but the Creator, when He ordered man to be a toiling animal, ordered the toil to be a source of happiness. Labor is much sweeter than idleness.

When one states that man was made for work, there should be made also the companion statement that work is a great, uniform source of happiness. To see a farm assume beauty under one's care, to behold a statue assuming elegant shape, to see a temple or a home rising according

to one's plans, to see a rose blooming which one has planted and cared for, to see a fire burn brightly which we have built, to have the people applaud our music—all these ends are ordered by Him who ordered the days of labor and solicitude. With most minds their work is their inspiration. When work is painful to body and soul, then despotism and cruelty have displaced nature. When young children work in the shops, and when men and women work like whipped slaves, and for a few pennies a day, then God's laws are as far away as they were from the bloody ships of Captain Kidd. We do not call the career of Captain Kidd "mercantile life."

So the toil of that woman who sung Hood's "Song of the Shirt" did not fall under the head of human industry, but rather must it take its place among the results of the world's crime. When one would make up an estimate of industry one must assume that the toiler enjoys the air, the light, the food, the clothing, the rest and sleep demanded by the man, woman or child. When a woman works fifteen hours a day for ten or twelve cents, we must not call that labor. It must be alluded to as torture, and in history must be

written down in the story of the inquisition. As Kidd was not a merchant, but a pirate, so much of industry is not labor—it is martyrdom.

Away from the wrongs of an age, labor is one of the glorious things of our world. Man's mind is dormant until he goes to work. When the lawyer, or statesman, or writer, or thinker, or artist of any rank or pay gets once fully at work, then does his mind come to him, his sleep and clouds vanish, and his life's flood sets in. An idle, lazy person has no brains; for sleepy brains are not a positive quality. In the new science and art of electricity the workmen recognize two kinds of wires—the live wire and the dead wire. The men are very careful when they have to work around a live wire. In the realm of mind these two terms may well be used.

The idle, lazy brain is a dead wire. As a promoter of sleep it has no equal. It was difficult in his late years to arouse Mr. Webster; but, could he by some means be once awakened, then all his deep insight, his grasp, his language, came back to him, and for an hour or a half day he and those who were listening to the orations were all in the world of intense and happy life.

When Theodore Parker uttered his funeral oration over the dead Webster, no listener moved in his seat or became tired or restless in the two and a quarter hours. The work of thought made life and made happiness, and changed the two hours into a time of blessedness.

Thus work is not simply a doing, it is also a being. It is an awakening. When Sir John Lubbock was traveling among the South Sea natives, he found them so averse to any kind of action that they did not love to talk upon new subjects. They had been asleep so many generations that the idea of a new truth became painful to them. Lubbock's happiness was their misery. They were dead men. Work, thus, is not a source of income only, but it is also an arousing of the soul. Often when the reader closes his book after having read for an hour in a great work, the question, What has he learned? is not half so valuable as the question, What has he been? He has been a live wire for the time. His language, his wit, his pathos, his reason, his virtues, have all been back and at home in his soul, and he can say to the book: "I thank thee for an hour of life."

It is rather strange that, when the curious are going among the world in search of the reason why so few persons attend church, they should omit one cause, like that of the South Seas—the indolence which can not endure the idea of hearing or doing anything. There are, indeed, many good and bad reasons for the absence of many from the world's church, but the enumeration of causes will not be complete until we have included that mental indolence which does not want to encounter any person or any thing or any idea or any music or any motion of any form whatever—an indolence which hates, not only a sermon, but everything except a full supply of nonentity. There are times when many a laborer, of high or low grade, needs an absolute isolation from all activity, but, after all these deductions have been made, one must still confess the existence of a multitude who are absent from everything, because of an absolute torpidity of spirit. The thought of any form of action is oppressive. The church is only one of the sufferers. These Asiatic souls could not water a dying rose bush, nor throw out crumbs to a sparrow.

Our country has pushed work forward as a revenue, but not as a happiness. When society shall think of work as a mental awakening, as an inspiration, we shall at once have a better world.

In that golden age, men and women will engage in great works, because such tasks will bring the greatest happiness. When we make out a role of amusements, such as drama, opera, concerts, dinners, games, visiting and travel, we should not end the catalogue without adding the word "work;" for only recall for a moment the happiness man extracts from his pursuit. If the conditions of civilization were what they should be, there would not be an adult mind living, that was not in love with some form of industry, and there would not be a blacksmith, who would not laugh at times over his anvil, and not a farmer, who would not hum a tune along his rich furrow.

The perpetual satirists of modern womanhood make daily flings at its fondness for lunches, parties, lectures, readings and literary clubs; but these critics ought to confess the promise and virtue in a social world, which has ceased to extract happi-

ness from sleep and an endless nothingness. Given a womanhood fully awake, and the transition becomes easy from ordinary aims to aims much nobler. A heart once alive can move from sphere to sphere. The modern womanhood can in an instant show power as the world needs. We are happy in the thought that it lives.

In speaking of the nobleness of work, John Ruskin said, years ago, that a part of the beauty of a column, or a statue, or a picture, is found in our admiration of the quantity of work which it contains. "The column of the Apprentice," which attracts so many visitors to Rosslyn's Chapel, of Scotland, is made admirable by the quantity and detail of the carving.

It is as rich in work as the book of Dante or the book of Milton. The column holds up a vast number of thoughts and emotions and would seem erected in memory of labor. A theory of Mr. Ruskin long ago was that no painter should ever throw in a foreground or a background carelessly. If his purpose is to paint a ship on the sea, the artist must paint the pebbles on the shore just as perfectly as he must paint the ship. Nothing in any part of the canvas must be slighted. Wherever

the eye falls it must see the beauty of labor. It must see that man, the thinker, actor and lover, has been in each inch of the painting. Work is the utterance of the soul.

If we ponder a moment, we shall conclude that Mr. Ruskin spoke truly and that his principle is of universal application. We love to hear a speech all full of thought and truth, and to read a poem whose thoughts, words and rhythm have all come through the shop of the finisher. When we read the "Elegy" of Gray, or the "In Memoriam" or "Virgil," we feel that here some workman has toiled over his task and has turned mixed and crude ore into pure gold. A stack of last year's straw is not so delightful as the reapers at work in a new field of waving wheat.

We all, indeed, live in a working age, but this industry is poured out too exclusively upon one subject—the making and securing of property. Young men hasten through college, skipping over great books and great years, that they may the sooner reach the busy scenes around money. It is a sad blunder to hasten by the lands where the Greeks and Romans exhausted centuries of work upon language, sentiment, eloquence, and all

beauty; sad to dash by these charms, that we may get to the market-place the sooner. Work is not only an accumulation of money, it is also a being. It is a color of the human soul.

Our energetic city has suddenly come upon a form of its weakness; its energy is all in one direction. It can pursue business, but it can not govern and adorn itself. It can not execute a law. It can not clean a street or superintend a contract, because there are no minds or hearts that are running in those directions. The general industry is all towards the affairs of the individual. But the streets would all fall under the general law of Mr. Ruskin, and can be made more beautiful only by an enormous quantity of labor and devotion. The homes of this city are neat and beautiful, because each home comes under the care of some personal soul; but all that part of the city which is public catches no love or care from anybody. It is more friendless than the old blind horse turned out to die on the commons, for the humane society will carry that horse a bucket of water and a bundle of hay; but as for the city, it has not even the humane society for its friend.

It is a neglected orphan, deaf, dumb, blind, and poor. If fault-finding could save it, we clergymen could make it a New Jerusalem in two days; if resolutions could make the place beautiful, the woman's movement last summer would have made untidiness a matter of history. What the city needs is some men who have the disposition and the power to be its friends. Somebody must come with love, to make the foreground and the background, and to reveal painstaking work. As the picture, the statue, the book, the poem, are made by work, so the city must be made by devotion. To ask our city to be anything, under the existing apathy, is like asking a Virginia contraband to take a whitewash brush and reproduce "The Angelus."

It is in vain to double our taxes. Money will not make a beautiful city. Three hundred million dollars were spent on the name of "Panama," but there is no canal. New York City is in debt a hundred millions, but its condition is little better than our own. The power of money depends upon the men who direct the money. Can money paint a picture? No, but a gifted soul may. Can money write a poem? No, but a Milton

can. Can money clean a city? No, but a General Butler can beautify a New Orleans, and a Baron Haussman can create for France a new Paris. Haussman was to Paris, what Angelo was to sculpture, and what Homer was to poetry. Whenever Haussman flung the people's money, beauty grew up where the coins fell; and now, France has a city, because it was able to produce a soul.

All of our cities are about alike in weakness and repulsiveness. This city equals any in merit. The theory of each is bad. The rulers of a city should be composed of men who can make deformity turn into beauty, and weakness turn into power. Millionaires having reached the fixed limit of five or ten millions should then become the creator of the city or the State. Their minds and gains should go toward something greater than a private fortune. How absurd it is to elect a saloon-keeper or saloon loafer to help govern a city! Why did we select a great art lover to collect and arrange our pictures for the World's Fair? Had we no chimney-sweep whom we could have employed? Why put educated ladies on the Woman's

Columbian Board? Could not an employment office have furnished a group of girls? When a city shall conclude that, like a piece of art, it needs skill, industry and love, then will it begin to meet the ends of its being.

Some of the States are drafting laws by which they may secure a part of the millions which the richest citizens leave behind when they die. But who is to spend this enormous income from great estates? Unhappy millionaires, if at death a part of their gold is to pass into the hands of a city council! The truth is, what a city needs generally is the help of the powerful man long before he dies. The men who are endowing our university with libraries, telescopes, laboratories, are as powerful in their mind and taste as they are in their gold. The services of these men are as valuable as their money. When the people of Paris found out the merit of Baron Haussman, they said: "If he will make a new city we will give him the gold;" and a new $50,000,000 was subscribed toward the great reconstruction.

Thus all over this planet, and in all its ages, the law of devotion and intelligent labor has held its sway. No person and no State has ever been

able to escape the grasp of this law. Its meshes seem like silk, but they are iron. Nature scorns and punishes all apathy. Nothing has ever come by way of indifference, and so old is the world now that we may assume that no good will ever come by that gate. It is indeed not a gate by which man comes, it is rather a swamp, a marsh, where he sinks.

Would that the heavy veil of nature could be lifted that we might all see the eternal Father at his work! Could such a vision be granted us, we should see an infinite Mind acting into all space, slighting nothing, but devoted and potent where an ocean rolled or a lily bloomed. In the absence of such a face-to-face interview we have to speak of the power of the sun and tell each other how its heat made the forests which, waving in the air a million years ago, are now seen crushed into beds of coal, and how that heat made all that life and verdure which bedeck our globe to-day. But the sun explains nothing. It simply tells us that there is a mind somewhere which is making the universe burst forth into beauty and tremble into life. Could we look back of the ocean, we should see some hand holding it; could

we gaze back of the coming cloud, we should see some loving heart pouring out great streams of color in the west. Sublime and mysterious as the universe is, one fact is clear—it is at work under the loving care of somebody. There is some angel painting the apple blossoms, and there is some angel carrying perfume to the rose. The man or woman who is indifferent is already dead. Nature hates such a loveless heart.

As man must bring his wisdom and devotion to bear upon his city, state and home, so must he bring it to bear upon his religion. The religion which prevailed five hundred years ago may not be noble enough to meet the need of the races which now live. Our times are restudying all the Christian and moral problems. It may be the past did not bring out fully the morality and philanthropy of Jesus Christ. It may not have seen clearly the relations of religion to common conduct. It may have thought the earth to be under a curse, as were the companions of Ulysses in the Island of Circe. We know that each new era is born to a new industry and a new affection, and that the passing religion must catch something of this new toil. As man must send art

onward more perfect than he found it, so must each epoch send religion onward in garments more beautiful than those in which it came. Man's labors will never end, not only because the tasks are each infinite, but also because labor is always an awakening of life. Labor is the hand which strikes the strings of the mental harp. Devotion is only another name for life. It is the tie that binds man to his calling. It is the chain of gold that bound Newton to the stars, the chain which bound Washington and Lincoln to our Republic.

The relations of all young minds to their life should be those of laborious devotion. It should be deeply felt that the sweep of years is the arena of a care and a labor that shall make the natural marble show its tints, and the crude gold its purity. Intemperance, the race-track, and each form of vice and dishonor, must be discarded as simply a quick ruin; and then one's language, one's taste, education, breadth, depth, kindness, and religion must be made the objects of an unchanging regard. Nothing equals life in the power to absorb work and devotion. It absorbs all and destroys nothing. The soul catches all this attention, and runs with it out into this world

and into immortality. Whoever cares little how he lives is already lost.

This is the birthday of an American, who, when a boy, began to lavish care and labor upon his visit to this world. Born in a mental desert he began to reach out like a palm tree toward riches, soil, and springs of water. We can now look back and mark his devotions. He worshiped his handful of books; he paid homage to all the greatness which had gone before him; he made reasoning an amusement and a pursuit; each year which brought new blossoms brought him a new survey of his world; each yellow autumn added to his pensiveness, each spring reawakened his hope; the time which slowly changed lonely forests into populous states, changed his young thoughts into great principles, and by the day when middle life had come, he stood up encompassed by doctrines of right and humanity which the world now sees were divine.

He attempted to mingle reason, sentiment, honor, justice, love and happiness, not only in his own spirit, but in the heart of the world; and seldom in human history have so many strings of the soul sounded in such perfect harmony. Never,

perhaps, was a better manhood created out of such unpromising material; but this man cared for his life; and, as the great pictures of art carry the labor of the artist, as the column in Rosslyn Chapel arose, carved in all its extent by loving care, this man carried with him to a noble grave all the rich mental details which could be worked out in a single lifetime.

There is one kind of selfishness that is admirable. It is not, indeed, a selfishness, but rather it is a kindness to the race—that self-love which leads the mind to take care of all its faculties and its liberties. This care is not an egotism, it is only a confession that the world and its God are great. When man says, "Let me see the flowers, let me hear the music," his heart is full, not of himself, but of the universe. All this self-development is a worship of the empire which encompasses the spirit. All egotism is thus displaced by the presence of the infinite.

This long argument over work, care and devotion leads to a conclusion which carries us beyond the boundary of time. If man is ordered by his Maker to pour out care day by day, and if he makes and occupies his years with such devotion,

it follows that He who made man is also pouring out upon his empire an attention, a love, a thought, that are infinite; and that, if not in these years, then beyond the grave, all the eyes of mortals that close here will open again upon a human family all worked up into a perfect finish and inwrought with the many images of all virtue and all happiness.

Radicalism—Root and Branch.

For behold the day cometh; it burneth as a furnace, and all the proud and all that work wickedness shall be stubble; the day cometh that shall burn them up; that shall leave them neither root nor branch.—Malachi iv. 1.

In one of the reading books which lay in many homes and cabins when our century was young there was a thrilling story called "The Rising of the Waters." A Canadian gentleman had built a little board hut on the upper bank of a river. It was to be the home of himself and two little sons while some workmen were surveying some forests and were felling some trees. At daybreak on a summer morning a rain began to fall. For a time it was a pleasant sight. The pattering on the board roof was good music to be heard. As the puddles began to form, the delight of the boys grew steadily. When, hour after hour, the darkness and downpouring increased, and awful lightning and thunder began to play a frightful part in the growing tempest, the boys grew silent and hid themselves under the cloak of their father. To this alarming gloom night set in and its terrors, and, fed by a thousand hill-torrents, the river began to roar

and to carry whole trees along as though in wrath. Toward morning the woodmen had to leave all their huts and betake themselves to the hills. This piece of prose, equal in power to Hugo's chapter on the battle of Waterloo, was called "The Rising of the Waters," and often it comes back to the memory of those who mark the slow rise and advance of reform. First come a few rain-drops, and after long time the skies grow darker and the flood begins to roar.

The certainty of ultimate victory keeps most great hearts from despair. They do not expect all things to act at once on the line of their wish. They are capable of grasping long periods, and of picturing a future, few of whose beauties have yet come. It is probable most great reformers have been men of powerful imagination, not of that imagination which composes poems and romances, but which can detect a great moral landscape lying beyond the actual scenes of to-day. We have no right to assume that the poetic faculty can do nothing but make verses or assist in art. It is needed in the daily life of the citizen, for it draws for him an outline of the rewards and works to which his labors are bear-

ing his heart. Poetry is only one of the forms assumed by this mental quality. It has a wider office—that of creator and guardian of man's life and man's world. It is necessary for the average man and woman to be hopeful, and to plant their hopes upon the gradual advance of intelligence and goodness.

It is said that our Legislature is drafting and reading a law to limit horse-racing and betting to sixty days in the year, and those must be days in the summer. We do not dare laugh at a group of philosophers who look upon gambling as a wrong so great that it ought to prevail only a part of the year, and then only in the summertime. Instead of laughing at the Legislature we may well rejoice that the feeling against the old popular vice has grown so large as to become visible—so large as to extend its goodness toward some months of the twelve.

In the Mosaic laws a man was not to be whipped beyond forty stripes. The mercy of that period lay in limiting the blows which might be inflicted. Many died from the effect of the forty blows, but more would die if the flogging champions could keep up the lashing indefinitely.

A few centuries afterward, when Paul was living, he was beaten with forty stripes save one. Mercy had given the lash another backset. It had to cut the flesh only thirty-nine times at one whipping. But there was no law to prevent Paul from being lashed five times. Thus creeps the progress of an age; and, if our philosophers permit gambling to reign and ruin for only two months of the year, we must "thank God and take courage." The prize-fight has been forbidden in all the States where intelligence has reached any degree of popularity.

It is a blessed day in morals when men make a beginning toward the study of a wrong. It is the first suspicion that is so difficult. In 1700, Sir Thomas Brown, M. D., discussed the question whether the Englishman should get drunk once a month. He gathered up the data with all the patience of an astronomer. He thought the nausea of drunkenness a medicine equal to calomel in virtue.

It was difficult for slavery to make its first appearance as a violation of rights. It was seen as a great convenience to the white man, then as a necessary result of climate and race; then it turned

into a missionary movement, and, at last, into a fraud. The rising of the waters became at last deeply impressive, and the slave-holders waded out.

One of our excellent local clergymen preached recently against such an amusement as shooting birds for a prize. All would have been well had not the clergyman entered into a sweet defense of the gentlemanly hunters who bring down a few birds for table use. He rejoiced in the sport of dog and gun. The sermon showed how difficult it is for a moral principle to make a start. The pigeons which fall at the shooting matches are all sold for the table. It remains for the pulpit to prove that to shoot a bird out in the weeds and pond lilies is any nobler than to rob it of life within the limits of a city.

Thus morality crawls along like a wounded snake, and reduces the stripes inflicted upon the birds from forty to thirty-nine. But morality advances, although at a snail's gait. The pulpit of Christ must stand upon the truth formulated not long since, that "the death of an animal may be a necessity, but it can never be an amusement." With this sentiment in the public soul, all slaugh-

tering of birds and game will be left to those men who are not touched by any tenderness of heart. As the whole thirty-nine stripes have passed away from the shoulders of our negroes, and from what Saint Pauls we possess, so the day is sure to come when the gun will give no pleasure to a true gentleman, and he would sicken at the thought of killing the dove which stands as an emblem of the soul, and of bagging the quail which sung "Bob White" in the harvest field of last summer.

These remarks are not those of fault finding. We all are, or all have been, in the same old bloody happiness. We all used to shoot, but we should all in our later years make a new survey of our old morals, and should gladly eliminate any lurking remnant of the old savagery. If there are men who have not yet reached any kindness of nature, men who can kill a deer or a fawn or a dove as cheerfully as they would pick up a ripe apple from the ground, let those men do the killing for the length and breadth of the land. It is high time for you all to go up a step higher in your forms of pleasure. Heliogabalus ate a plateful of nightingale tongues. The birds were slaughtered that he might show Rome how great a king he

was; that his divine body was superior to all those little angels which in Italy made the plaintive midnight music. Would you not all have said: Let those birds live and sing in the hedge; bring me on a plate some bread and honey from the fields of Virgil, some ripe figs from the gardens of the Cæsars.

In the long course of events it will come to pass that there will be no insensate men to act as butchers for the world. What then? With the coming of that day the eating of meat will also cease. With many thousands in our land already that form of food has lost its charm. As the last thousand years have wrought great changes in man's thoughts and being, so the years to come will bring changes greater still, and it is almost certain that the far-off tables will groan with all the riches of the orchard and the fields. In the golden age man will eat amid breads, fruits, music and flowers. The dove, the quail, the nightingale will not be there in death to mar man's sweetness of life.

Much as we admire the modern human race, we can not but perceive that man stands here to-day much encumbered with his inheritance.

He eats meat because such was the practice of his more savage ancestors. Education is not good only as a means of learning the branches called reading, writing and arithmetic. One of its greatest forms of usefulness lies in the fact that it helps us escape from our ancestors. It is well, indeed, that we had ancestors, and one may recall with gratitude the art and literature and law that came down from antiquity; but this gratitude need not make us forget that we inherited egotism from the classics, pugilism from the Spartans, murder and war from the Saxon, mendacity from the Arabs, and business habits from the Pirates. It is one of the holy offices of education to pass the modern mind through a fire which may burn out this old dross and send man onward in a greater purity.

And some one will say: Did not the God of nature command the animals to feed upon each other? The lion kills the dog; the dog the rabbit. Yes, but the answer is: Man was not made to be a brute. His problem is to find how far he can drift away from the brute forms of life. An ancient discovered that the spirit of the brute tendeth downward, while the spirit of

man tendeth upward. Man must not rely upon the brute world for his lessons in virtue. He must look into his own soul and evolve his career from his own time and divinity.

The last charge against these humane and spiritual ideas is that this teaching is all poetry. The charge is true. It is all poetry from first to last. But this also is true: Our world is founded upon poetry. The globe itself floats in a sea of ether. As it turns over, on one side it sparkles like a crystal ball, on the other side it is dark in shadow. On the brilliant side men work, on its darkened side men sleep. While the ball rolls it passes under the poetic sun, and asks that orb to make for it a poetic spring, summer and autumn. Out of this request came the forest, the fields, the grains, and the fruits; and, after years have passed by in this excess of beauty, man appears in these woods and fields and adds to the sublime aggregation that awful and rich mystery of life which no science can describe and no history contain. Out of the beautiful woods and mountains of Judea comes a Christ, chanting a group of beatitudes which surpassed in sweetness all previous eloquence and song. All poetry,

indeed! but the quick impulse to a new civilization. Ah, poetic world! thy light is composed of a thousand colors, thy scenes are all a mystery, thy sounds are all music. Touch thee where man may, his eyes are full of wonder, and the greatest truth seems only the greatest dream.

The poet Statius, whom Dante so loved, attempted to describe only one little fact of the human career, and he stood amazed by one simple phenomenon—that of sleep. He says: "Sleep is a hidden grotto in a dense woods. Man passes into it. Motionless figures stand all around his couch. The silent clouds envelop it and keep away the roaring of the sea. The angel of silence goes about with folded wings and forbids the winds to move the branches rudely. She forbids the foliage to rustle. She softens the distant thunder. The mountain streams all move more silently. The god of sleep is in the bower. One hand is under the hair of his left temple, the right hand falls and lets go the horn which it held in the long day." Poetry! Of course; our world is all composed of poetry, and the words "benevolence," "civilization," "education," are only the names given to man's best pictures

and his grandest song. Poetry is not the overstatement of the truth, it is the effort of the soul to reach the reality. The crossing of the Delaware by Washington, the inauguration of Lincoln, are scenes as poetic as any in the works of Milton or Shakespeare. Into much more of such poetry our world is hastening. It is carrying us all with it in its grand flight. Manhood and poetry are one and the same.

Radicalism is the final philosophy into which we must all empty our hearts. The word is derived from the Latin term for the root of a plant or tree. The farmer and gardener know that of many noxious plants it is a waste of labor simply to mow off the tops. They must be taken out by the roots. This is radicalism. A legislature may temporize and may take away one stripe and leave thirty-nine to cut into the shoulders of a saint, or it may make a part of the year free from the gambler's art; but the individual citizen need not wear a legislature about his neck, nor a city council. Burdened by such mill-stones he can not do otherwise than sink. He must within his own soul be a radical and make his whole year poetic. He must follow a divine dream all day

and all night. It is much to man's honor to be up with his age, but it is more to his fame to be in advance of it. To be behind the age is infamous. That is the perfection of barbarism. If our State feels that gambling ought to cease a part of the year, it is well to keep up with the State; to fall below such a State would be a moral calamity. In going below the State one might find himself in an unhappy country.

In our age and in all times the most beautiful of all things is the individual. Our age ought to excel the entire past in the creation of the noble individual. Education, climate, industry, and freedom are his to be used and enjoyed. He need not wear any chain upon his spirit, except that gold fetter which God fastens to every wrist. We may be, indeed, helped by a party in politics, or by a church in religion, but we must not be fettered by such organisms. It used to be said that a party has no soul. Each party has a soul, but that soul is not as sensitive and noble as that heart possible to the individual. The soul of a party is always diluted in intellect and sentiment. In forming our government there was a difficulty in finding any principles that would suit the

whole thirteen colonies. It was easy to find the great soul of a Washington or a John Adams, but it was difficult to find the soul of the whole thirteen colonies from Boston to Charleston and Richmond. When a half-score of artists differ as to the color which should cover a wall or a ceiling, at last they all agree on a tint. Thus all the old parties, unable to be adorned by a complete soul, are often seen to wear a mental tint. In the great Middle States when the hard maple trees had not fallen victims to the all-destroying ax, the farmer and his sons were wont to count much on the sugar and nectar they would extract from the trees in the days between winter and spring. But often when the bright sunny morning had contributed a pint of sweet sap to each crock and trough and bucket, a shower of rain would fall and fill the vessels to the brim. With sad faces the family would go out after the shower to taste the contents of the trough or bucket, to learn whether they would better attempt to boil down the compound or throw it all out. Thus the little soul a party possesses soon becomes so weakened by successive dilutions that the whole compound should be emptied out. The attenu-

ation has become infinite. The individual must make his escape and study truth once more in root and branch.

The one great hope of our times lies in the advance of the individual. These isolated minds are unencumbered; they are so light-armed that they can soonest reach a height. On a certain night in Greek history it was necessary for the army in a hostile land to pass through a long ravine. Woe to the troops if the enemy should be on the crags above! The Greek captain sent far in advance some of the light-armed soldiers, and these had soon preoccupied all those heights. Thus in our day of trial and great danger there must spring forward the unencumbered individuals who can outrun the heavy crowd and hold all the moral heights.

After these advanced individuals have multiplied in number and have grown in courage, they create a new party in Church or State. The party will, in morals, be less, indeed, than they, but its merit will be of a deeper tint. Having issued from many individuals of marked good, the new party will be like a national currency from which the state has taken away more of

rags and silver and into which it has poured more of gold. Thus each free and lofty individual is the poem of his day; not running in advance of its truth, but only in advance of its stupor and its vice. Being free of foot, he has outrun his creeping race. The individual must wear but loosely all party ties. It is said that many men drink because they dislike to be so unsocial as to decline to touch glasses with a friend. Singular age, in which a man will become a drunkard by general request! Often a political party is only a request which has become so swollen with office conceit and vice that it orders the weak minds around like a heartless tyrant. It charms like a serpent; "it stings at last like an adder." Against it the isolated individuals must arise as against a foe to all that is good upon earth.

All good begins in some one individual. Many persons were wont to gaze at the stars, but forth came the one Galileo. Each cause, each science, each reform, starts in some solitude, and then gradually expands toward society. Galileo must have been thankful for his first friend. Over his grave now the human race bows in friendship. Thus individualism is the fountain of the river.

Radicalism is the gate through which the individuals all come. In its good meaning it is infinite goodness and happiness—the place where wrongs are torn out by the roots. It is the line where earth joins Paradise.

One cause of our city's unrest lies in the fact that so many individuals have been reared who can now feel deeply its vices and follies. Thus far the children of degradation and wrong can outvote the men of the new era. Not a few whose minds and hearts are in the new, are standing with their feet mired in the political mud of the past. There are thousands of others whose virtues are not a positive color, only a tint. We must wait until the individuals shall have become more numerous and more intense. The radicals must never be disheartened, for if they can not shape the world external they can enjoy that world that is in their own thought and practice. If the individual can not close the saloons, he can have the happiness of saying: "I do not drink." If the law permits thirty-nine stripes, he can say: "I abolish them all, both as to man and beast." Thus, while the world is creeping toward a better condition, the individual can fly to it on dove's wings. While the church is full of false

doctrines, he can, simply by shutting his eyes in some solitude, be instantly with God; and while the earth, all in all, is black with its vices, he can breathe the aroma of the better land. Inasmuch as the individual, having only a few years, can not wait for the world to become humane and just, he must adorn his own days with those virtues, and thus create his own beautiful civilization, just as the traveler at twilight enjoys his own song. As the world will not die with you, it must not live with you. It moves too slowly; you must hasten, for your time is short. You are light armed. You can climb the mountain and see the morning while the valley is still dark.

The Christian Church is fortunate in the fact that it stands attached to a person whose radicalism attacks vice and wrong in root and branch. In Jesus of Nazareth all wrong dies and all love lives. In him tears cease. There politics turns into poetry, as life turns into immortality. But the Church could carry only a little of him, because a party can not carry a deeply-colored virtue, but only a tint. But there stands the Christ perpetually, and the society which once came from him, bringing thirty-nine stripes, soon went back to him, and returned with thirty-eight.

Thus it went and came, until the stripes were all gone from Paul's shoulders. It came away from the Master once with a contempt for the black man. It kept going and coming until the black man was free. It once was but a little kind to the children; it went back to its origin until at last it took all the little children into its arms and joined the Master in the words, "of such is the kingdom of heaven." Thus, under the repeated touches of Nazareth all poisonous plants die, root and branch.

This moral scene resembles that story about the "rising of the waters," only it reverses the feelings of the heart. In that night in old Canada the waters silently rose to man's alarm and danger, but in civilization this flood rises to man's joy. All good and true hearts exult in the long moral storm. As we lie on our pillow at night, we wish the rain drops would grow in size and number. The fainting heart needs the help of the tempest. The river which creeps onward hour by hour is the stream of human happiness. The lightning is welcome, the rolling thunder is music. The father and the two sons need not fly in terror from these waters. All human feet should hasten to touch this healing, peaceful wave.

"The Gentleman of the New School, Rutherford B. Hayes."

The wisdom that is from above is first pure, then peaceable, gentle, easy to be entreated, full of mercy and good fruits, without changes and without hypocrisy.—James iii. 17.

The gentleman of the old school no longer proves satisfactory; his place will soon be filled by a man of the new school. The word "gentle" has added much to its import since it came into duty in the Latin times. The word *gentilis* then stood for the best kind of manhood of that period, but then the best manhood was often very poor. In almost all times and places before the Unites States came into being the most of opportunity for education, culture, and politeness lay in the family. The family implied the school-house, the best manners, and the highest religion. All the commonest people and the enormous multitude of slaves were outside of refining influences. To belong to a *gens*, a group of families, was to have more advantages than a slave could enjoy. To be attached to the family of Abraham, Isaac, or Jacob, was in the old Hebrew world more than equal to having in our day a diploma from Oxford

or Cambridge. So in the Latin times it was a great advantage to be born a member of some *Turquinia gens* or *Claudia gens*, or *Julia gens*. It was much like saying in our day, "He is an alumnus of Yale or Princeton."

Such membership in early or late times has never made the worth of the members absolutely certain, but it has always made it probable that the person thus related was superior to the wild man of the woods. Cicero defined the *gentilis* man as "one belonging to a family which had never been in slavery, and which had received no injury from its remote ancestry." The presumption followed that education and good manners had run along in the channel in which the family had flowed.

The family power and fame reached a wonderful dominance in the Roman period, and it reappeared in Europe after the disintegration of the Roman Empire. All the old castles in Europe and England tell us how the family or the *gens* went onward, carrying what there was of literature, education, reason, and good manners. The massive walls, the moat, the drawbridge, bear witness to the efforts of old ancestors to

escape overthrow and subjection. In Dante's day this war of families was still raging, and was busy in making war, confiscating old castles and ordering enemies into exile. A *gens* man in those years was not much like the gentleman of modern times, for the world has since become spiritualized, and now the gentleman has actually the many virtues in the large which once were admired even in the small. In England the word remains much as it stood in the times of Cicero, and a drunkard or a glutton or a gambler may be a gentleman, because he may be a member of a high *gens*, and not be a man whose ancestors lived by hard toil or were men of the woods or slaves of a lord.

In our republic the term has been spiritualized, and now the word gentleman means one who acts as though his family had been noble for a thousand years; he acts as though long time had emptied its experience and goodness into his heart. He is the son of many a noble race which has acted nobly. As Jesus was called the Son of Man because he stood for the ideal youth of our world, a son because he held the power, the enthusiasm, the righteousness, the

kindness, which attach to the ideal manhood, so the modern gentleman is that ideal soul which seems in Cæsar's day to have absorbed all the good from the Julia *gens*, and from the Fabia *gens* of earlier days, and to have stolen rich colors from the Capulets and Durantes which gave the world its Dante, and to have passed through the castles of Germany and England only to extract the virtues which bloomed within those walls. He did not pause amid those high opportunities that he might emerge a rake or an idler, great in the fox chase and in vice, but that he might gather up all the qualities which make a perpetual goodness and a perpetual beauty. Of such souls our age can now show a large number, because a republic is a field favorable for their growth. An enlightened republic is a kind of nation favorable to the production of gentlemen. But it must also be said that the Western monarchies have become so similar to republics that they, too, can grow a kind of soul not easily possible in the older times.

A republic is made the better soil for this form of manhood, because no soul can be ideal unless it grasps the rights of all humanity.

Many of the so-named gentlemen of the old school were such only by comparison. They showed a little white, but only on a very black background. When the wife had to keep silent, and at times was the recipient of a blow or a kick, when a serf was soundly flogged at the caprice of the master, when war was a regular pursuit, then the term gentleman possessed no deep spiritual import, for that import is impossible where there is no tender appreciation of human rights. Cicero loved his daughter tenderly, but his wife had no rights that he felt bound to respect. Dante was an intense friend to his friends, but he was bitter toward political opponents. Shakespeare gathered up all kinds of conspicuous personages which had run across the world between Cæsar and Henry VIII, but he did not make the perfect gentleman conspicuous in his drama. Shakespeare was a central point in which all paths met, and if the path of gentility is not seen on this Shakespearean map it is because it had not yet been opened up through the woods. In those plays the perfect gentleman was almost as rare as was a steamboat upon the Thames.

The human race has been unfortunate, not only in its efforts to create a noble manhood, but also in its efforts to keep what it has gained.

By the time the Greeks have reached some moral worth, like that found in the characters of the Platonic school, the Persians are seen on the border, ready to trample the Greek flowers under foot; by the time Rome has become able to point to a Pliny and a Tacitus, the northern barbarians are beginning to move southward to trample all the Latin pearls into the mire. In the meantime the savages are overthrowing in Britain the civilization begun by the enlightened Julius Cæsar. Not only was the progress of the higher manhood arrested, but the old grand languages were broken up into wretched dialects, which had to be made into the new tongues or jargons which are now spoken in Europe. To find a good has been in all times difficult, to retain a good, a task equally arduous.

The coming of the actual manhood could not but wait for the advent of human rights. There must always be a wide intelligence before there can be a noble character. The mind must be able to make a survey of the world, and see the

whole net-work of human rights. It is not essential that a gentleman be a good judge of art and music. He may be color-blind, and in an art gallery mistake "The Autumn on the Hudson" for "The Springtime in England;" he may be tone-deaf and not know "Home, Sweet Home," from the "Marseillaise," but his intelligence of men must be broad, and his feelings kind in an infinite degree.

The present Emperor of Russia is, perhaps, a sincere man, but his sincerity does not aid him in this contest for the fame of gentility. He has not moved in the high families of the human race and garnered up the splendors of the widely scattered *gentes*. He has not come through all the Athenses and Florences and Londons and Americas. He came to his throne by way of fanaticism. He felt called by God. He persecuted Baptists, Catholics, Stundists, and Jews, because God wishes them put out of the way of the true church. It is said that he did not wish to be Emperor. He lamented that he had to be Emperor. He would have declined the crown had not his spiritual advisers made him believe that God had called him to take tender care of

the Greek Church. Out of this one mental cloud come all the cruelties which so disgrace the Russian dominions. Alexander III thus stands not a gentleman loved the world over, but a character torn and shattered like a tree riven by lightning. He wants to be a noble man, but no wide study of human rights draws for him an ideal; the path thitherward does not run near his palace.

If we compare with that King of the North the ex-President who, a few days ago, passed from this country, we shall see at once how the teachings of our land help the mind toward an actual gentility. To a taste for all art, all education, Mr. Hayes added a most delicate sense of human rights. Intelligence as to where justice lay, and then a tender love for that justice, helped him to reach long ago the spiritual import of the word gentility. When a perfumed air drifts over a southern road along which the traveler rides at nightfall, he does not know from what special flowers the odor comes. It may be many a variety of flowers has combined with the grasses and with the forests of gloomy pines in making the overhanging world all fragrant. It may be the far-off ocean poured the first ingredient into the cup,

and then passed the compound onward to receive other forms of sweetness from all the scattered chemists of Nature. Thus in the formation of a heart like that of Mr. Hayes many elements were poured in by many hands. We can not name them, nor count them, but chief among these fashioners of the soul must be reckoned that justice which does the right by each form of life.

Without this sensibility of rights, the true gentleman is impossible. Calvin may have desired to do his duty; such may have been the wish of many a Roman Catholic persecutor; such may be the wish of Alexander III, but all these desires are inadequate. Gentility comes, not when a man desires to do his duty, but when he also knows what his duty is. It is a beautiful combination of intellect and heart.

No sooner had ex-President Hayes died than Southern men met in council and hastened to confess that the ruler of the North had always done the best possible by the men and the homes of the South. He had not only cherished good desires, but he had so studied the world, so thought, that his desires were not made bloody by fanaticism, but they were made beautiful by intelligence.

As soon as this citizen had been relieved from his duties as President, he accepted places of duty, but only of that duty which pertained to the betterment of human conditions. Great educational movements and great humane movements called him to new tasks, and he always accepted the calls. His life began well; it continued as it began; it ran evenly to the end. It was free from fanaticism, from indifference; free from the egotism which loses the public in the universe of one's self; full of sympathy with the many-sided progress of mankind.

An approach to such a character has always been possible, but it was easy for John Milton and Lord Bacon and Shakespeare to come short of it, because they were encompassed by all the hardness of a despotism. An enlightened republic makes the character more attainable, because a republic is founded upon the nobility of man, woman and child. In this republic there is immense respect shown to woman, because that study of rights which has been preserved here for a hundred years has created a taste for all the equities of social life. It would be a misfortune if study could develop a taste for literature

and pictures and music, and could not enlarge the taste for the equities of society. That century which has led our people along in many of the common forms of taste has led them forward in their sense of human rights, and has turned many a man from the pain of being an animal into the happiness of being a gentleman.

And beyond a doubt the same republic, working in its second century, will create an army of gentlemen greater than all the standing armies of Europe. In that far-off day when these characters shall throng the Legislatures and fill Presidential chairs and assemble in Parliaments and sit down upon thrones, the standing armies of the world will be dissolved.

When we were all young and at school the dear teachers were wont to tell us that a gentleman was a youth or a man who walked softly and who shut a door without making a noise. He was gentle like a dove. The inference drawn was in favor of a nature not very far removed from ordinary stupidity. The definition was true as far as it went, but it did not go very far—not more than one step in the long way of man's being. Man's footstep on a floor is of no conse-

quence when compared with his footsteps among men. If the Russian Czar would only walk softly among the rights of the Jews and Stundists; if he would only not shut all the doors of liberty and hope, what a gentle soul he would indeed become! Gentle! not like a harmless dove, which can wing the air like an arrow, but gentle like an intellect which has flown through all the great homes of earth and has extracted from all the great families their wisdom and their goodness.

All terms are elastic. The word Christian is often used to distinguish an Englishman from a Mohammedan or an American from a Turk, but the word Christian is not thus exhausted. It moves on until it may describe for us the fervor of John Bunyan or the peace of Mme. Guyon.

So the word scholar may apply to a hundred shades of attainment between that of a common schoolmaster and that of the two Scaligers. When the younger Scaliger was only eighteen he knew several languages, and was soon called "The Colossus of Learning." Thus all great terms will hold little or will hold much. As the Nile river runs low or runs high, so great words run feebly or run full. Among these terms which

are subject to such vicissitudes must be placed the word "gentleman," it being, indeed, applicable when a man speaks in a low tone and respects the laws of the drawing-room and all social laws, and applicable also when a mind studies the happiness of mankind, and when the heart feels as though it were a loving mother of the human race. If we ponder over things, we can not but conclude that the Nile of gentility has not enjoyed its great June rise, that flood which shall pour untold wealth into the valley of mankind. We hope the rain is now falling in the mountains which will make this rich inundation.

Our Western race seems to have come to an era of enlarged terms. All the cardinal nouns and verbs of our language are swelling like the lily-buds in spring.

The word "liberty" has opened so as to admit all complexions and conditions; the word "religion" has expanded so as to admit millions once shut out from the arena of love; "power" has expanded so as to add the steamships to the oar of the galley slave; the word "benevolence" has expanded until it implies good will everywhere

and forever. Into this transmuting and purifying age the word "gentleman" has been tossed, and soon it will not mean a man who could ride well after the hounds in old Virginia or in merry England, or could write a love letter in the style of Addison or Cicero, nor will it stand for a modern graduate who can handle an oar or a bat like a Greek athlete, but it will burst its old confines and mean a perfect body occupied in each drop of blood by a great and beautiful intellect. Is this to expect too much of our race? The drift of all things compels us to see a great future for man. The advent and reign of a new manhood is not only possible, but it is near.

Whoever recalls the whole life of ex-President Hayes, sees the lad in his first years, sees him at college, sees him on the banks of the Ohio in schools of the law, sees him afterward at home, as perfect there as any domestic picture earth can show, sees him in power and afterward in private life, can not but feel that it is not difficult to be a gentleman.

It is only to run in one of those ways of wisdom which are full of pleasantries and peace. Our literature helps point out the new path, our art helps, our religion helps with its tender love,

our Nation helps with the eloquence of its great ideas. If mental and moral progress moves on through the next century, persons then living will possess and behold a more delicate and more widely spread nobleness that can be seen in these times; for although our earth and our race are old, a high nobleness is yet young. If so beautiful in youth, what will this gentility be in the high noon of its career?

Inasmuch as public men are the lawful themes of remark and the lawful objects of study, it is not necessary for us to close our eyes to the high nature of that resolve which led the President-elect to make a long journey that he might stand by the fresh grave of a faithful servant of the nation, and might help lament that goodness, however marked, is always moving toward the tomb. To the call of friendship, the call of humanity was added. A sensitive ear could not easily be deaf to such a pathetic invitation. In the Florence of Angelo's time all men paused a moment on the street when a funeral cortege was passing. Death was greater than business or pleasure. It was the king whom all must salute. When the President-elect journeyed across states,

when he commanded all the work around him to hush while the coffin of a public man was being borne toward its place in the snow and grass, he acted within the borders of that high gentility which long, long ago began to draw its richly colored line between the refined citizen and the barbarian.

Few are the young men who yet realize what a power and what a happiness are contained in the simplest ideal, manhood. The reason of man's being is sought in wealth or in notoriety or in what is called by the fascinating name of pleasure. But it is quite certain that those reasons of existence are poor when compared with the possession of a character which is beautiful to have and to reveal, and which is an ample passport to the world on either side of the grave. Not many can be poets, not many can be orators, but millions can have what poetry and eloquence can only express. After an orator has expressed the genius of a country, others must come to live and act the nation's life. Orators, therefore, need not be numerous. One man can utter a sentiment, but it is worthless until the millions have planted it in their hearts. The Scottish chief blew his

horn in the mountains, and then out of every ravine and thicket and cave came the brave soldiers of Wallace and Bruce. How empty the bugle-call, were there no rush of troops! How empty the oratory of a nation, if there is no rush of men to obey its high mandates! The men who utter eloquence must divide honors with the men who obey it. What our age needs is not that each public man be an orator, but that the state, the city, the church, the home, shall contain the men who are living a life befitting so advanced a period.

The New Testament writer known as St. James could delineate a high manhood. It was "pure, peaceable, gentle, full of mercy, not fickle nor false." But, after a few years had passed, none came to live the higher life. The savages rolled down upon the cultivated races, and when Christians and Romans emerged from the ruins, they, too, had lost the moral worth of St. James, and of that One who had created and inspired a group of saints. In the late years of our nation so many noble men have lived and gone down into noble graves, gone in such a richness of character, that the heart may well hope that an age of a high humanity is about to come. The remem-

brance of many who have recently left our world is the memory of lives well lived—lives in which kindness and intelligence and action were grandly mingled. These lives have not resulted from Christianity alone. Religion alone may create only a fanatic. To explain them we add to religion the wide learning of the age and the sense of light born of the republic. Religion alone is a poor outfit for a traveling soul. The barbarous tribes are deeply religious. Knowledge alone will leave the heart poor. Liberty alone France possessed in her reign of terror. It is when a religion like that of Jesus joins a wide and deep intelligence, and when both act in a nation dominated by all the rights of man, the highest type of character becomes easily possible. The present time may forgive an American if he should fail to become a Methodist or a Presbyterian, but there can be no forgiveness for him should he fail to become a gentleman. In defense he can not plead the inadequacy of evidence, the mystery of doctrine, the old cruelties of the church, or the errors of the holy books. The arguments in favor of gentility are clear as the sunbeams and are unanswerable forever.

It is well known that our land is producing more noble characters than any other nation ever produced, yet it is also well known that a vast swarm of young men are extracting nothing from our education or our religion or our profound study of human rights. Their ideals are low. They study the laws of the toilet, they become skillful in their judgment of liquors, they know all the paths of vice; if there is anything disgraceful they find it, if there is anything infamous they love it. This crowd, although large, is not as overwhelming as it was when it sunk Rome. Then all the sons of statesmen and scholars and orators became gamblers and drunkards and gluttons. In our day it is necessary for a youth only to wish to see moral excellence and, behold, it rises up all around him like the beauties of land and sea on the horizon. We stand encompassed by beautiful lives and impressive graves. The musical voices of the living are joined by the musical memories of the dead.

The youth who has high aspirations must close his eyes to the littleness of an age and save his mind and heart for the vision of goodness and greatness. As artists on their noble studies of

nature do not sit down to sketch a malarial bog, or some piece of deadness or repulsiveness, but go to where a mountain of pines rises up from a flowery field, or to where the smiling ocean lifts the soul toward infinity, thus the youth who hopes to make high use of his stay upon earth must look long and with rapture upon those fields of human life where humanity unfolded itself in more colors than a whole summer-time can contain, and in a breadth and depth which no ocean can equal.

Our New Era.

And he that sitteth upon the throne said: Behold! I make all things new.—Rev. xxi. 5.

When Paul was making a sojourn in Athens, he marked this peculiarity of all those citizens and visitors who enjoyed any leisure—they spent their time in hearing or telling some new thing. They would meet daily in the public temples or common resorts and spend hours over the facts or theories of the time. A recent traveler in Greece says that the higher natives will surpass all other races in their willingness to sit early and late at a table to discuss the morals and politics of the whole world. The passion for political thought seems to link modern Greece with that of Socrates and Plato.

It may be that Paul in his zeal for the young Christianity felt a little contempt for those Athenians; but he should have admired their mental drift, for, if he had just espoused a new religion, he ought to have commended that Greek spirit which was always looking for the newest thought and truth. The Athenians soon gathered around Paul and persuaded him to go up to the hill

of Mars, and in that quiet place tell them all about his new Galilean theology. Great changes have come since that conference took place, but all these changes have come through that longing of the mind after new things.

We must not forget to make a distinction between the world's childish delight in novelties and its hunger after new truths and new things. It is always easy for a virtue to become a vice. A little child, eager for a new toy each day, is an object at which we may laugh or complain; but we can not complain or laugh at a Newton, who was eager to learn something new regarding the stars; nor at Columbus, who was eager to learn something new about the ocean which rolled at the West. In the conduct of the playing children we see only a foolish fickleness, but in the longings of the astronomer and the navigator we see one of the noblest qualities of the human mind. It is better, perhaps, not to designate the rapid changes of childish taste as a vice; it is rather the infant stage of a love for the new. Later years temper and guide this passion, just as the poets of the world are nothing else than the dreaming children of the earth carried onward to

a high standard of thought and language. When the little child rushes to its mother and tells her that it saw some lions and bears in the back yard, or saw some Indians stealing children from the park, that child is not wholly out of harmony with the John Milton who saw angels firing guns in Heaven, or with John Bunyan, who saw Giant Despair making life so sad for Christian and Hopeful.

Bunyan's giant caught these two travelers sleeping on his ground. He locked them up in a dark dungeon from Wednesday until Saturday, "without one bit of bread or drop of water or ray of light." At times the old giant went into the den and beat his captives with a crab-tree cudgel. On Saturday Christian remembered a key he possessed, called "Promise," and with that he opened the door, and away they both ran. This is a childish dream carried up toward a mental perfection—a dream full of truth, for all older ones know that the key of promise will help them away from the old Giant Despair.

The fancies of young children and much of the fickleness of early life are the seed or the promises of that love of new things which at last

is the glory of our race. Man was created and placed in a very imperfect world. It must have contained little indeed. Could we reproduce the far-off scene which lay between the two poles a million years ago, we should see a spectacle of human poverty of which we know little. To reach some faint hint of that old emptiness we might even to-day repair to the African bushmen and see a picture of the human creature before his fancy had begun to work.

Those bushmen do not assemble like the Athenians, to tell and learn some new thing. They would not lead a Paul away to a Mars Hill that he might regale them with a sketch of a new Jesus and a new faith. They have only a small language. They deal most in gestures and must build a fire when they would talk at night. Their language is to be seen rather than to be heard. They have not reached the power to build a house. They have not yet reached the intellect that can dream of wonderful things with our little children, or with our old Miltons and Bunyans. With them life is not infinite. It is very limited and very small. They do not make any progress, because they are incapable of think-

ing of any new condition. Many of them eat to the uttermost, and then attempt, by some narcotics, to sink into sleep. They love unconsciousness more than they love the vexation of thought and life.

Could we go back and see the human race through its whole extent in time, we should find one of its great turning points to be in that day in which men first began to inquire of each other about some new thing, and in which the heart began to dream of vast and blessed changes. Happy day to the primitive human race when some angel came and sung out from the sky: "Behold! I will make all things new!" With that voice in the sky, humanity began to toss itself forward. Its heart turned toward the new.

Those evolutionists who make man a natural result of other animals, and who identify man with the fish and bird, leave us all bewildered by the fact that no animal except man ever dreams of a new thing, a new surrounding, a new happiness. Man is the only form of life that loves the new. Before man there is always rising the picture of a better world—not of heaven only, but of a better earth. All dumb brutes are finite; man struggles with the infinite.

There is a bird in Australia that makes a little garden, that plants seeds, that makes a sitting-room in which birds may assemble; but this dear little creature has no dreams of a home better than the one it builds; it has no dreams of an America beyond the sea; it is never troubled with any thoughts of the beyond. You can not even ask it about God, or life, or death, because its mind is not capable of an inquiry. Man is the only animal to which you can speak of the future. His world reaches backward and forward; and thus he separates himself from all other creatures and touches the infinite. If you speak to the horse about eternity the words are all lost; speak to man about it and he weeps. Thus between man and all other creatures a gulf lies which materialists have not bridged.

Modern civilization comes from a source far more hidden than the fountains of the Nile. At least the source of the enlightened humanity is more hopelessly hidden, for Africa could be examined mile by mile and foot by foot until it should be compelled to give up the secret; but it is impossible now to traverse the realms of old races, and find what stages it passed through on

its way to its historic condition. In this absence of fact we are permitted to believe that when man had advanced so far as to dream of new things, then his progress set in in a full power. Man's civilization has slowly emerged out of his mental superiority in this one particular—the power to project a new future. The human race has been created by its dreams. In its poverty it has been able to think of wealth; in its slavery it has been able to lay plans for liberty; in its taste it has been able to think of more and more beauty; in its many tears it has been able to think of more happiness. Thus the dreams of which we often make sport are the dearest hopes of our race. Even if man's individual "ship" does not come in, the ship of his race comes. "The Castles in Spain" hide in those playful words the real and noble mansions of many a nation. Man's dreams reveal his power. They are the early dawning of his brilliant day.

Go back along any of the great paths and we soon find the human mind growing eloquent over its future. The result is the same whether you open a holy book or only a volume in common

literature. At some page it breaks out into a rhapsody over human progress. Isaiah stands for the Hebrew commonwealth and empire: "Ho every one that thirsteth! Come ye to the waters, even he that is without money. Come, take wine and milk without money and without price. * * * My promise shall not return unto me void. It shall accomplish what I please. Ye shall go on with joy and be led forth in peace. The mountains and the hills shall break forth before you into singing, and all the trees of the field shall clap their hands. Instead of the thorn shall come up the fir tree, and instead of the briar shall come up the myrtle." Isaiah went so far as to picture a day when all the wild beasts should put aside their ferocity and be led along by a little child.

The substance of such a vision is all to be found in the philosophy of Socrates and Plato. In Virgil it springs up again in nearly the words of Isaiah. Virgil sang: "A great age will come. A high quality of years will be born. A more divine race will appear, and iron will yield up its place to gold. The serpents and the poisonous weeds will perish. The fields will grow yel-

low with the ripening corn, and the sap of the oak will be honey."

In the Dream of Scipio, written perhaps by Cicero, all this triumph of man is seen beyond the river of death: There Scipio sees his parents and friends and loved ones in an image grander than life and in a nobleness that made earth seem humble. These and many similar passages all united in declaring man to be a child of destiny— a mind that can urge its world always onward and can make all things redouble their value.

Against Henry George's theory of non-ownership of land, some one quoted a sentence from a writer of the former century: "Give man the secure possession of a bleak rock and he will turn it into a garden; give him a nine-year lease of a garden and he will turn it into a desert." This old sentence illustrates the fact that man did take his desert world and did make a garden out of it. It stands all beautified in Greece and Italy and France, beautified everywhere because man, the dreamer, has lived in it and with it. Although life has been too much like a lease for man's perfect peace for all hours, yet nearly all talent and love have acted as though they were to

dwell here forever. When man is in his full power his heart acts as though it were to beat forever. Owning this world he turns the barren rock into a garden, and all this great change comes through his perpetual dream of a new greatness and a new beauty.

There was given to man in the beginning a very simple world, but its possibilities were infinite. We must, therefore, conceive of society as marching from one to infinity. New ideas must come each day. There can be no such thing as a fixed politics, or a fixed social life, or a fixed religion. When the sun sets each evening we bid farewell to the world of that day. It will never return. The rising sun of the next morning says: "Behold! I shall make all things new." The world will waken to new thoughts. The kings have attempted to make the human race stand still, but not all the power of empires has availed to keep crowns from falling and liberty from springing up from the dust. The Calvinists attempted to make their creed perpetual, but what flourished so triumphantly in a past century dies suddenly in this period. The Roman Catholic Church is carried along by the same irrepress-

ible growth of the race, and, boasting of being founded upon a rock, finds that its rock moves. The laws of the universe do not know any difference between the Protestant and the Catholic, the republican and the democrat. It cries out to all: March from A to B; and soon the ground trembles beneath the footsteps of men. All the known powers of money, church and state can not keep humanity still. One might as well put a heavy stone on the shadow of a tree to keep the sun from moving.

What, then, is conservatism? Conservatism is the desire to keep society from moving to a worse condition. It is also a desire to keep man from running madly when he ought to move slowly. It is also a desire to remain in a safe place while in great doubt. It is often a sending out of a dove to see if the deluge has ceased. Conservatism has no meaning whatever when it is arrayed against progress. It is, in such cases, only a dignified name for stupidity. Much of modern conservatism is only a profound satisfaction taken by a man in a selfish or stupid life. If you would find the lawful arena of conservatism, read in the "Vicar of Wakefield" that chapter in

which Moses was sent to town to sell the family horse. The family was in great poverty, and had to part with its domestic pet. In the evening Moses returned. He had sold the animal for £3 15s. and 2d. This price was low enough to make the family weep. But the worst had not been told. Moses had not received cash for the noble pet, but he had taken a box of green spectacles which were said to be worth the alleged sum. Moses ought to have possessed conservatism enough to make him bring back the horse unsold. Thus, conservatism is a wall between society and the insanity of crime or blind folly; but when a new and true idea comes, this wall is to be torn down, and we must all move out and move on. The sweetly new is a voice from the sky. It is the dove returning with an olive leaf in its mouth, thus telling us to leave the old, dark ark and move out into the fresh, sunlit world.

The early phrenologists found in the brain a department wholly devoted to wonder. Impelled by that quality of the mind, the little child is forever asking questions of its patient mother. It wonders: What are the stars? What is on the moon? What makes the thunder and the light-

ning? What makes the snow? What makes night? Who taught the birds to sing? Who painted the flowers? Who made God? What is sleep? What is death? Oh, marvelous and divine island in the soul's ocean! Oh, enchanting land beyond any described in fable or history! Long after man has passed out of childhood his wonderment runs on and on, and, should he live a hundred years, he passes all his last days in deep wondering. The scene becomes too great for him. In his limited circle he struggles with the infinity around him. If he climbs a height he sees more, indeed, but this new height makes the horizon more sweeping. The questions which childhood asks increase in all after years. The heart simply does not utter them because it has no longer a mother to whom to run. In an infinite and silent wonderment mother and son at last meet.

This is the corner of the brain which at last makes poetry and then baffles it. One of the poets says:

"Where lies the land to which our ship must go?
Far, far ahead, is all her seamen know.
And where the land she travels from? Away,
Far, far behind, is all that they can say."

Another poet asks:

> "Oh, where will be the birds that sing
> A hundred years to come?
> The flowers that now in beauty spring
> A hundred years to come?
> The rosy lip, the lofty brow,
> The heart that beats so gayly now?
> Oh, where will be the beaming eye?
> Joy's happy smile and sorrow's sigh
> A hundred years to come?"

Out of this perpetual wonderment of the mind comes much of the fact and splendor of humanity. Armed and inspired by this wonder, man starts out as a barbarian and comes in at last with a civilization. The Greek wondered if there were not a more perfect face, a more perfect form, and out of his longings came a high art. The Greek woman wondered if woman must be a slave forever. Out of her anxiety came a Sappho, a poetess and writer to rival the fame of Pericles. Christ wondered if there might not be a nobler human career, and to-day his name is worn by all the greatest nations. A sailor once wondered if there might not be a hemisphere to the west. His wonder at last secured three ships and afterward pulled the old thick veil off two continents.

Encompassed by such a long series of scenes, we can not but conclude that the highest duty of society is to compel its flagging soldiers to march on toward a better future. We must always appeal to our fainting hearts and tell them that God and nature have ordered an advance. We must be young even in old age, because, when a man is ninety, his church and state and city are still young. Each day they begin a new life. A new socialism is here, a new orthodoxy is here, new books are here, new art, new songs, new prayers, new beauty. The man of white hair must live and die in a new world. Only his body can be old. All of the great things longed for come, and, being noble, they take their place among the treasures of civilization. America is the land which Columbus longed for; and its freedom to-day is that of which the Washingtons all dreamed. In our country are to be found now the garnered longings of years.

There is a vast difference between a great new age and an age of novelties. There are young men who keep up with the age by ordering a new kind of coat. Its corners are more rounded than they were yesterday. These youths

carry a lighter walking stick and hold it in a new way. So are there ladies who keep up with the age by purchasing a new kind of hat. Of these matters and persons civilization takes no note. It does indeed remember that the Greek men and women did not change their style of robe, head-dress and girdle once in a thousand years. This release left them time to become great in intellect, and the important fact is, that, in that land of manhood and womanhood, changed a poor body for a better one, and a common mind for one more gifted, low art for high art, and the mutterings of savages for a language and literature rich beyond all description. The heart fond of novelties is only an infant's heart when compared with a soul that gathers up the mighty truths and feelings of a new period.

On the coast of the German Ocean women and children, and men also, are constantly walking to and fro looking in the sand for the lumps of amber cast out by tide and storm. Here, in this great republic, a large company of minds has walked to and fro on the shores of a new ocean, and valuable is the wealth they have

found. It has come from both war and peace. Never walked the wondering, longing mortals upon sand so rich. They have found liberty, education, rights, a religion of deeds and love, all the arts in beauty beyond those seen by Phidias or Zeuxis, music far beyond what the past ever heard, and then a public taste for a goodness and beauty higher still and much more abundant. The divine voice, "I shall make all things new" has been sacredly kept to our age. A new civilization has come rapidly, as though weary of its long delay.

To you who live in this part of the noble earth much of these material and mental riches has come. You have not strolled on life's shore in vain. You have found amber in the sand; but whom will you elect as guardians of these treasures and longings of the new West? What men will you choose to execute your ideas of well being and well doing? What men will you appoint to utter all your noblest thoughts and to embody them in the city's public and private life? What men will express your taste or your eloquence? Can the depraved take care of the splendor the noble have created? The answer is

loud and distinct. A new and splendid age needs a new politics. It is a crime to gather up goodness and beauty from all places and times and then ask the saloons and city bedlams to fashion our politics. More than we need new statues, new pictures, new music, new temples, new parks, we need a new municipal life. A great age must create a great politics. The men who make an era must save it and love it. A party should rise up out of the new time, that the new time might stand guardian of its own mental treasures. We early perceive two large religious groups in religion—the Protestants and the Catholics, and two large political groups, each of which four groups could contribute some mind fully adequate to speak and act for the time. Civilization does not indeed know anything about the lines that divide men into parties in church or state. Civilization can take note of only intelligence and virtue, but human brotherhood sees and feels these lines, and, therefore, the new politics would best look upon human friendship as being one of its latest and best principles. Each of the great groups should contribute its most noble and typical mind, and

these minds, working together, should take care of the civilization they love and have helped to create.

This angel of the sky having said to all the races which have come and gone, "I will make all things new," having said these words to the first artist who attempted to carve or paint beauty, having repeated them to the first orator who wished to speak, and to the first poet who attempted to be the mouthpiece of the human heart, having flung the rich promise to the first full soul that ever attempted to express a sentiment in song, having cheered the first citizens who ever dreamed of founding a republic—this kind angel, crowned and loving as the Creator himself, comes at last to each faithful man when he is dying, and while earth is receding whispers to him in that moment, when all the dear things seem passing away forever, and says, "Behold, dying heart, I will make all things new!"

Tributes

Tribute Verses.

By Frank W. Gunsaulus.

Where gentle waves come slowly into shore,
   Beside the sea-green splendor, loved and praised,
Sleeps his last sleep the poet-priest, who bore
   Man's soul to heaven, in dear hands upraised.

He swung no censer fragrant with sweet fire;
   His was the incense of God's fairest thought;
He held the chalice of the soul's desire;
   His faith with jewels all its gold enwrought.

His priestly robe, all beauteous with gems,
   Was holy eloquence, and truth, and love;
He knew how poor are earth's best diadems;
   His were the riches of the life above.

Our poet-preacher, in his words of prose,
   Made life a lyric, and its dreams sublime;
Far from his musing and his hope there goes
   Eternal music for the sons of time.

No son of thunder, with a lightning stroke
   Smiting an ice-field in his furious blast;
His was the sun-burst, as from heaven it broke,
   Sure of its triumph when the noise had passed.

Light, white as Heaven, warmth, as soft as tears,
   Came from his genius like an April day.
So, melting dogmas with their twilight fears,
   Summer hath conquered in the breath of May.

Hard were the bands that held the feet of Truth,
  Weary of cold, and frozen into creeds;
His sunny soul hath kissed her lips and youth;
  Lo, Truth comes bearing harvestings of deeds.

His was the fragrance when the storm is done—
  Breath of the lilies when the sky is clear.
Through all the tumult, God had this strong son
  Telling our doubtings: "*The Divine is here.*"

One to this prophet were the good and true—
  One with all beauty in the earth and sky;
His was the faith that gave this world its due;
  His was the love that laid its honors by.

He loved the Christ whose beauty was more dear
  And sweeter far than strains of angel's lyre;
For this alone—Christ filled life's deepest tear
  With God's own glory and divine desire.

Far on the edge where seas of doubt roll high,
  This soul was calm, 'midst surf and storm unvexed;
Far o'er the waves, beneath a clouded sky,
  Moved a fair soul with doubtings unperplexed.

Ye called him vague? What soul, who stands and knows
  All man would feel and all that man may find,
Waits not in silence? For truth's morning rose
  Opes leaf by leaf within the faithful mind.

Never did he with trumpet call the brave
  Round some rush-light that soon must die away.
He spake: "'Tis dawn!" when o'er the earth and wave
  Quivered the promise of a new-born day.

His was John's Gospel of the love divine;
  His was the logic of the human heart.
His was the sight, intuitive and fine,
  Finding the Savior in life's common mart.

Where, asking questions, Socrates had found
  Wisdom and silence in the open mind,
There, in old Greece, he lived in thoughts profound;
  Near the Ægean was his hope enshrined.

What hours were they, when on the streets of Rome,
  Walking with him, philosopher and seer,
Horace or Virgil led our poet home,
  Nor asked a verse to make his presence dear.

Both Greek and Roman, intellect and law,
  Found in his Christ their whole demand fulfilled.
O for the Vision and the Face he saw,
  When adoration bade the creeds be stilled!

Moan, autumn winds! His autumn-time was here;
  Ruddy and golden all the fruit he bore.
'Midst harvest sheaves and leafage brown and sere
  We say: "Farewell, but not forevermore."

Sermon

Delivered by Rev. John H. Barrows, D. D., Pastor of the
First Presbyterian Church, Chicago, at the
Funeral Service held in the
Central Church.

The power of an endless life.—Hebrews vii. 16.

The grieving multitudes gathered in this beautiful hall—the monument and memorial of the love which David Swing inspired in your hearts—are only a small part of the greater multitude who cherish his name and his life in affectionate and grateful remembrance. But we do not mourn for one who has gone out of existence. He has rather just entered into life, the full and endless life, whose ennobling, inspiring, restraining and consoling power he so beautifully proclaimed. It might have been said of him, as was said of Agassiz, that, "to be one hour in his company was to gain the strongest argument for the immortality of the soul." And these flowers, children of that beauty which he loved, the sweetness of music, these words of tender prayer and the tears which may not all be kept back, also speak, now that he has gone, not only of our affection but of our faith in the rationality and goodness of this

universe, created and governed by him who has brought life and immortality into full light through the Gospel of Christ.

Sometimes, in life, Professor Swing gave to his friends an impression of pensive loneliness, as if his heart-hunger for affection, which years and sorrows only increased, had never been satisfied. Enough of love is expressed in this meeting, at his burial hour, to content any soul. Our thoughts at this time might be: "Forever silent is that voice which, with its magic like that of the fabled music of old, built those modern walls for the service of God and man." The good gray head which all men knew, is gone from our sight. The deft spinner and weaver of the brain will offer no more fabrics for our delight. The beautiful home by the lake shore, where the father and grandfather was the center of love, is darkened, and the library in which he found companionship with Plato, and Dante, and Milton, and all the chief sages and poets, will miss the master's hand.

But these shall not be our meditations, but rather, how thankful we are for such a gift kept for us so long; how many and good are the les-

sons of his character, and how abiding the fruits of his wisdom. When great men have died, it was his wont to speak of them from this pulpit. He not only surveyed the wide world of letters and of action, enriching other minds with his thought, but how tenderly he always spoke of the illustrious dead, as one by one they sank from sight—Sumner, Garfield, Phillips, Beecher, Blaine, Phillips Brooks, Tennyson, Whittier, Browning, Dr. Patterson, and the rest. What a genius he had for appreciating the good and great, and how little disposition to believe evil and to point with snarling criticism at supposed imperfections!

We covet his skill and his temper in speaking our thoughts to-day. No one in our city was more esteemed by all classes of men for his humanity, which reached not only to the poor of his kind, but to the dumb animals. His modesty, his wisdom, his scholarship, his gentleness, drew to him men and women of many types. Old controversies had worn themselves out, and men valued him for what he was. He was our most famous citizen, or, with Mr. Moody, the evangelist, and Miss Willard, the reformer, he was one of

our three most famous citizens, and he is mourned to-day by devout and loving souls throughout the Northwest and all over America. It was to this place that other men of fame, coming to our city, flocked on Sunday, somewhat as they used to go to Plymouth Church in Brooklyn, or as they are now found in Westminster Abbey. Our friend, your pastor and teacher, will be mourned beyond the seas, by good men in London, and in other lands, and even in far-off Calcutta the tears will fall in Peace Cottage when Mozoomdar learns that his friend has gone before him.

But here the Catholic and the Methodist, the Baptist and the Congregationalist, the Presbyterian and Episcopalian, the Unitarian and the Jew, feel that a brother has been taken, and the city will seem impoverished to many thousands, even though they feel that his life on earth will continue, since he has joined "the choir invisible of those select souls whose music is the gladness of the world."

It is natural for us, in comparing him with other men, to say that he ranks with Frederick W. Robertson and Dean Stanley, with Bushnell and Beecher, in the temper of his mind and the

quality of his thought; but I prefer, without any comparison, to think of David Swing as a genius, unique, original, doing faithfully the work to which he believed he was called in the peculiar circumstances of his life. That life is very familiar to those whom I address. We call before our minds his early career—his father a pilot on the Ohio, a man of stern temper but of strict integrity, on whose tombstone are written the words, "He was an honest man;" the meager advantages of his younger years, his going up to college from the farm at Williamsburg, where he had read a few borrowed novels and Calvin's Institutes, and gained a good start in Latin; his successful student career, his companionship with men who became famous, his success as a teacher of the classics, his call to this city, and the pastorships of the Westminster and Fourth Presbyterian churches, the breadth and originality of his preaching, the heresy trial, his acquittal by the presbytery, the renewal of the charges before the synod, his withdrawal from the Presbyterian Church, the organizing of the Central Church, the building of this hall, the widening of his fame and influence, and the twenty years of his faithful preaching.

At the Miami University he roused the enthusiasm of all, and whenever he lectured or preached, the college and village poured out their throngs to hear him, as the great cities did in later years; and those who heard him at the beginning remember well that his ideas were as unconventional and broad from the start as in later times, and the temper of his mind was the same, while his literary style, fashioned by his genius and his familiarity with the classic poets, was the same Virgilian prose as that which has captivated so many thousands.

He will be remembered as a preacher of a new type. He stood before you luminous with a heavenly light, his features made lovely by his thought, discoursing of the life of man, "the life of love, the divine Jesus, the blissful immortality." He found in the Bible, to use his own words, "the record of God's will as to the life and salvation of his children." He did not preach like others, but according to the bent of his own genius. His discourse might not harmonize with Professor Phelps' definition of a sermon; it was not always a popular speech on truth derived directly from the scriptures, elaborately treated

with a view to persuasion, but there was a quiet power which moved many minds, as fiery exhortation or elaborate exegesis does not always move them. With ethical enthusiasm, with luminous intelligence, with gentle sympathy, he made known his faith in God's goodness and man's possibilities. His intellectual refinement was extraordinary, and it seems almost an irony of fate that this rude city of the West should have held the most cultured and æsthetic of American preachers, as it certainly seems strange to millions that out of Chicago one year ago there blossomed the fairest flower of art the earth has ever seen.

And here, through all these years, David Swing taught the people to love God and man. "We find in the Christian church," he said, "the ideal service of our Heavenly Father. It is one among ten thousand, and, in its leading head, Christ, it is spotless." He had a zeal for righteousness, and this came with his blood, for he was descended from the Protestant Germans who were driven out of the Palatinate. He was a reformer who did not come over in the Mayflower. But, though not of New England parentage, he knew the meaning for liberty of that

little ship which, as he said, carried "a continent and a republic."

But he was no fanatic, demanding impossibilities or advocating any rigorous asceticism of conduct; he loved all the humanities and the gracious pleasures of life, while he denounced with quiet earnestness all public and private sins. His civic patriotism was not less marked than his genuine Americanism, and his last sermon, given here only three weeks ago, told what he thought of the recent troubles which have imperiled our liberty. And we shall do well to listen again to the last words he ever uttered in his pulpit:

"Oh, that God, by His almighty power, may hold back our Nation from destruction for a few more perilous years, that it may learn where lie the paths in which, as brothers just and loving, all may walk with the most of excellence and the most of happiness."

It was excellence and happiness which he strove to advance in every way, and he helped to teach us faith in ourselves as we are brought under the power of truth and goodness. By his life and words he showed that the art of Athens and the diviner art of Jerusalem may have a

home among us. As he felt deeply that men are to be aided best through hope and through generous praise, he would not fix his mind on the evil only. He said: "If we come to think that all are worshiping gold, we, too, despairing of all else, will soon betray ourselves by bowing at the same altar."

He seemed free from the greed of gain himself, and stood and shone as a beautiful intellectual light in our city. You who are members of this congregation are glad that you furnished the golden candlestick from which his life streamed out, and that you were yourselves the medium through which that light first passed to others. He called our thoughts away to the better aspects of the age, and while men were scanning with eager envy the deeds of the millionaires, he bade us mark "how our scholars hurried to the far West to study the last eclipse of the sun, and how a score of new scientists met on that mountain-top to ask the shadow to tell them something more about the star depths and the throne of the Almighty." Who else in our times has preached more continuously and persuasively the gospel of a kingdom of God on earth?

I need scarcely analyze the qualities of his mind, they were so palpable to the community. His extraordinary mental resources are well known, the poetic and, perhaps, mystic cast of mind, his love of music, his love of art, his delight in beauty, his familiarity with all that is best in literature, and, I may add, his good judgment of public men and measures, his level-headedness and lack of that foolish credulity in believing almost every evil of successful men which marks a certain narrow, fastidious, and pessimistic type of character. After the great fire he proved himself in practical ways a most efficient helper of the needy, giving himself, in company with a dear friend, to the work of caring for the destitute. He had a faculty of drawing to his side the men of civic might and influence, and if you will read his declaration and argument made during his trial for heresy, you will discover in him a power of clear, discriminating statement, and of forceful reasoning, which may surprise any one familiar only with the more imaginative workings of his great mind.

Professor Swing was not aggressive and belligerent, but if any human brother was ill-

treated, whether the Jew in Russia, or the negro at the South, his voice was quick in protest. He was not belligerent, I say, but he was splendidly persistent, holding to the truth as he saw it with a loving but invincible tenacity. It was not the noisy persistence of Niagara, but the quiet persistence of the sun and the punctual stars. He appeared to be without any ambition in the ordinary sense; he did not husband his literary resources, but poured out his thoughts with marvelous facility, never rewriting or repeating a discourse. What he wrote came from his pen without interlineation; and his memory was so tenacious that he required no memorandum book for thoughts and facts. He always knew where to find what he required. He deemed it a blessing that his old sermons were burned up in the fire, since he was delivered from the temptation to fall back on what he had done.

And you will know that he was a man of deep and quick sympathies; many of us will cherish the words he wrote to us in sorrow as among the sweetest and most comforting that ever came from a Christian heart. He was deeply attached to his old friends, and especially to this

city, where for nearly thirty years his voice has been heard in behalf of righteousness and love. He, whom we mourn, loved Chicago as it loved him, and though he once made a European journey, his heart never traveled, and he always preferred to see the Old World through the eyes of the poet and historian, and to dwell here among his old friends.

And you all remember how his wit and humor were as remarkable as his affectionateness and his imagination. He may have been tempted to satirize too keenly at times, and too frequently, the theological conservatism against which his life was a protest; but surely here is a weapon which good men have a right to use, and he employed it as the friend of God and man. I scarcely know of anything better in its way than his recent picture of the slowness of the human mind, even in this age of express trains and telegraphs. "Our moral world," he said, "is dragged by oxen. It has no railroad speed. The railway carries men's bodies rapidly, but it never interferes with the old slow speed of intellect. The intellect of the church always travels in the oxen's cart." But we bless God that it does travel, and

an ox cart in twenty years will make the circuit of the globe.

And what shall I say of our friend's permanent influence? If tolerance in religion be the best fruit of the last four hundred years, according to the words of President Eliot, written on the vanished Peristyle, then David Swing's contribution to the tolerant spirit was a large addition to our civilization. Who has done more to make us love those who do not think with us, and to eradicate the notion that one's own form of goodness or faith must be accepted by others, if they are to share our hope in God and immortality? He was acute and broad enough, as some are not, to perceive that the truest spirit of tolerance flourishes, not only among those who believe but little, but also among Christians who believe very earnestly the general creed which Christendom has proclaimed through more than eighteen centuries. This man helped to bring us out of the backwoods theology, which was extremely useful in its time, but was contentious and fitted to a rougher generation, and was not sufficiently ethical, and was not just either to God or man.

He suffered, and younger men have breathed freer air because of what he endured in behalf of spiritual breadth and freedom. Thousands of Presbyterians will now applaud what he said at his trial. "Much as I love Presbyterianism, a love inherited from all my ancestors, if, on account of it, it were necessary for me to abate in the least my good will toward all sects, I should refuse to purchase the Presbyterian name at so dear a price." He helped forward the movement for revising the Westminster Confession, and the more logical and important movement for displacing it by a shorter, simpler, more scriptural statement. He helped to make possible such an exhibition of the grandeur of religion and the brotherhood of all religious men, as that which last year, in his own words, made this lake shore "almost roseate with the passing chariot of the Infinite."

Professor Swing is lovingly praised by many who do not share his theological views; and his influence was large, and will grow larger, over many thoughtful minds that prefer to remain closer than did he to historical Christianity. They have learned, in part from him, to look on the

other side, on what I may call the ethical and literary side of Christian truth. He was influenced more by the poets than by the theologians. It has been said by Dr. Munger that the greater literature is prophetic and optimistic, it is unworldly, it stands squarely upon humanity, its inspiration is truth, and it is corrective of poor thinking, of that which is crude, extravagant, superstitious, hard, one-sided. This influence will continue to emancipate and illuminate the Christian mind. More men will yet feel that they will live a truer and more Christly life by cherishing gentler thoughts of other good men, and by a larger faith that the spirit of God is working everywhere. You love to hear his voice, and, therefore, listen to him once more. " We may love our garden and home tenderly, but we must not trample down the field of another; but each morning when the dew hangs upon our vines, we must confess that it glistens as well in the parks of our neighbors, and sparkled before we were born, and will be full of sunbeams after we are dead."

Now that he has gone, how many of us wish that we had known him better! And yet, many

felt that he was their friend, and that they knew him well, though they may never have sat at his table or conversed with him familiarly of high themes. Their souls have had sympathetic communion with his spirit, and every week they have talked with what was best of him. For several years it was my fortune to live within a few miles of the poet Whittier, and I never thought it needful to intrude myself into his home in order to know him; for had he not spoken his choicest thoughts to me for twenty years? Had I not fallen in love with his "Maud Muller" in the hayfield? Had not his "Barefoot Boy" been my friend? Had I not pitched my tent of imagination on the Atlantic beach with him, and had I not felt his summer-heart even when snowbound in the icy solitudes of winter? Had I not watched with the "Quaker Poet" on election eve, when the fate of freedom was in jeopardy, and with his childhood's playmate had I not felt the Mayday flowers "make sweet the woods of Follymill," and had I not heard "the dark pines sing on Ramoth Hill the slow song of the sea?" Had not his psalm been to me like David's? And why should I look at the features of the "Hermit

Thrush of Amesbury" to know the music of his soul?

All this is true with many of our friends. It was true of David Swing, and it will remain peculiarly true now that he has gone. He still speaks to us, and we may know his inmost heart; his soul lies open before us on the printed pages, and if that which is keyed to universal truth is not to be outgrown, why should not men and women read for generations the thoughts of David Swing? Why should they not read him as they do Sir Thomas Browne and Jeremy Taylor and Emerson? Who can hope to clothe in more beautiful garments the sweetest forms of heavenly truth? Who will ever write of the goodness of God in language more lucid and melodious than his? His "Truths for To-day" are truths for the twentieth century, and his "Motives of Life" are more lasting than Karnac and the pyramids. Though his greatness was literary and ethical, rather than theological, still he has influenced the popular creeds more than many theologians.

We bid farewell to a gracious spirit whose outward form we shall not see, and, while we mourn an irreparable loss, we count also his ineff-

able gain. He has crossed the bar, and it was peaceful and beautiful. He has met his Pilot face to face, and has entered the haven and found the heavenly shore in the great mystery beyond, many-peopled with those whom he loved and who were glad to welcome him. The happy immortality which he preached is a dearer delight to him than to most men. He has found selectest company there, whose thoughts were sweet to him on earth. If we could have followed his spirit's flight we might have seen something to remind us of the vision which King Arthur's friend had of his passing out of sight—

> "Then from the dawn it seemed there came, but faint,
> As from beyond the limit of the world,
> Like the last echo born of a great cry,
> Sounds as if some fair city were one voice,
> Around a king returning from his wars."

He has had a choral welcome there. All the chief friends who stood by him at the time of his sorest earthly discipline greet him yonder, and what multitudes besides! May the power of that endless life into which he has entered abide with us! A leader of thought, a prophet of the gentle humanities of Jesus, has fallen, and the old places which he loved here are desolate.

The October leaves will cover paths where he used to walk, winter will spread her white mantle over the earth, and spring, which he so loved, will come again and clothe the field with grass and blossoms; but he will not see them, nor the summer flowers, which seem to live in his speech. But we believe that his is an eternal springtime, or a beautiful, unending summer, and that more than all the loveliness which he knew on earth shall be his forever. A still living master in Israel has written: "There is only one gathering place of the great and good which shall never be left desolate; only the shade of the Tree of Life shall be always refreshing; only the stream from the Fountain of Life shall flow on without end."

The Poet Preacher.

A Sermon delivered by Dr. Emil G. Hirsch, Rabbi of Sinai Temple.

Among Biblical heroes, none has whetted the imagination of later generations to the degree that Solomon has. The bare outlines of his life as given in the Biblical record seem but a shadowy fringe to the glory of the sun which loving fancy dreamt had risen with this monarch's reign to bless Israel. He was accredited with wonderful gifts. He understood the whispered speech of the stars, the soft pleadings of the forests; he knew the secrets of the birds as they were warbled forth from bough to bough; what the ants in their council of war buried in the deepest of their hearts, Solomon was believed to have unraveled; the rivers ran but to tell him of their message and their ambition, and to inform him of the commission with which they were charged; he understood all the languages that were spoken under heaven's dome, and had power to command energies generally jealously guarded from the possession and ken of human minds. And more than this, it is said in the legends recording the

wonder-deeds of this Jewish king, that when he brought the holy ark into the temple, the very cedar wood which clothed the walls began to bloom again, and, as long as Solomon reigned, the freshness of this transplanted denizen of the heights never waned or even gave signs of withering.

All comparisons, of course, halt; and still, for one who knows these legendary and fanciful portraits of the Eastern monarch, the suggestion is ready at hand that one who had like gifts has departed from our midst. Solomon, famous for his wisdom, had powers not greater than in the providence of God were given unto him to do honor to whose memory we are gathered here this morning. Like unto Solomon he knew the speech of the trees and the tongues of the running brooks; like unto Solomon of the fable when he entered the temple, the very cedar wood began to bloom, and as long as he was present in the sanctuary the freshness did not pale and the perfume did not grow less. A miracle was wrought by his very tongue, and stone gave response, as it were, to the pleadings of the softer human heart.

The first hours of pungent grief always are heavy with the dull sense of a great loss. But perhaps the loss is but apparent, and the gain is all the more permanent. Ours, then, is the duty to measure our loss and balance it over against the permanent possession left in sacred trust with us by this life now closed. And yet we must confess that none there is who can do justice to its fullness of gifts and powers. Yea, we must be modest and remember that perhaps posterity alone can gauge the influences for good this life sent forth in this large country. While we merely may lay the finger on the roots, our children will find shade and refreshment under the crown of the tree developed into beauty.

Is not genius like those mighty rivers whose sources are the constant anxiety of geographical explorers? However far we may penetrate into the caverns of their icy birthplaces, the actual spot whence they bubble out and the real secret of their mighty sweep eludes forever the grasp of the diligent searcher.

Who has laid his finger on the cradle of Rhine or Danube? None. Who can tell us why the Nile carries its strength? None. Who,

why and how Congo was ushered into life? As yet, none. Like these rivers, genius forever is an unread riddle. However far we may push back in our climb up the heights to the sources, there remains mystery unsolved, for genius is powerful reflection of light divine, is revelation of God himself.

And so, in this our search for the mighty sources of that river which has given refreshing waters to many thirsting lips, and has wooed forth flowers along many a bank and strand, we are confronted with the old despair, if despair it be, that genius' birthplace is curtained off from the eye of man; it is in the holy of holies where God's presence abideth and into which even high priest can not penetrate except with downcast face and in humble and unknowing reverence.

None can tell whence the power came to our friend gone from us. Nevertheless, there is boot in the expedition up the heights; although the actual source be forever withheld from our knowledge, we can trace the progress of the river after it has freed itself from the mother embrace of the Alpine range. We would not presume to lay bare the curtained cradle of his

strength and might and beauty—we would modestly inquire into the currents contributory to his reservoir of power and might for good in our generation.

The law seems to be well nigh universal that genius, at birth, is not beckoned to broad roadbeds, but has to thread its way, a narrow rill, down rough and steep mountain slopes. Our old Talmudic sages proverb this observation when they say: "Have ye heed unto the children of the poor, for from them shall go forth the light of truth." The exceptions to the rule prove the law. It is generally from the gloom of poverty that the brightness of genius shines forth — ease and affluence are not necessarily adverse to the formation of character and untoward to the steeling of ruder metal into elasticity, but certain it is that, where the divine fire is slumbering, the fans of poverty woo the blaze to break forth, while the softer zephyrs of affluence seem more frequently to be fated to lull to sleep the smouldering ember underneath the ashes. So many of our greatest men in Israel were kissed awake by the light, midst the dusk of contracted outward circumstances. And outside

of Israel, in America, the galaxy of fame is studded with stars whose first beam fell not from vaulted window of palace, but from the low opening of cottage and hut.

As a rule, it is not the city, again, with its luxurious wealth of refining influences, but it is the country, apparently poor in all those things which make for culture, that wings to flight innate poetic inspiration, and voices to preach and prophesy natural, sturdy, ethical enthusiasm. Most of the poets of America were children of the open country—held communion in their early days with the laughing brooklet and the growing flower, the green meadow, the sweet-scented clover, the struggling corn, the swaying wheat, the waving forest, the singing bird, the silence of wooded dell and the mystery of the tangled ravine; not in the bustle and din and confusion and distraction of town, where commerce drives her chariots and selfishness celebrates her triumphs, does it seem possible to nursery these tender children of light and love, of budding song and burning righteousness. In the purer, even if poorer, surroundings of country hamlet— in its hard school of struggle, in the farmer's

experience, appear to lie the conditions favorable for the growth of wider sympathies and the quickening of the mind toward truth and beauty. Our lamented friend and teacher adds another name to the long roster of men come to eminence from self-respecting poverty, who had slaked their thirst for refinement, though the wells of their early country home promised but a scant flow of these living waters. He had indeed the gift of Solomon. He understood the speech of tree and the sermon of running brook. The dialect in which the queen bee marshaled her golden cuirassed host was not a foreign tongue to him, as was not the jargon of the ants legislating for their busy clan. He was the bosom friend of flower; he had mastered the secret of nature's changing robes; he had often been a guest in the chamber where are stored the garments, lacy or fleecy or ermine-seamed or flower-garlanded, of the seasons. Whence to him such wonderful knowledge? From his early days, from the schooling of the hours when he, a farmer's boy, followed the plow and handled the hoe and the rake. Yea, no academy in town could have given him this understanding; to the last of his days,

in all that he uttered and in all that he thought, breathed the fresh fragrance, the purity of the country sky. Here one of the sources, though not *the* source, of his power; for behind this knowledge of the language of nature was his mind, a revelation of the divine and, therefore, mystery shrouded from human analysis forever.

The farmer's boy, reading and interpreting nature's signs and symbols, became a poet. Hard science reads the inscription of the stars in terms of a fearful struggle—each planet whirled along by the impulse of self-preservation, opposing with all of its volume the attraction of other heavenly wanderers—and as the planetary system is kept agoing by the lubrication of struggle and strife, so science, wherever her torch lights up the nooks and corners, points us to a battle field—a warfare that knows no truce—a bristling camp deaf to the sweeter carol of peace, or the consoling choral intoned after the fray and fight is o'er. For the sciences can only analyze, and analysis is dissolution—decomposition. A flower before the bar of the sciences is calyx, pistil, stamen, anther, pollen, carpel. The flower as a whole, with its message of beauty and of peace, science

knoweth not and regardeth not. Where this scientific spirit of analysis prevails exclusively and points the compass for life's ocean, the meaning of world necessarily is set in a minor key. War unending, never eventing into peace,—should this not burden a human soul? What is this universe then but a vast machinery without purpose, without harmony even—a chaos spinning along, we know not why and we can not tell to what issue?

But what the scientist disregardeth, for it is not his concern to pay it court, that the poet remembereth, and where he, whose eye is weaponed with telescope or spectroscope or microscope, sees but the fearful scars of an endless struggle for existence, the poet, his eyes turned inwardly, beholds beauty and harmony. The love-tipped tongue of the poet sings the anthem of peace. The world is not enfolded in darkness, but is afloat in an ocean of light. Love's tokens abound everywhere, we need but open our eyes to its beaming, playful, helpful and hopeful beckoning.

The farmer's boy who had learned in the schooling of his poor home—poor in externali-

ties, rich in the eternalities of life—to read aright by the key of love and light the hieroglyphics of sky and soil, could not become the exponent of a creed of despair, nor the messenger of the call that we are doomed. He had to herald that view of life and of nature which exults that man from good proceeds to better, and that the heavens are constantly unfolding new miracles, as the fields are intoning new melodies, in swelling chorus praising a just and good God who leadeth all unto peace and final harmony.

Professor Swing's creed was that of an optimist, and one of the roots of his unshaken and unshakable optimism is his early life that led him to know nature, as few are privileged to know her, in the glory of the flowers in the garden and the greatness of that mysterious goodness which awakens from the seed the blossom and fruit, and again husks in the bud and fruit the seed for a new life—an unending life. And if his farmer-boy days thus led him to solve the equation of world in terms of ordered beauty, his book studies later confirmed the impression of his early years. Know ye that there was not in the whole of America a greater classical scholar than he upon

whose lips Sunday after Sunday the thousands hung with hunger of soul and in reverential admiration. The farmer boy of our western Ohio valley was a great student of Athens and of Rome; knowing his Virgil as but few knew him, and his Plato as but few understood him; at home in the Roman senate as in the Greek areopagus—Æschylus his daily companion and Æneas the bosom friend of his hours of study! A miracle, this, almost, and yet truth and fact. Not that there are not greater philological scholars in this country or elsewhere, but philology is always busy with the dry bones. It construes and scans. It compares broken syllable with fragmentary accent. This "dry-as-dust" method has been the curse of classical studies in Germany, and is beginning to stretch forth its octopus-like arms for new victims in our own schools. For soon will arise those among us to trumpet their find of an abnormal dative whereto to moor a new philological system! I am afraid lest, while they are rattling these dry bones, the living spark of classic culture be hidden from their blind eyes.

Among this tribe of word anatomists Swing can not be reckoned. For him classic culture was

an organic whole, and in the temple of this many-mansioned Nautilus he was a reverent minister. Greece, the people of beauty, had won his affection, and if any there ever was that appreciated the graces of the Greek muses, it was he. Beauty he had found in furrowed fields, and beauty's echo set ahumming his heart's harpstrings, through Homer and Æschylus and Sophocles and Demosthenes and Plato and Aristotle. This universe is a cosmos, beautiful harmony, is their jubilant affirmation. His studies in literature confirmed and complemented what the impressions of his early days had suggested. His mastership in classic lore is the second root of his optimism.

Poets are always optimists. Pessimism never yet has found a poetic voice. Perhaps one or the other may have enriched literature with dirge or lament. But even benighted Lenau in Germany and Leopardi in Italy do not disprove the contention that the poetic temper is essentially hopeful. The true poets have always clarioned forth the creed that through the apparent strife events harmony, that night is prelude and pledge of more radiant day. Beauty, and the creed that all things are for the good, are factors of one equa-

tion. Our friend who was at home in "the garden," and "the academy" of that wonderful people to whom we owe most of the elements of our culture—indeed found corroborated by the genius of art what the rougher touch of rustic tool had before taught him to read in the dialogues of the heavenly company, in the epos and lyric written in flowers and in ferns on the stretching and waving slopes of his home valley.

Student of antiquity as he was, Professor Swing could not become a pessimist. The farmer boy, greatest of classical scholars, had been touched by the live coal from the altar dedicated to a belief in progress toward ultimate harmony, and in the intrinsic essential goodness and beauty of life, and in the unfolding purpose of God through individual experience, and His guidance of the nations across the span of the ages.

That as a theologian the man so prepared would not make of religion a mere archæological museum of antediluvian specimens stands to reason. Loyal he was to the last to the church of his early days. Not that he treasured the dead formulæ of creed as unbroken vases of truth, but he became the mouthpiece and translator

for thousands of what is and was the most valuable possession of his sect. Strange it is, but nevertheless one may say it without fear of contradiction, it was the suspected heretic who brought about the recognition by an ever-increasing multitude of thinking men and women of the best his mother church had been the guardian of.

Say whatever you will about Calvinism; say that it is somber and suspicious of men; that it is narrow and uncharitable,—this one pretension history verifies, and those that are free from bias must own that Puritan texture is woven of a strong moral fiber; that in the hard discipline of life, of self-discipline, curbing alike his love and his passions, the Puritan trains himself to be true to the supreme and eternal law—"Thou oughtest." In the ungainliest garble of the Calvinistic creed, there is, to him who looks beneath the surface, stored away a wealth of ethical dower which softer creeds and less cramped definitions lack, or at least are not as insistent to emphasize.

In this sense, the farmer boy of the Ohio valley, the student of the Miami University, the classical scholar, the poet of the world of beauty, devel-

oped to be perhaps the most loyal son of the church which first led him to God's altars and taught him to stammer the sacred words: God, love and immortality and Savior. Through all of his later, as of his earlier sermons, rings and runs an ethical spirit, bold and deep and sweet withal. And when he found that his church was apt to cling to externals and sacrifice the eternal verities of its historic mission, of his own resolution he left his parental communion, but it was with a heavy heart. He himself, perhaps, was not fully conscious of the gap, which widened as the years lengthened, between him and his early religious affiliations. It was not he, at all events, that delighted in the breach. Swing is the exponent of the inner forces quickening within the Puritan form of presentation, and as an iconoclast, if iconoclast he be, he belongs to those,—as Oliver Wendell Holmes said of Emerson—that have no hammer. He removed the idols with such tender touch that the very removal seemed an act of worship and of reverence. The prophet may be weaponed with hammer—the poet is with harp. Which will succeed? Who knoweth? Each one has mission and scope and duty and call, but cer-

tain it is that the harp's invitation will be more readily accepted than the hammer's clank, and that the softer transmission and the tenderer transition will be less of shock than the bold surgeon's knife which cuts atwain the new-born child from the old yet loving mother.

The poet sang the fulfillment of the prophecy of his own religious youth in tones so sweet that none knew, and perhaps he not himself, that idols were falling and altars were crumbling, that a new world was rising—and still it was he who sang the birth song of this new world which necessarily is the burial song of the old, but in the angel's measure, " *Gloria in Excelsis,* peace on earth to men of good will!"

As a theologian, Swing merely carried out his poetic mission; he was the reformer who conciliated, led on but did not estrange—he was the focal point where two worlds met, each receiving from him rich tribute of love, reverence, light, but each hearing from his lips the call for new and higher possibilities. It is often thought by many who are thoughtless, that liberalism, to be liberalism, must be negative; that the true liberal must deny God, Providence,

immortality. And it is often deemed strange, if not an inconsistency, by men who are not Christians and never have been under the influence of an early Christian education, that liberal men in the Christian pulpit will continue to speak of the Christ and will not cease laying the immortelles of reverent affectionate love at the feet of the thorn-crowned prophet of Nazareth. Such pseudo-liberalism of mere denial betrays only the ignorance of him who professing it in self-sufficient conceit would criticise as inconsistent or disloyal the positive assertions of others, who, to say the least, are as liberal as he—yea, more liberal than he, because, while he does not understand, they do understand that the pathway of progressive truth is evolution and not revolution.

Is there so much new truth, after all? The unfolding process of liberalizing is, indeed, but a process of deepening and broadening the old river, which at first, indeed, was a narrow rill, but is, even in the moment of its juncture with the ocean, still the child of the earlier days and of the distant mountain peak. The Rhine is one from his Gothard birthplace to the Holland burial place—is one, if narrow at first and broad

at last—is one throughout the length of his winding course. And so is the current of truth and liberal unfolding of truth but the sweep of *one* stream. Truth digs its own new channels and feeds them from the parental stream.

We do not announce a new truth—we preach the old truth, if possible deepened and broadened and burnished and purified. But before we were, the prophet had professed. It was not we that found or formulated the announcement of the better life; Isaiah and his school had sounded it before we were born. All the principles of society to be re-constituted to-day are contained in the sermon of Isaiah and his like.

Historical continuity is the condition of liberal, truly liberal, work for fruitage. This condition the liberal may not disregard if his labor be other than the mere removing of ruins and the making of room for others. In this spirit our poet preacher of beauty plowed and planted. As a poet he could not make the universe equal to a tantalizing zero, or a negative. He read its higher value as the revelation of God; without attempting to define God or to confine him, he found him in the play of those wonderful forces

round about us. And in the steps by which humanity scaled the heights and arrived at its present position, he recognized the working of him, not ourselves, making for righteousness. He

"Doubted not that thro' the ages one increasing purpose runs,
And the thoughts of men are widen'd with the process of the suns."

The poet must be God-intoxicated, and God-intoxicated was Swing. His liberalism therefore was of true fiber. Atheist is not liberal. Atheist at best is the scavenger that removes mud and dirt and filth. But to plant the flowers more is needed than the dung-hill and what the dung-hill holds. To woo the flower into beauty there needs much more than the phosphates — there needs the seed of the flower. Has atheism ever scattered seed or ripened fruit? It owns what the garbage box can furnish and nothing more.

Yea, the truest, the most liberal men are God-intoxicated. Many churches may idol a God that is not God. If atheism is content to be protest against this fetichism one may bear with it, though not with its illiberal arrogance! But when

atheism would lay its heavy hand on the altar of nobler truth and on the truer service unto the living God, shall sound forth the warning: "Stay! lest thy hand be paralyzed," as was the hand, in the story of the Bible, of him who touched impiously God's own ark. God is. Such is the witness of the ages, their song and prophecy. And this God the liberal—this God our Professor Swing did preach Sunday after Sunday. This beautiful world is not the play-ground of blind chance, but is the symbol of a mind all engrasping, and the sign of a love all enfolding.

And this life can not be the end, is the second stanza of the poet's lay of hope. This is also the assurance of the thinker whose philosophy would complete the segment visible into the whole circle! Kant, a second Columbus, in his discovery of a new continent in the ocean of thought, a new world conception, vaticinates, for all his pure reason, of the immortality of soul; as indeed every poet has sung it from the heart; every troubled and perplexed mind crying out in the night for the light has found in this hope comfort. Our immortal friend, messenger of beauty, could not believe and did not believe that after this life

there would be less of beauty—or less of light; that sun and day would issue into primeval darkness and gloom. If thought alone had not whispered the brighter conception, his sense of beauty would have led him on to know and feel that the stars will twinkle on and the sun will shine on in the beyond, wherever we may be.

But as in his God belief he did not dogmatize, so in his immortality belief he did not presume to draft the architectural design of that heavenly home or to regulate the details of admission or exclusion. He was impatient of all such arrogance. His poetic soul uttered its deepest convictions, and in imparting them to man and world he found stay and staff and satisfaction.

And he believed in Christ. Why should he not? Who would deny that that name tokens for millions the best that world has ever seen or will see? But the Christ he taught was not a fact so much as a force. It was not a Christ that once had risen from the grave, but a Christ that is still rising from the sepulchre. His gospel was not a redemption that once had taken place, but a redemption that is to take place now, every day. The Christ, as preached by Swing, is one way of

stating the belief, which is certainly ours, in the continued life of love in man and through man in humanity. Christ to the Christian is the sublime formula hallowed by age and haloed by reverence. The sterner reformer, perhaps, wielding the ax which Abraham laid to the fathers' idols, might not have used the old term. But blessed be his use of the old term, for had he used another, many ears would have been deaf to his message that now were opened to the sweeter call of the better future through the Christlike life and the Christlike power for all the eternities. And he believed that in the personal Jesus was foreshadowed the peace of all good to be; he was certain that the words which fell from the lips of the prophet of Nazareth contained in an intensity shared by the words of no other mortal the essence of the divine, that the one life in Jerusalem and the one death on Golgotha were type of the life of humanity and its death unto a newer and nobler life.

Christ is, after all, an ideal. Each one has his own God, and each one builds his own Christ. I have a Christ in whom I believe, and so have you. We may perhaps not call it with a Greek

name, "Christ"—we may use the old Hebrew word "Messiah"; but whosoever would from the imperfect proceed to the perfect, must be filled with the messianic spirit! Swing construed for himself his Jesus. The critical scholar of the German school may, perhaps, have shaken his head and had this to object to and that to find fault with; and the old orthodox, perhaps, may have joined the liberal of the Dutch and German universities and pointed out here want of logic and there want of definiteness. What mattered that to the poet? The artist painted a Christ so perfect that whoever beheld his face was lifted up and inspired. The Christology of Swing, as much as anything that he did, belongs to the domain of the arts, and Canon Farrar, writing his book on Christ, as conceived by artists, might add a chapter on the Christ conception of Swing.

Happy the age that treasures his Christ conception. Happy the generation that is eager to behold this bright ideal outlook and uplook into the possibilities of a redemption of man as pointed to by the poet whose harp is, alas! now broken, and whose song is, alas! now hushed in silence.

The theologian was but the frame of the man, and the man eclipsed in his glory the theologian. Not that Swing was not yeoman or did not take yeoman's part in attack or defense. His rapier was sharp at point and at edge, but so good a fencer was he that when he thrust the opponent felt no pain.

He was a great humorist, and withal a keen satirist. The poet of beauty makes light of the faults of men, of the small touches of black that at intervals discolor a beautiful field of glow. The world is beautiful, and life is unto beauty, and God leads the world unto justice, and Christ rises from the grave to free men from the shackles of slavery. Why, then, lose patience with the faults and follies of men? Let us laugh them away. This is the natural conclusion of the poet temperament, and so our poet preacher laughed the faults of men away and the frailties of women. In his polemics, his humor and his satire, keen and sharp, and yet unoffending, stood him in good stead. Who has characterized the ingrained stolidity of current theology better than he did even in his last utterance? It travels in an ox-cart when all other

thought is whirling along in an electric chariot. An ox-cart may be said to circuit the world in twenty years—but an electric chariot covers the distance in eighty days perhaps, and we would rather go with the electric chariot than with the slow and steady ox cart. So might be piled one upon the other countless quaint but telling effects of his humor, all classic in construction and barbed to have results which the bolder attack of passion can not boast, even in its greatest successes.

It almost goes without saying that our lamented guide and teacher was never so eloquent as when he pleaded for justice; that his sympathies bubbled forth a crystal spring to refresh those that were down-trodden. As Jews, especially, owe we a debt of gratitude to his memory. He spoke for us when there were but few to speak. He pleaded with those who degraded their Christianity, who, professing to be Christlike, were demonlike, robbed human beings of all that could help their humanity. When the tidal wave of misery, sent on its errand by Russian cruelty, swept across the ocean to our shores, he bade the refugees welcome, denouncing with flaming tongue

a system of church and statecraft which could rob of home and almost of life millions of our brothers.

And so he pleaded for the negro in the South, for the evicted in Ireland; wherever persecution raised her hydra head and from serpent tongue hissed forth its poisoned message of distrust, he pleaded for the larger love.

He was a patriot. His sympathies embraced the world, and yet he understood full well that the large universe is a great stellar family in which each planet has its own orbit and its own elliptic, the ideal being the center, the sun, around which each one in its own path, but in company with the others, doth travel. So humanity is not made up of bare men—it is made up of men in historic communities and under historic conditions; is made up of men that have a family, that belong to a town, that are gathered in a state, is made up of men that belong to a nation. And we belong, this he felt, to the American nation—one of the missionary nations of the world if she were true to her divine appointment—the ensign bearer of liberty and of love. Ah, he loved this America and gave the best he had to

give of thought and of passion to the glorious banner of the Union.

His sermons may not have been models of theological construction. They may not have passed muster where the professor of homiletics reviews the exercises of pupils; but children of beauty, they carried conviction and thus directed aright the better inclinations of the human heart to love humanity and still not to forget country, family, state, nation and city.

And he had also a peculiar mission and position among us in these days of social distrust and social strife. We are all inclined to believe that the rich man, as such, has been and is in unholy league with all the satanic powers of hell. In the middle ages it was current superstition that stone might be turned to gold by alchemistic practices. There may be many to-day that argue that one who scales the height where money and wealth are found treasured, must be the confederate of Mephistopheles or an adept in Mephistophelian arts and sciences. It was his mission to show the other side of the picture; that not necessarily with wealth goes want of character; that wealth is an opportunity to which some are true, as poverty is an

opportunity to which some alone are true. He had been schooled in the hard college of a hard struggle in early days—struggle for bread, a struggle for the bread of life, physical, mental and moral, and certainly his sympathy was with the strugglers; but as he had risen why should not everyone rise? He believed in energy of self. He believed in the saving power of sobriety, in thrift, and in economy. He did not believe, and no one believes, that there is a royal road to ease and to peace, which we need but travel to make the goal; and thus, as the speaker of a society representative in its composition of the best in the city, he spoke to his friends of their duties to those outside of their circle. But to those outside he emphasized the knowledge, too, that not, as their distrust would lead them to believe, was the million always emblem of want of character or sluggishness of sympathies and of heart. His last message to us is indeed an appeal to be true to the American principles of liberty, of right and of duty—of regard one for the other. Perhaps in the din and in the confusion of the battle now raging, so sweet a voice as his would have been drowned. Perhaps a sterner clarion note is needed

to stir the rich to action and the poor to reflection; to despoil the impostors that now shame the sunshine of our liberty, perhaps a stronger light is needed than that soft beaming beacon of love and of beauty which was his; but in his swan-song is undying accent of truth. It is for us to translate that note into the louder appeal of duty and obligation, would we save our institutions in this hour of danger. By those who heed Swing's words our country will be lifted on the road to its final triumph—the solution of the social problem on a basis of equity and justice.

Is, now, his going from us a loss? It is, and it is not. I saw a picture this very summer in honor of a great sculptor, charmed on canvas by as great an artist of the brush. Surrounded by his very works, lies on the bed of glory, the couch of death, the sculptor who framed into life in chaste marble the children of his genius. His breaking eye is kissed in the last lingering light of the setting sun by a fair nymph, the latest of the artist's productions. What did the painter intend when in this wise he gathered around the death-bed of the sculptor all the works his fertile chisel had executed? Certainly this: the author of these children of the muses—their father in

the flesh—may be transplanted, but they that with kiss send off him who made them, the nymphs, remain to beautify and inspire, to lift up others by informing them of him who hath gone. The great and good man's love remains and his works abide. Swing is not dead to us.

He does not belong to that long procession of the great and the glorious that I beheld this summer on a canvas made prophetic by the imagination of a great painter—a long procession of the mighty of earth—Alexander, Napoleon, Frederick the Great, all riding on in stately pageant over the bodies of dead and dying, and above them—these monarchs and despots who sent unto death the thousands, the very flower of their nations—over them with averted face and weeping eyes stands the Christ. In this procession Swing has no place. He was a man of peace. How beautiful on the mountain tops are the feet of him who announces peace on earth. He belongs to another procession over which the Christ hovers, but to bless and not to weep; to those that made man better, not by the baptism of blood, but by the waters of purity and love and devotion and beauty. His works remain. He has not gone from us, and the immortality he so often put

into sweet rhythm he himself is proof of. Is he not immortal? Some one has said, and has said it rightfully, Swing is the great gulf stream— a gulf stream of influence. This influence will travel on as does the gulf stream, speeding becalmed ships, warming cold climates, tempering the winds for those in the grasp of a torrid sun, but preserving his individuality in the mighty flow—in the ebb and the tide of the ocean. A gulf stream of influence for the best, for the truest, the liberal thought of religion was he; a child of the muses, son of beauty, translating the speech of nature unto us, and transmitting the messages of the ages unto us, foretelling the glories of the future, speaking of the rising love of redemption, of the beauty of the household of God the Father, the unending life of each and all, he is now, as he was in his life, the torch-bearer of a better outlook into life, and of a broader love to bind man to man, the children of one God rising into the glories of one messianic kingdom. "Thy kingdom come" was oft his prayer. He has helped make that kingdom nearer, more real to us. Blessed be his name. זכר צדיק לברכה. "The memory of this righteous one is a blessing." Amen.

Memorial Sermon.

Preached at Plymouth Church, Chicago, by Rev. Dr. Frank W. Gunsaulus.

How beautiful upon the mountains are the feet of him that bringeth good tidings, that publisheth peace, that bringeth good tidings of good, that publisheth salvation, that sayeth unto Zion, Thy God reigneth.—Isaiah lii. 7.

WE need a line from the most rich and literary of the poets of the Hebrew nation to initiate in our hearts, and especially in our speech, any fitting recognition of the unique and precious treasure which our city and our land have lost in the death of David Swing. It is necessary, also, that it be a verse of that poetry which describes the ministry, not so much of a great ecclesiastic clad in pontifical robes, or that of an urgent contender for some revered proposition of belief, as that of the prophet who, in the echoes of yesterday and the din of to-day, perceives the soft and chastened eloquence of to-morrow, if in any way the passage may serve as a prelude to our thought of him who, for a quarter of a century, stood in the twilight, in the name of the ample dawn.

The words that will accord with our grief and harmonize with our grateful sense of what God

gave this city when he gave us David Swing must also be full of a sincere and calm optimism. They must radiate with that rapturous faith in the triumph of goodness which rang like a vital note through all his music. They must carry his glowing assurance that the history of man is the history of a divine progress. For this faith was the sky under which his eye beheld the contest of energies divine and diabolic, the eddies in the stream of man's life that so often appear to testify to a receding river, and, beholding them all, he never faltered and never feared.

Words from any literature that may suit the hour when we strew rosemary on the grave of David Swing must open the mind toward that gateway into the realm of ideas which is called the beautiful, for, with him, as with the great novelist, "beauty is part of the finished language by which God speaks." And so I have chosen the passage from Isaiah which I have read: "How beautiful upon the mountains are the feet of him that bringeth good tidings, that publisheth peace, that bringeth good tidings of good, that publisheth salvation, that sayeth unto Zion, Thy God reigneth."

He himself has said: "There is no tribe or race which is not aware of such a something as the beautiful." Every race whose stream of blood entered or influenced the veins of this prose-poet contributed its highest æsthetic instinct and commandment unto him. To his spirit, as to Emerson's, "beauty was its own excuse for being." He allowed no argument in favor of what was ugly; that which was beautiful for him needed no apology or praise. All his mind's powers ceased to question the right of the beautiful to be and to rule, at the moment this unfailing eye found it beautiful; and, at the instant of his discovery that a thing was not beautiful, all his own beauty of soul, with playful irony, stinging sarcasm, and wealth of moral enthusiasm, set itself for its destruction. He went through our work-a-day world with a serene faith, like that of Keats, that "a thing of beauty is a joy forever;" and his vision of the immortal life was the seer's picture of the survival of the beautiful. Throughout his childhood, youth, and for twenty years of his public career, he lived in the valley of the Ohio, of all valleys the most sure to stimulate and enrich this æsthetic sense. All through his

sermons and essays we find pictures of what nature gave to this singularly rich and suggestive mind. They were criteria for years to come by which beauty might be recognized. They were facts so fair, and the fancies they inspired were so glorious, as to make his pages of essays and sermons true to nature and the soul in their truest moods. The aching seed and the April shower, the rich, black valley loam opening its wealth of motherhood for the seed, the rose that hesitantly met the earliest hour of June with fragrant kisses, the bees, gold-corseleted, that live on the lips of clover bloom, the long, green lines of corn, the yellow, wavelike valley of wheat, the rosy fruit of autumn, and the white snows of winter—all these come and go, as we think of the youth sitting by the old fireplace and watching the play of splendor in the flame, or, as in the brilliant day, he labors or dreams in the field, or, at night he broods beneath the white magnificence of stars.

It was all culture of the sentiment that says, "life and conduct must be beautiful." At college, this child of Athens, who had been born nearer the Ohio than Ilyssus, found his own native Greece and wandered along the edge of the

blue Ægean with Socrates and Plato, heard Sophocles recite his tragedies and beheld Phidias carve the Parthenon frieze; for he had a singularly inspiring teacher who, then and there, gave a new life and career to this soul who loved the beautiful. In his own childhood's home with those he loved, he had learned what his whole life illustrated, and what Mrs. Browning has so often repeated on his lips:

> "The essence of all beauty, I call love;
> The attribute, the evidence, and end;
> The consummation to the inward sense
> Of beauty apprehended from without,
> I still call love."

But the Greek youth, nursed on Hellenic food, was predestined, and now he was reinspired by his study of Greek literature and Greek art to be the apostle of the beautiful. To him evermore the *beautiful* became *good*. He found the ethical side of beauty. Professor Swing's spirit was too spacious and too nearly full-orbed, not to find within itself the experience which responded to and identified itself with the ebb and flow of the tide of life and thought and achievement in all the great nations. He had too sincere and truthful a sense of the imperial value of righteousness,

not to reflect, at some times very vividly, at *all times* quite faithfully, the quality and message of the Hebrew people to mankind. Yet the quality of his nature, the attitude of his mind, the method of its approach to truth was that of the Greek, rather than that of the Hebrew. None knew better than he that God had called these two peoples, each to an unique task, in the bringing in of the kingdom of God, which, to David Swing and to us, means the consummate achieving of the dream of civilization. The Hebrew wrought for righteousness; for this the nation was called to be a *royal priesthood.* In quite another manner, as characteristic of God's providence, as truly emphasizing the gift of the genius of the Greek, did Jehovah call the Greek to a *royal priesthood* also. He called the Greeks to be an intellectual aristocracy, as he called the Hebrews to be a spiritual aristocracy, and both did he call to minister unto all humanity. In each case the unique and precious stream flowed between banks of patriotic conviction.

The Greek was called to be an artistic nation; his Sinai revealed the law of beauty. God called the Hebrew to be "an holy nation;" his Sinai

revealed the laws of righteousness. It is certainly true that David Swing was a preacher of the message of the Hebrew—righteousness; but he approached it, he loved it, he championed it as a Greek. To him righteousness was the moral side of beauty, and, looking upon his career and its gracious influence, we repeat the Hebrew's words: "How beautiful upon the mountains are the feet of him that bringeth good tidings." It was this Greek spirit that made him able to so speak the "good tidings" that his preaching was literature. He knew the holiness of beauty.

So great, however, was the moral uplift of his nature toward a perception of and a yearning for the supreme beauty—"the beauty of holiness," as the Hebrew poet names it—that he was always telling us: "It must be inferred that there is a moral æsthetics which outranks the physical forms of beauty. The moral kingdom does not destroy the other empire. It is the old story of 'empire within empire,' 'wheel within wheel,' but with this caution that moral beauty is the greater of the two kingdoms. Moral æsthetics is what our age now needs." This is what the Hebrew singer had in mind, when he sang: "O worship

the Lord, in the beauty of holiness." To this the heart and eloquence of David Swing responded for eight and twenty years in our great materialistic city; but it was a Greek, clad with the splendor of a Christian knight, who uttered his plea with all that sobriety of statement, that artistic regard for the beautiful which made him the finest essayist who has stood in the pulpit of the nineteenth century. As we hear some more Hebraic gospeler utter his Ezekiel-like oracles to some valley of dry-bones, or listen to some evangelist or reformer hurl his warnings or maledictions against iniquity, remembering this sane and refined soul, we say with that most Grecian of recent anthologists:

"Where are the flawless form,
The sweet propriety of measured phrase,
   The words that clothe the idea, not disguise,
Horizons pure from haze,
   And calm, clear vision of Hellenic eyes?

"Strength ever veiled by grace;
The mind's anatomy implied, not shown;
No gaspings for the vague, no fruitless fires,
Of those fair realms to which the soul aspires."

The unique and unimagined value of such a man, holding so high a place in the moral culture

of this community from 1867 to 1894, can not be overestimated. When he came hither, filled with the results of years of scholarly investigation, calm with the vision given only to men of genuine idealism and cultured faith, fearless in the superb equipment of his learning, and trusting the whole world and its interests to the influence of truth, as only the scholar and the Christian does, we were just out of the thunder and moral dissipation of a civil war; huge fortunes had come as by magic to men who scarcely considered the ideal values in opportunity and influence which lie in a single dollar; we were at the beginning of a movement, in an industrial age, which has reaped enormous profits by the employment and direction of human beings along the ways of material progress; a city, draining its unexampled vitality from a vast empire, was rising like a huge vision before the cupidity and greed, the hope and reason of the West. What a gift of God it was that then there came to you a *soul*, a human heart cultured to the perception of the valuelessness of mere money and the supreme value of great ideas and noble sentiments, a brain that was certain of nothing so surely as that righteousness is moral

beauty, and that this beauty is, or ought to be, supreme! David Swing, at the opening of an age of gigantic material advancement, through years of persistently regnant materialism, in a city of tremendous practicalism, has been one of the most heroic and noble figures of our time; for he has been the scholar in the pulpit, the Christian in society, the philosopher in our literature, and the beloved citizen of the ideal commonwealth in all our public and private policies. He has embodied in himself the mission of the Christian scholar.

What is the Christian scholar? The Greek ensouled with the genius of Hebrewdom.

He is the one being to whom life must always appear both as a vision and as a duty. The order of progress, now and ever, is, first, "the new heavens," and then, "the new earth, wherein dwelleth righteousness." Life, as a vision into which have been gathered every noble idea, every true sentiment, and every worthy purpose, with all their victory and their hope—a vision awfully grand with the announcement that it hangs in the heavens to be obeyed, glorified with the assurance that it is to be realized on the earth—this is the

truest gift which years of instruction and study may give to the scholar's soul. The scholar is the deliverer of men. He is the sworn acquaintance of something still more venerable than their revering age, something more ancient than their prudence, and into their solemn cautiousness concerning tradition it is his to introduce the permanent which declines, because it needs not, their endeavor to preserve its pedigree or to enforce silence. The scholar sees the reality beneath all appearance, and it is his prerogative and fortune to furnish to the untrained his trained eye, that they too may know that there is a sky above and a river-bed beneath the flow of things. Wherever such a soul goes, there goes hope. He has had the experience of nature in his science, the experience of man with ideas and principles in his study of history, the experience of man with himself in his fearless study of the soul; and "experience worketh hope." To the hopeless man who has seen his flag go out of sight as it fell beneath the feet of wrong, he comes, to lead him out of the atmosphere of momentary defeat to a larger induction, and to bid him up and on. Wherever such a soul goes, there goes resolute-

ness and self-respect. Such a man, prophet and oracle, has been David Swing.

It was the Christian scholar's message of the infinite beautifulness and desirableness of truth which he came to give.

His very manner and voice, his presence and attitude, made his message more powerful as a rebuke to our pretentiousness and self-satisfaction, and a stimulus to our affection for high ideals and God-like sentiments. He seemed to brood wistfully, and often, with the whole statement before him, carefully written out, he paused, hesitating to handle truth which had cost so much and was so dear, with anything but reverent care. He had worked an immense deal of ore into coin before he rose to speak, and he knew its worth too well, and man's need too surely, to jingle it before human cupidity as a common thing. But before he concluded his address, it was all our own.

> "He spoke, and words more soft than rain
> Brought the age of gold again."

That voice filled its strange stops with the peculiar quality of his view of life, the "sweet reasonableness" of his message, the native music of

his melodious soul ; and no melody of earth ever seemed so varied in harmony or so increasingly beautiful as its utterance. When I heard him, I confess myself to have been under such a spell as only the finest orators may create, while I was saying to myself that this is not oratory at all. His was the eloquence of self-command, of affectionate confidence in his latest-loved truth, whose beauty he was then showing to us, lit up by a perfect faith that the angel he modestly championed would easily make her way in the world.

In the hour of his supreme power what resources he had, what forces came into his grasp! He had a finer humor than Beecher; it was radiant atmosphere, never tumultuous with stormful glee, but kindly, genial, an air in which the laughter rippled o'er the soul as the water moves when a swallow flies close to a quiet pool. In that radiance, buds of thought opened, seemingly without his touch, and unripe purposes grew golden in the warmth and glow. He had perfect mastery of sarcasm and irony. They never mastered him. In these rare moments of superlative power his good humor kept the sharp edges from cutting a hair, while the blades

flashed everywhither. Just at such an instant in his appeal, sober common-sense, the strongest faculty, or set of faculties which he possessed, uttered its behest, while fancy and memory played about the message as sweet children about a gracious queen. More than any or all of these, was the man who stood so quietly there —the dear friend, the high-minded advocate of the good, the true and the beautiful—urging us to a security of faith, a sanctity of life, and a reasonableness of conduct, like his own. Thus he became his own best argument. It was the eloquence, not of speech, but of beautiful character. What Lowell quotes to describe the speech of the Concord seer may be quoted to describe him:

"Was never eye did see that face,
  Was never ear did hear that tongue,
Was never mind did mind his grace,
  That ever thought the travail long,
But eyes, and ears, and every thought,
  Were with his sweet perfections caught."

It is often said that Professor Swing was not a reformer, and that he possessed none of the qualities and, therefore, had nothing of the career of those heroic men who root up ancient and wide-branched wrongs and create a reign of right-

eousness. He was a philosopher, not a transformer of institutions and laws. The fact is that such a soul's contribution to the evolution of goodness in the world is always of the highest importance. Ideas will always gather champions. Such a service as his is too likely to be underestimated, because it is so fundamental and so great. With a strange hesitancy as to accepting the conclusions of Darwin, our preacher's mental method was that of an evolutionist. He trusted the development of involved ideas. The revolutionist always attracts more attention and offers the picture of a more easily understood courage. But there would never be a revolutionist, if the evolutionist, whose plea is reason and not a sword, whose appeal is to ideas that render battles useless, were heard.

In the thick of the fight for some instantly demanded righteousness, David Swing was not a Luther, fiery-tongued and dust-covered as the fray went on; he was rather an Erasmus, the temperate, calm scholar who had already whetted the sword for a Luther's strong hands and held its fine blade ready for his service. But he was never beset with the cautiousness of Erasmus.

No Erasmus would ever have held the moral sense of the same community for all these years. He was Erasmus and Melancthon in one. His shy and clear-eyed soul reminds one of our own Emerson, whom Wendell Phillips, in the angry warfare where he was using Emerson's ideas as fine Damascus blades, called "that earthquake scholar at Concord," of whom also Lowell has said: "To him more than to all other causes together did the young martyrs of our civil war owe the sustaining strength of thoughtful heroism that is so touching in every record of their lives." From his benign place of culture David Swing has supplied epigrams which have become battle cries to many souls, who, in the turmoil, are fighting the good fight, to whose successful issue he made the contribution of victorious ideas. He lit the beacon and has kept it burning, so that, in the contest of right against wrong, of intelligence against ignorance, of nobility of character against the vulgarity which exhibits its coat of arms or its wealth, the soldier of truth might not mistake a foe for a friend, or lose the path of triumph. His was the thinker's heroism—the finest in the life of man. He feared not the consequences of

any truth; he feared only a comfortable lie, or a popular blunder. He was more than a Falkland with a Matthew Arnold to praise him, and to forget the lonely hours of Sir John Eliot and Hampden. He never cried peace where there was no peace. He always, somehow, got his word of cheer to the beleaguered army of truth, even if he were not with them at the hour of their captivity.

With the thinker's courage he trusted to the predestinated dominion of ideas, not only the fortunes of society, but also the future of the commonwealth and the hope of man. Not the lightning that smites and cleaves, still less the thunder that rolls and amazes, his was the soft and pervasive sunshine, bearing the secret fate of the summer and traveling with the molten snows, falling silently upon the icefields that gleam and shimmer as they slowly drip into the harvests of the future.

He has lived for living ideas and generous sentiments, the exquisitely true statements of which are so generously left on his pages that they are sure to be in the hearts and on the lips of the men of to-morrow, and all this because of his serene faith in the native supremacy of the

good, and the true, and the beautiful. This exalted and broad faith has given him breadth of interest and largeness of theme, and an unerring touch, as he has dealt with life's variety of problems. Above controversies, he has been so lofty as to provide for controversialists who would fain find the truth, the keys which unlock her treasure-houses. Our text describes him—" beautiful on the mountains," where a large view enabled him to see valleys of life running into one another, roadways, seemingly opposed in direction, gradually and surely tending toward each other. Oftentimes he would come down close to the hearts of the mistaken and debating searchers for truth, and usually he came to show them that each possessed some truth or ideal needed by the other, and that the pathway to righteousness and God was wide enough for them both.

Such a supreme faith in the good and the true and the beautiful made his eye quick to discern its presence or absence in all places. He was therefore a wise appreciator of art, in which this Greek loved to behold a Hebrew lesson on righteousness, a penetrative and comprehensive critic of literature, whose treasures lay at his

feet, a patriotic and sympathetic thinker in politics, which he would have baptized with Christian idealism, a true and broad-minded champion of religion, which he knew to be the noblest concern of all human life. One could not read with him "The Grammarian's Funeral" of Robert Browning, and see the face of David Swing, as he lived and toiled with the scholarship which made the renaissance victorious, without thinking, if he had actually been one of that age, he would have found such a grave also. But our Professor was more than one who "ground at grammar."

The mighty renaissance with which he had to do, and in the study of which the importance of his personality, its spirit and its gentle strength appear, has proved itself the greatest event in the history of religious thought since the Reformation. The Oxford movement, under the fascinating leadership of Newman, never reached beyond the English and American Episcopal churches and the Roman Catholic church, in whose fold the leader found a home. At that hour there was afoot, under Maurice, Kingsley and Stanley, a movement in England, inspired by Coleridge, fast putting on robes of poetry in

the lines of Tennyson and Browning, which, at a later hour, was sure to find responses here in the hearts and minds of such men as Beecher, Phillips Brooks, and David Swing. Earlier than either of his great contemporaries, Professor Swing saw that this was the renaissance of the Greek spirit in theology.

A lover of that ancient Rome where Greek literature still ruled her orators and poets, our Professor never could sympathize with mediæval and theological Rome. The Almighty God and his government, as treated by the theologians of Rome, for nearly two thousand years, whether Catholic or Protestant, were only a huge Roman emperor exalted to omnipotence and an empire where Roman justice and power alone were supreme. Orthodoxy had been partial to these thinkers, for Rome had been the seat of orthodoxy. Orthodoxy had, therefore, been fragmentary; outside of her accredited formularies were other truths quite as necessary for a full statement of Christianity. For example, the view of the atonement called orthodox was sympathetic with ideas of divine government borrowed from the Roman government; and as that government's

view of justice and humanity was not exhaustive, so that theory of the atonement was partial, if not untrue. Against this, as well as against views of the inspiration of scripture and the theology which dogmatized as to the fate of the wicked, the Greek spirit rose in him to utter its word; not to fight, for this is not the business of ideas, but to utter its life as a flower expresses itself in fragrance and beauty, to initiate a genuine renaissance, a re-birth of hidden and forgotten truth. The whole movement of theology in the nineteenth century has been a re-uttering of this Greek spirit. Augustine, Athanasius, and Cyril of Jerusalem have yielded to Origen, Chrysostom, and Clement of Alexandria. Our Greek poet-preacher, uttering his too long delayed truth in preachers' prose, has proved himself a worthy successor of him who was called "golden-mouthed" at Antioch, and him who was named by Jerome, "the greatest master of the church after the Apostles."

As Emerson left the church whose life he inspired as has no theologian of our age, so David Swing retired from what was a battlefield, to give all sects the benignant and untroubled illumina-

tion which was the radiance of his soul. Without the impulsive eloquence and massive movement of Beecher, but with more than Beecher's calm and propriety of utterance; without Phillips Brooks' vision of the whole human heart and his abounding religiousness of devotion to Jesus of Nazareth as the revelation of God, David Swing performed a service like theirs, to all religious interests, in emancipating the mind of our time from the establishments of piety and the formularies of a partial faith.

Such men are always called heretics. The truth is, they are the men of faith. They are those who do not believe less than the reactionary who would try them, or the conservative who distrusts them; but they believe more—not the same things and more things beside—but they believe *more*. When David Swing denied that God was limited to the methods of government mentioned by the Westminster Confession, he had a larger and more truly evangelical belief in God than his opposer. To-day the church of his boyhood comes to his grave, and one of her most eloquent orators embalms with odorous spices the heretic of yesterday. Intolerance is the only rad-

ical unbelief. No man has so little real faith as he who believes that God's truth needs his police duty to keep it alive, or to protect it from being stolen.

When these men first spoke, critical wiseacres were pointed to the ruddy east; but they answered that some one's house was on fire, and forthwith they sought to extinguish the flame. It was the dawn—inextinguishable and glorious. Fearlessly, that movement which reddens the whole Orient may be trusted. It will journey on to complete the noontide. Looking at it, one sees that it is God's presence in man's deeper, larger faith.

"And on the glimmering limit far withdrawn,
God made himself an awful rose of dawn."

His interest in theology sprang from such a root as gave him a profound interest in the problem of society. He confronted it with the same principles, asked of its dogmatists the same questions, and answered its demands with the same faith. Just as he declined to believe in and preach a gospel of despair which left a less loving God than Christ on the throne of the universe, so he declined to believe that the best civilization

will permit capital to grow rich by child-labor, and lawlessness to destroy public order. His unmoved faith in God, and man under God's love, is at the basis of a dream of a better society, just as it was at the basis of a truer theology.

The idea of God was Christianized in his deeper confidence; the same transformation must come to the life of man here below. As the vision of Christ, saying: "He that hath seen me hath seen the Father," changed the conception of God, and made man a worshiper of the universal Fatherhood, so Christ in the life of man will change methods and bring about a universal brotherhood. What makes for a true theology makes for a true sociology. "No Christ-like soul," he says, "will consent to walk along through life or to heaven without wishing to drag all society with it to the sublime destiny."

This deep faith made him the lover of men whose personal creeds were divergent from his own and whose methods he could not have adopted. It was enough that they were bringing in the better day. Full of admiration for the philosopher and scientist, he nevertheless said: "It is not Comte or Tyndall who must plead

with the begrimed miners of England; it is Moody and Sankey." He could trust any man whose soul was acquainted with the large truths of the Nazarene, because he trusted them. "The truths of Christ's reform," he said, " possess that impulse which comes from their lying outspread, not only in the light of earth, but in that of eternity."

Perhaps his proclaimed vision of Christ was not inclusive of all the lines which love and worship have made for yours; but I never heard him more earnest than when he said to one who wished to substitute a paganism for Christianity: "Even could we draw from the classics or Hindoo world a complete definition of manhood, we would seem to need a Christ to enable the human race to realize the dream betrayed in the definition." "The cross is only an essential prelude to the new life." Perhaps his humor lit up the true features of some doctrine so dear to you that you mistook the kindly light for his repudiation of truth. Doubtless he saw more clearly those truths of which little is said in creeds; but this, at least, is true: the confession of faith he perpetually uttered and preached is made up of the

sweetest hopes and the most frequently spoken commandments which moved the lips of Jesus Christ.

Of unique and pervasive beautifulness of nature, of large and living scholarship, of most thorough religiousness of mind, of genuine American fiber and faith, he lived with us and died among us, the most beloved of our citizens, if not the most distinguished; the most poetic of the prophets who has not left his life in his verse; the most genial and philosophical of American essayists, who was always a priest of goodness; our soul's friend, to whom we say: "Hail and farewell."

Rev. Thos. C. Hall's Tribute.

A great sorrow has fallen upon many hearts this week. A former pastor of this church has been taken to his rest. A beautiful and sunny life has come to a peaceful close, and the memories and sweet associations of a long ministry now gather about an open grave. Professor David Swing was too well-known a figure among you to need any description or eulogy from my lips; but I would not do justice either to my own or to your feelings, were I not to pay a tribute to the love and gentleness of the life that has passed away. It is most striking, that, in all that is being said of Professor Swing, the remarkable intellectual gifts which were his are passed over so largely, in order that men may emphasize again and again his love and sweetness. These qualities of his were not born of ruddy health and prosperous condition. Pain was his familiar companion, and carefully had he to watch himself that his work might not suffer, but he seldom spoke much of himself. His high classical attainments and complete familiarity with the Latin

poets are rarely met with to-day, but he spoke very modestly of them, and they were only means to the end he had in view. His message was of a full sweet forgiveness through a Father's redeeming love, and he couched that message in words of singular beauty, and illustrated it from an imagination quick to all the perfect in nature or in art. There was Christian refinement in every finished product of his pen, and the glow of a loving heart was felt through all his periods. No one was more adept in the art of gentle satire, but it was chastened and controlled as few men so possessed succeed in controlling their gift. A charming humor played over much that he wrote, but it only seemed to enhance the seriousness and depth that will make his writings a fund of moral inspiration for all time.

Professor Swing saw clearly. His mind worked rapidly and thoroughly. He did not permit himself to become entangled in his own explanations. He saw many things a good while ago that men are only now dimly perceiving. He gave his message, found his place, and leaves now a great city incalculably poorer for his departure. He was a splendid citizen, and loved Chicago. In a con-

versation with him, had not long ago, I lamented some things that make our streets unattractive. He acknowledged the weakness, but with that characteristic hopefulness that made him so strong in doing his work, he said: "You are young. You will see our work tell on these streets as it gradually tells on the character they figure forth." He had great faith in the power of love and in the receptivity of the human heart for its healing power. He believed in love lived out, not simply professed, and, if sometimes impatient with creeds, he seldom lost his power of sympathy with the heart behind a creed, no matter how distasteful the creed might be to him.

Nothing was more noticeable about Professor Swing than the extreme quietness and unobtrusiveness of his manner. He did not seek notoriety, nor did he seem much to value praise. He desired only opportunity to give his message and to serve. And he served faithfully. He was a pastor to many hundreds who had no more claim upon him than that they had read his sermons or knew his name.

Into many houses of mourning he came with his own personal message of love and hope and

confidence. He thought kindly of all, and his gentle judgments were the sincere outcome of his charitable view of life and men. This quiet confidence in the real underlying goodness of humanity was no mere sentiment with him, but was born of a profound conviction that God was really redeeming humanity, and that into the poorest, meanest life there was being inbreathed a diviner and a nobler being. This was the ground conception of his philosophy and his theology. Not that he overlooked sin or underestimated unrighteousness and wickedness, but that he fixed his eye upon a redeeming love shed abroad in the hearts of men through the message of Christ's gospel. Indeed, his heart was often stirred by the treachery and unrighteousness that surrounded him, but he would soon find rest again in the hope of the future and his confidence in the final outcome. In speaking of this to me one day, he said with much impressiveness: "Why should one judge life by its lower phases, or one measure your faith by its low water-mark of depression? I may lose confidence in humanity for one hour out of the twenty-four, but it is the other twenty-three hours of faith in humanity, in which I will do any work for it."

He often spoke of the necessity of living on the level of our nobler inspirations, and, amidst the trials and difficulties, many of which were unknown to all but an inner circle, he wonderfully succeeded in keeping his teaching keyed up to a very high pitch of lofty inspiration born of a divine faith. In his later days he had a certain sense of loneliness. Many of those whom he had known, and known intimately, had passed before him through the silent portals that have closed forever on his own spirit. And he had planned to associate with him, this winter, a few of the younger men, who gladly would have gathered about him to share his experience and learn from him. But the Great Master desired it otherwise, and his spirit is lonely no more, but rejoices in the fellowship of unnumbered believers and is ever present with his Lord.

The lessons of his life are many and very sacred. Many of you will lay them to heart as you learn them from lips more competent than mine to interpret them to you, but the broad, full message of a saving, redeeming love, working out, in sacrifice and praise, its mission and its task, is the lesson he would most have you, mem-

bers of the church to which he once ministered, lay most to heart. He believed in Christ as the friend of the friendless, the teacher of the ignorant, the Savior of the lost, and the hope of a despairing world. It was as Christ was formed in him the hope of glory, that he became a teacher of his time, and a prophet of a fullness of salvation to be worked out through Christ.

Tribute of Rev. Dr. H. W. Thomas,

Pastor of the People's Church.

In whose heart are the highways of Zion,
Passing the valley of weeping, they make it a place of springs.
—Ps. lxxxiv. 5-6.

It can never cease to be a strange and impressive fact, that the years of man on earth are so few. He comes not to stay; but to "pass through" this wonderful world. He would gladly linger beneath its skies, rest by its streams, work and study longer upon its great tasks and problems.

But he is hurried along from youth to age; from cradle to tomb. The countless generations of the past have looked out upon the same continents and oceans — wandered and wondered beneath the same stars; have laughed and wept, loved and sorrowed—"passed through" this scene and mystery profound — passed on to the infinite beyond; and of all the millions living now soon all will be gone, and other lives will have come to fill their places.

Such a strange order and conditioning of the conscious life of man, naturally, necessarily, gives to his thought and work a forward looking and

movement. He can not, if he would, go back; the path behind him is cut off; closed to himself, but open for others. Only in memory may one live over the years that are gone. History may prolong the backward vision of what has been in the long past; but one can not be a child, a youth again — can not stand again in the glad years that are gone. The only path upon which the feet can move lies before, stretches on into the ever strange and new of the coming to-morrow.

Not alone is it impossible to recall the years that are gone, but impossible to change them, to do anything to make them other or different from what they were. When one reads of the wars, the slaveries, the persecutions, the wrongs and sufferings of centuries ago, the soul rises up in protest, and would gladly go back and fight the battles over again; rescue a Joan of Arc or a Bruno from the stake, or change the sad ending of a William of Orange. But man stands powerless to undo the sad yesterdays of his world; he can atone for his own nearer wrongs only by making better each to-day.

This cutting off of the past, this impossibility of going back and undoing what was, holds man's

whole life and being in what is, and projects it into the larger possibilities of what may be, gives a forward looking to those "in whose hearts are the highways of Zion," that, "passing through the valley of weeping, they may make it a place of springs."

And when the mystery of this strange fact of the few passing years of man on earth is studied more deeply, whilst it is still true that one can not go back and undo what has been, there arises the larger thought and fact of the continuity of individual and world life in which the good is conserved, the evil left behind.

In the individual life and consciousness, childhood and youth are not lost, but carried forward into the years and strength of manhood and womanhood. Our childhood, our youth, is still a part of ourselves; play has changed to labor; the "a, b, c's," the "one, two, threes," are with us in the books we read and the numbers we calculate; lisping speech has become a language; obedience in the home has opened the way to the larger world-order; lessons of truth and right have become great principles in the life of morals and religion.

And what is so evidently true in the individual experience is true, in another sense, in the larger life of our one human family. Each passing generation leaves to those who follow in its steps the paths over which it has journeyed, the work it has done in conquering land and sea, its progress in the industries, arts, sciences, language, literature, and the institutionalized forms in which these have taken shaping. The childhood of the world was carried forward into its youth, and this into its manhood. The millions who "passed through" this strange scene of learning, doing and becoming, "had in their hearts the highways of Zion," and helped "make the valley of weeping a place of springs."

Civilization has been carried along the great "highways" of all industrial and business pursuits; homes, cities, schools, temples of justice and religion have arisen; the great inventors have facilitated labor and travel; the lovers of liberty have toiled to make men free; the lovers of art have filled the world with the beautiful; the lovers of music have filled the world with song; the lovers of justice have tried and are trying to adjust the inequalities of the social order;

the lovers of reason have striven to make this a rational world; and the lovers of religion have toiled and are toiling now to make the earth a vast world-home of souls, of brotherhood, of love and prayer and hope immortal.

Whatever may be the thought or hope of man about a life beyond death, race-continuity of the millions in this world for ages to come is not doubtful. So great is the rejuvinescence of the life forces of our human world, that its youth is ever rising out of its age. War, famine, pestilence have carried away countless millions; the earth has to be re-peopled nearly three times in each century; but, through all, race-continuity endures, and with ever increasing numbers.

It took Germany one hundred years to recover from the "thirty years war," but Germany is greater to-day than ever before; and, with Alsace and Lorraine gone and forty thousand German soldiers camping in her midst, France rose up and paid a billion dollars in gold. In the third of a century since the rebellion a new generation of men and women, young and strong, have come into the great life of our own country.

Facing this fact of race-immortality, a great and near motivity comes into the life of man.

He "passes through" the strange scene; but he lives on in the life of children and country. Men die; institutions live, industries live, thought lives, truth lives, right lives; love, hope can not die. Hence there is the great inspiration, the altruism of the continuity of race life, race immortality; the othering, the enlarging, the prolonging, the re-living of self as a conscious part of world or race life.

Nor is this larger vision poetic, speculative. How can reason cease to be reason, or love cease to be love? How can they drop out of or cease to be a part of the true, the good that is eternal? Oh! not for a day, but forever, is the thinking, loving, hoping life of man; and not far away are the blessed dead, but more deeply and divinely than ever alive, and living in the deathless realities of the real, and, like Moses and Elias with the transfigured Christ, coming back and sharing in the great events and interests of the world in which they once lived and toiled.

"Are they not all ministering spirits sent forth to minister to the heirs of salvation?" "Seeing, then, that we are compassed about with so great a cloud of witnesses, let us run with patience the race set before us."

It should not seem strange that in this forward-looking of a world there are those, "in whose hearts are the highways of Zion," and that, "passing through the valley of weeping they make it a place of springs." All nations and religions have journeyed to some ideal of the better. With the Jews it was embodied in their Zion, their Jerusalem. The prophets hastened on before to climb the mountain tops and catch the light of the greater years; the priests lingered behind to organize, to build temples and minister at altars, to found and conserve institutionalized forms. As the prophets caught the larger truths and life of the spirit, the highways of Zion were in the soul, not in ritual observances; and they would make of all the earth a Zion, a Jerusalem, a vast empire of souls filled with righteousness. To such a Zion all the paths of a noble loving life were great "highways" along which all souls might gladly journey; but the Scribe, the Pharisee, the narrow dogmatist would close all the shining highways of a great rational religion of humanity in this tearful world, and leave open only one narrow dark way to a little walled-in heaven for a few little souls; and for these, not because of any per-

sonal worth or merit, for what they had tried to be and do, but saved by a divine decree, and imputed merit and righteousness of another.

A great preacher and prophet of God, one "in whose heart were the highways of Zion," and who " passing through the valley of weeping made it a place of springs," has gone from our city and our world. No more will he stand in the pulpit to which the many thousands have gladly gathered in the last twenty years. Our dear Professor Swing has "passed through the valley of weeping." This is his first Sabbath in the tearless land. His poor body, that can suffer no more, will be carried by those who stood by him in life to the church where he has so long taught the great truths of a great religion; but that voice is silent now.

Of this great preacher it can be truthfully said, "in his heart were the highways of Zion;" not the little Zion of priest or sect; not the highways of narrow dogmatists; but the Zion of God, and the highways of the true, the beautiful, the good.

He saw the great truths. To this man of God was given the clearer vision. He saw the great truths of Christianity, hidden and almost lost in

the maze and obscurity of the old Latin theology. He saw the doubts that were burdening the faith of his age. He saw the highways of reason and a rational religion. He heard the voice of God saying: "Son of man, prophecy, speak, teach;" and, prophet-like, he was true to the vision, counted not the cost, thought not of the trouble that was to come—that the old vessels could not hold the new wine, and that he must go out from his old church home and find a free pulpit in which to be a free man—free as the truth makes free—and lovingly to preach the truth as he saw it.

The prophet is always far in advance of the priest. Standing on the mountains, he sees the new morning, while the priest stands down in the shadows, and is trying to make fast, and to bind religion to the thought of some long ago. Professor Swing was the prophet; Dr. Patton was the priest. The one stood for the "truths of to-day;" the other for the mistakes of yesterday.

The prophet stood in the clearer vision of the divine; the priest stood for a confession of faith formulated two hundred and fifty years ago, when the church was busy burning witches. The priest had back of him these old interpretations or

declarations of what the minds of that time thought to be true. These were held up as authority, and the statement was boldly made that the question of their truth or falsehood was not in debate. The only question was, Did Professor Swing believe them? If not, the doctrine was that he had no right to remain in a church built upon them and pledged to their support.

Technically, legally, such a position may be well taken; but it makes the thought of the past a finality, cuts off the possibility of progress, leaves no room for the growth of ideas, no place for the new and larger faith of man in all the great and better years of the future. In everything else there may be progress; religion alone must stand still. And, more than this, such a position not only binds the reason of man to a special interpretation of the Bible—in effect puts it in place of the Bible—but it emphasizes this special form of faith as the essential thing in religion—makes creed greater than life.

And thus the great trial for heresy came—had to come. Standing in the light of truth, the prophet could not unsay what he had said. Standing by the altars of creed, of authority, the priest

demanded strict conformity to law. Good men sought the mediation of larger toleration and personal liberty, but in vain. With all his greatness of intellect, sweetness and beauty of life, Professor Swing was pushed out of the Presbyterian Church as a heretic, and Dr. Patton was honored, extolled, petted and rewarded as the "defender of the faith."

And each, from his standpoint, was right. The true man can be true to himself and to truth, only as he stands by what to him is true. The great preachers can not be bound by majority votes and decisions. They must be free in the world of truth, and stand with open face before God. Such was Professor Swing, as simple, as honest, as humble as a child, and utterly incapable of mental trickery or duplicity. He could not deceive himself as to his own real beliefs, and he would not deceive others. Judged by the standards of orthodoxy, he was not orthodox. He did not claim to be. He did not accept as literal the story of the fall of man, did not believe in the doctrines of original sin, substitutional or penal atonement, and endless punishment; but he did believe in the great truths of the new theology, lived in the great spiritual

verities of religion, and felt that a great Christian Church should be large enough to hold the thinking of its children, and tolerant enough not to oppose their highest conceptions of truth.

From Dr. Patton's standpoint the church had the truth—had all it ever could have. Orthodoxy was the only and final statement, and this it was the duty of the church, at any and every cost, to defend. If really sincere in this, there was only one thing to do. That one thing he did do, and, in doing it, if his theory be accepted, he performed a high and sacred duty and was worthy of all praise.

But is the theory correct? Is there no truth outside of orthodox churches? Will these churches continue to claim a monopoly of salvation? Great changes have come in the world of thought in the last twenty years. The new theology is taking the place of the old. The heresy of yesterday is becoming the orthodoxy of to-day, and the larger and better faith is finding its way into nearly all the great pulpits. Will the churches turn out these prophets of the new age? Will the prophets be true to the voice and vision of God and the growing thought and need of a world? These

are the questions that are still troubling the orthodox churches. They have claimed too much. They hesitate to make concessions, and yet are powerless to stay the great world-movement of the new truth and life. Even the conservative Gladstone, seemingly not knowing what others have written and said along the lines of his own thinking, has come to the higher view of the atonement.

Professor Swing has helped to make plainer "the highways of Zion"—the highways of a great reasonable religion; helped to make easier the path for other feet, and to bring nearer the great church of humanity, in which all minds shall be free to learn and to grow, and all hearts shall rejoice in the blessedness and joy of a religion of love and hope. In that great soul there was room for Jew and Christian, Catholic and Protestant, Orthodox and Liberal; for he saw all as children of the one Father, and saw a good life as the meaning and end of all these forms of faith and worship. Hence he had only kind words for all.

In the heart of this great preacher were the highways of the beautiful. He loved nature and

art, loved continents and oceans, mountains and valleys, lakes and rivers, flowers, trees, the sky and stars above. He saw, in all, the presence and goodness of God. To him the vast world was a beautiful home. He loved pictures and statuary, music and literature. In that great soul were all the highways of love and kindness. He bowed down at the altars of life, and could not harm or hurt the meanest creature. He loved bird and animal, friend and stranger, man and God.

"Passing through the valley of weeping," such a noble, toiling life has helped "make it a place of springs." From a mind, clear as crystal, have poured forth streams of purest thought and literature; from a heart of love, springs of kindness have made gentler the life of man, and flowed on down to bless the poor brute world, and fountains of life have risen up to the throne of God. He has lived and pleaded for everything good; has been light in darkness, comfort in sorrow, hope in despair, to minds and hearts unnumbered, unknown.

Great preachers add honor to cities and nations. Milan had an Augustine, Florence a Savonarola, London a Spurgeon, Brooklyn a Beecher, Chi-

cago a David Swing. That name, stricken from the pages of a Presbytery and Synod, was written quickly and forever in the heart of humanity. We are lonesome, the world is poorer, that he is not here. It was so unexpected. We hoped he might live and work on to the end of the century. He belonged to us all. There is such a feeling of absence, of vacancy, of something gone,—as if some sun-crowned height on which we had often looked had suddenly dropped from its place among the mountains; but, in form transfigured, glorified, he will not be far away, but near, in the deathless world of memory, of love and hope, till the valley of weeping is passed through.

We sorrow with his family and with his church, and pray that some one will run forward and lift up the banner carried so long, but dropped in death by this great preacher and teacher. Noble friend, prophet of God, caught up to the heavens, farewell, till the night is passed and the morning dawns.

An Estimate of the Character and Work of David Swing.

By Rev. Frederick A. Noble, D.D.

"Your fathers, where are they? and the prophets, do they live forever?"—Zach. i. 5.

For a period of more than twenty years David Swing has had a conspicuous place in the life of Chicago. Like the merchant princes who have grown up here, and the manufacturers of wide renown, his name and fame have come to be closely identified with the name and fame of our city. Few are the intelligent men, especially in this land, who have known of the activity and growth of this vast metropolis, who have not known something also of the celebrated Music Hall preacher. He spoke to large numbers from Sunday to Sunday, and the printed page prolonged his voice and carried his words afar.

Now that his remarkable career is ended, and his work is done, save in such subtle and abiding influences of it as death has no power to arrest, it seems good to pause long enough by his closed casket to acknowledge his excellencies and to pay such tribute as is his just due, and to come

to some well-grounded conclusions touching the value of the services he rendered to religion and society. So much was done in this pulpit when announcements reached us, in turn, that Beecher and Spurgeon and Brooks had ceased from their labors and passed into the heavens. Pursuing a similar course with reference to Professor Swing, I shall attempt this morning to tell the story, in brief, of his life, and to make as intelligent and candid an estimate as I may of his character and work.

Many things in the make-up and method of Professor Swing are much more readily understood when it is known that he was of German descent. Like all of the higher type who are Germans, or who have German blood in their veins, he was cosmopolitan in his appreciations and sympathies, and could easily enter into fellowship with the representatives of every nationality; but there was a peculiarity in the working of his mind and the expression of his thoughts, which differentiated him from the pure Scotchman, or the pure Englishman, or the pure Frenchman, and indicated kinship with the marvelous people whose modes of apprehending and pre-

senting truth are at once searching and picturesque, subtle and poetic, and whose genius has illustration on the one side in the mystic creations of Jacob Bohme, and on the other in the sublime productions of Goethe.

But the German strain which left its impress on his intellectual and moral nature brought him neither social distinction nor wealth. Like Carlyle, like Livingstone, like Paton, like Garfield, he was born to poverty. Not to abject poverty. For as Mr. Blaine showed, in his great oration in commemoration of his murdered chief, there is a wide margin of difference between the poverty of those who, while straitened in outward circumstances, are yet self-respecting and intelligent and virtuous and aspiring, and those who, not having anything, are quite content to remain as they are, and who from generation to generation live on in a state of dependence and often of degradation.

To add to the embarrassment occasioned by limited means, his father was swept away by the scourge of cholera which visited Cincinnati, the place of Swing's nativity, in 1832; and the child, so full of unknown promise, was left a half-orphan while only two years of age.

It calls for no extraordinary exercise of the imagination to picture the struggles through which this mother, said on all sides to have been an exceptionally earnest, faithful, and devoted Christian woman, must have passed in order to keep her home unbroken, and her two cherished boys, David and his brother, comfortably sheltered and clad and fed. God is on the side of such mothers, because such mothers are on the side of God; and somehow they are led through their trials, and in due time society sees them emerging from darkness into light. Like another Cornelia looking into the upturned faces of the two Gracchi and declaring them to be her jewels, one can think of this Ohio mother as often looking out upon the breadth and splendor of wealth about her, and then taking these two sons by the hand and exclaiming in quiet triumph, "These are my possessions."

At the end of five years, the Cincinnati home was abandoned, and a new one was formed out in the country. Three years later, or when young Swing was ten years of age, there was still another change of location, and, in virtue of this change, the lad was to have eight consecutive years of experience on a farm.

Farming in the West is so unlike farming in the East that one brought up on a hillside of New England can not be sure that handling tools, and managing cattle, and sowing and reaping, and building fires, and mending fences, and going to mill, mean exactly to him what they mean to one whose agricultural training was on the prairies or in the river valleys of this wide and fertile interior of our land. But all that is best and most significant in the experience they share in common. East or West, the boy on the farm lives the larger part of his active life out under the broad open sky. He grows familiar with the varying hues and shapes of clouds and the sweep of storms. He smells the fresh odor of the mold when the furrow is turned, or the hoe finds its way to the roots of weeds. He observes with delight the unfolding of vegetation from the time when the seed swells and bursts through the crust of the earth till maturity has been reached. He watches the procession of the flowers, and very soon is able to predict what new beauty in each succeeding spring day will greet the eye, and what new fragrance will be in the air, as he goes forth to his toil. He gets on good terms with the birds,

and quickly understands in what order swallow and bluebird, and sparrow and thrush, and robin and oriole and bobolink, will make their appearance in tree-top and glen. He becomes familiar with the moods of horses and sheep and cows, and in instances not a few comes to have a deeper insight into human nature from what he knows of brute nature. The whole realm of the exterior world, with its suns and its stars, with its revolving seasons and growths, with its varied forms and forces of life, is open to a youth whose daily tasks take him to field and pasture and garden, as to hardly any other youth. Some of the sweetest and most pathetic of his songs Robert Burns would never have left us, had he not followed the plow, and seen daisies ruthlessly turned under the sod, and poor, timid little mice scampering away in fright, because their nests were invaded and destroyed. Those eight years on the farm meant much beside mere physical health and strength to the live brain of David Swing.

The eight years of farm life, however, came to an end, and at the close of these years, in addition to the other things he had done, and the other benefits he had gained, the young man

was found to be fitted for college. The work had been done by a Presbyterian minister, who, quite likely, had put the thought of going to college into the boy's head, as well as helped him to realize it. Miami University was the institution chosen for pursuing a classical course. It is needless to say that the college at Oxford forty years ago was not what it is now. When this boy entered it, it had been a college only sixteen years. In the nature of the case it could not afford such amplitude of facility for education in all departments and branches as some of the older and more richly endowed institutions of the East; but people who decry colleges because they are small and young, and think it foolish to have attempted to establish so many of them, especially in states and territories west of the Alleghanies, know little of what they are saying. Had it not been for this small college, or for some other small college not far away, where expenses were light, and with teachers in its several chairs well able to go to the heart of ancient learning, and to deal intelligently and courageously with the modern problems of life, it is a question which hardly admits of more than one

answer, whether this active-minded and aspiring young man would ever have found his way into academic halls. It is certain that all about us there are men by the score and score, who are eminent in their professions, and who are making splendid records of usefulness, who never would have got their start without the aid of the small colleges. Perhaps there is no moral which the life of our dead preacher points more distinctly than this.

In the way of early biographical details, it remains simply to say, that after young Swing had graduated he studied theology, for a couple of years, under the direction of the Rev. Dr. Rice, of Cincinnati. Before completing full preparation for the ministry, however, he was called to occupy the chair of Greek and Latin in his *Alma Mater*. This chair he filled for something like a dozen years. He might have remained there to the end had he been willing to stay; for his teaching was exceptionally successful. He reproduced ancient scenes, and handled the great thoughts of the great minds of the old Greek and Roman nations, with an appreciation and an enthusiasm which kept his

own soul aglow, and fired with high heat the souls of those who waited on his instructions.

Twenty-eight years ago Professor Swing came to Chicago. From the day he arrived and took up his work, till the day he died, his name has been a household word in this community, and his sayings and doings have been recognized factors in the development of our common life. For almost three decades he has been a voice in the midst of this people, giving out the truth in such form and manner as he conceived it to be truth, sometimes expressing and sometimes molding public opinion, but always commanding attention. Among his adherents his popularity never waned, and the interest strangers took in hearing him increased rather than diminished. His career was unique, and his success was phenomenal. It is easy to recall the names of men who have maintained themselves on independent platforms, but there is no case exactly parallel to this.

What now is the secret of this unique career? In what quarter shall we look for the explanation of a success so marked?

We shall miss it immensely if we attribute it all to his liberal views, and to the interest which

the outside world, through its newspapers and platforms, and otherwise, is wont to take in one who is supposed to be at irreconcilable odds with orthodoxy. This was one element, and a very controlling element, of the esteem in which he was held in the popular heart and of the attachment with which multitudes clung to him. But it was only one. He had merits quite outside and beyond all those which men are in the habit of associating with that courage of conviction which is sufficiently defined and robust to dissent from commonly accepted views in religion. He was a man of rare gifts and rare acquisitions.

1. To begin with, much is to be set down to the purity and loftiness of his character. He was not sweet-tempered merely, and loving and kind and helpful merely; but he was a man so clean and elevated in his life, so ideal in his thoughts and words, and habits, and tastes, and associations, that it seems almost like an impertinence to commend him for the possession of high moral qualities. These qualities were so much a part of him, they entered so vitally into his personality, that one can not think of the man without thinking of him as the embodiment and expression of an imposing uprightness of soul.

Such character, as a certificate of sincerity, and a re-enforcement of what one says and does, can hardly be over-estimated. When William M. Evarts was once asked to account for the strong hold Dr. John Hall had taken on the people of New York, his prompt answer was, "His superb character." Character tells. The loftier the character, the more positive and far-reaching the influence of the man who possesses the character. If the character be defective, especially if it be defective to the point of falseness, the words one speaks, though they be brilliant as flashes in the northern sky, will be wingless, and as weak as the chatter of a group of imbeciles. One can think of a man in an eastern city, who had exceptional abilities and a large following, and who broke away from the old faith and set up on an independent basis, but who came to quick collapse because his character was discovered to be bad. One can think of a man in a western city, who has marked capacity of thought and speech, and who has sought to make of his free opinion a working capital; but his questionable character has wrecked him. Professor Swing had an unimpeachable character.

2. In addition to this high type of character, Professor Swing was magnificently equipped for the kind of pulpit work he was to do. He had a cast of mind peculiar to himself, and to many people exceedingly interesting; but this was not all. He had a well-disciplined mind, and a full mind. He knew things. Science had brought him treasures of knowledge. History had poured her vast wealth at his feet. Literature had opened its choicest pages to his eager search. Philosophers and poets and quaint and unheard-of authors had taken him into their fellowship and whispered their secrets in his ear. Remember, he had his early out-door training, of which he made much, and his college preparation, which was exceptionally good because he made it so; and his four years in the university were years of golden opportunity coined into a splendid record; and his two years of special theological study and training with an eminent minister; and then, plus all this, he had twelve years of life in a professor's chair, which he used to such advantage in his own discipline and development, that Greek and Latin came to be to him almost like a mother-tongue, and Homer and

Æschylus and Vergil grew well-nigh as familiar to his thought as Shakespeare and Milton and Whittier. His sense of the value of these old classics was cropping out continually in his sermons. His fondness for the Greeks and their tongue was the fondness of a mother for her children. Here is a paragraph from one of his tributes of admiration: "The Greek language is still almost an unsurpassed tongue. Eighteen hundred years have added only a small area to the scope of that vast speech. There is scarcely a question of the present day discussed, that was not reviewed by the Greek thinkers and stowed away in their manuscripts. Their essays upon education, upon health, upon art, upon amusements, upon war, read almost as though they were written yesterday. Even that question which seems our own, the creation and property of this generation—whether women should vote and follow manly pursuits—is all fully discussed in 'Plato's Ideal Republic.'"

His information was both thorough and wide, and he was master of it. He knew what had been the achievements of thought in Egypt and India. He knew the art of Italy. He knew the

story of inventors and explorers. He knew the triumphs and problems of modern research. He knew what all the great writers of romance have said and taught.

These vast stores of knowledge he turned to account in his preaching. In a single discourse one might often detect contributions of fact, or reference, or incident, brought in from almost all the lands and ages, and from almost all the realms of investigation and study. In this way, he maintained an unflagging interest, and kept whatever he was saying bright with the flash of jewels gathered from afar. He did not attempt to illustrate his speech with touching anecdotes, like Spencer and Guthrie; nor to punctuate his writing with over-many crisp, sharp sentences, like Spurgeon and Parkhurst; nor to create dramatic situations with which to surprise the mind, like Parker and Talmage; nor to force all the varying moods of the heart, and all the wide experiences of life to aid him in impressing his thoughts, like Luther and Beecher; nor to bring forward the stories and characters and striking events of the Scriptures to point his periods, like Hall and Taylor; nor to put a torrent of energy

into his words to sweep them on from source to sea with the irresistible and awful might of a swollen river, like Robertson and Brooks; but, for all this, he kept his utterances so alive with present-day interest, and so illuminated with light of star and reflection of flower, and so warm with a half-suppressed passion, and so fresh and beautiful with the garments of fancy which he wove and threw over all his forms of thought, that nobody ever grew weary or dull of mind under his presentation of a truth. If his sermons were not so much sermons as essays—essays on the model of Aurelius, or Plutarch, or Emerson, or Lowell—it is still true that the wonderful fascination and power of them, or a share of it at any rate, must be sought in the masterly skill and wealth of learning and poetic coloring he was able to give them.

There is a lesson here for all who contemplate entering the ministry. It is the lesson of thoroughness of preparation for the great work. If a man has nothing in him, and no capability of having anything put into him, and is nevertheless determined to engage in the ministry of Jesus Christ, let him rush into it. The quicker he goes

in, the better; for the quicker he goes in, the quicker he will get out. But just in the ratio in which men have natural fitness for the high business of preaching the Gospel, and are sincere and earnest, and consecrated, do they need to take time to discipline their minds and fill them with knowledge. Had I the ear of theological students, I should say to them: Read, read, read. Read the great histories. Read the great poetries. Read the great essays. Read the great biographies. Read the great romances. Read the great results of science. Read other things? Of course. This goes without saying. But read, read, and still read.

3. Professor Swing won the confidence of large numbers of the best people of the community, and brought them into close affiliation with his teachings and suggestions, by the profound and wise and helpful and unremitting interest he took in social and ethical questions. His word stood for pure, manly living in the individual; for sweet homes; for refinement and culture and noble aspirations in social circles; for good schools and good books and good music and good pictures, and good habits; for high standards in business

spheres; for clean politics and patriotic devotion to the welfare of the state; for temperance, and liberty, and humanity, and justice; for a fellowship which should bind into one, as with cords braided out of the love of God in Christ, the weak and the strong, the poor and the rich, the low and the high, and make them all feel the sacredness and beauty of human brotherhood.

In no crisis in our city or commonwealth, when sharp, ringing voices were needed on the right side to keep men level-headed and stanch, did he ever falter. When the red flag was lifted up, and mad agitators wrote what amounted to "divide or die" across their banners, and the authorities were thinking more of the votes they might want in some coming election than of the peace and order they had solemnly promised to maintain and the protection they had sworn to afford, he threw the influence of his own name, and, so far as he could, the influence of the congregation he represented, into the scale against anarchy. When waves of poverty and distress suddenly rolled in upon us, a year ago, and threatened to whelm us under their weight, he uttered the most searching and courageous and

helpful words which found expression in any of our pulpits. He went to the root of the matter, and, while urging the people to whom he spoke to give of their abundant wealth to help the needy, he did not hesitate to tell these wretched, starving people just why they were wretched and starving. They had been sowing to the wind of idleness and unthrift and self-indulgence and intemperance, and they were reaping the whirlwind of want and woe. In the discourse delivered by him only a few weeks ago, from his desk in Central Music Hall, his first for this new year of work, and his last—forever, he handled the whole subject of our recent strike and riot in a way to show how clear was his insight into present conditions and perils, and how firm his grasp on the principles which must be accepted and followed, if peace is to be preserved, and labor and capital are to be reconciled for good.

Whatever he did not find in it, Professor Swing found in Christianity these two things: He found the highest rule for the government of individual conduct, and he found the highest system of political economy which the world has ever known.

Here is a passage from a sermon in "Truths for To-day:" "It would seem that Paul, in his chapter upon Charity, was expressly describing the perfect gentleman. 'Charity suffereth long and is kind. Charity envieth not. Charity boasteth not itself, is not puffed up, doth not behave itself unseemly, seeketh not her own, is not easily provoked, thinketh no evil, rejoiceth not in iniquity but rejoiceth in the truth; beareth all things, believeth all things, hopeth all things, endureth all things.'"

Having said this, he goes on to show that our philosophers and political economists and statesmen have made, not only a very grievous, but a very foolish mistake, in permitting their prejudices to come in and interfere with turning to the Bible to find the foundation-stones on which to erect a system for the regulation of the relations of man to man in society. "It has long been a custom," so he says, "of philosophers, to pass in silence any lessons of civilization upon the pages of scripture, and patiently to seek and deeply to love everything in Aristotle or Plato— a blossoming of prejudice only paralleled by the Christians who despise everything from Plato or Aristotle." This conviction deepened with him.

He saw no rules to guide individuals and no basis of good citizenship at all comparable to those furnished by Christianity.

By his identification with moral causes, and his uniform and earnest advocacy of righteousness in all the relations of life, this man helped to create a wholesome public opinion in Chicago, and to keep thought and life at a higher level. Immorality has been made to seem grosser, and meanness meaner, and selfishness more contemptible, and official corruption more criminal, because of words spoken by this great and scholarly preacher. What is not less to his credit, he has had the courage to look men of wealth in the face and tell them what, in virtue of their wealth, they owe to education, to art, to philanthropy, to the state, and to the uplifting of the masses of ignorant and degraded and vicious humanity with which they are daily jostled on the streets. The tonic energy of this teaching will be missed in the days to come.

4. Beyond all this, Professor Swing held with a tenacious grasp to some articles of faith which must have a place in any system of Christian theology, and some of which, indeed, are vital and fundamental to any system of religion.

Like all men who have any intelligent thought and convictions on the subject of their own existence, and their relation to the universe and the powers of the universe which are about them, he had a creed. It was not so long a creed, and it did not comprehend so much as the creeds of some other men. On the other hand, there are creeds not nearly so long and not nearly so comprehensive. To accept one of his own latest statements, he believed in God, and in the immortality of the soul, and in the love of Christ. This is not all there is to believe, nor all that it is rational to believe; but when a man accepts God in his personality and fatherhood, with all these conceptions imply, and the great doctrine of immortality as something inherent in the soul and necessary to any exalted and worthy idea of our natures, and the love of Christ as being the purest and warmest and most transforming love which ever finds its way into the human heart and mingles with the currents of human life, he has a basis of truth on which he can stand and do a certain kind of very effective work. Such a man, at least, can be a breakwater against incoming floods of materialism,

and possibly hold back some doubting soul from rushing on to the extreme limit and plunging over the awful abyss of absolute and utter negation. There is no age and no condition in which the assertion of things spiritual is not worth much to mankind. We are of the earth, earthy; but we are also of God, and may be godly.

This man who has just gone out from us never wearied of avowing his faith in things unseen and eternal, in mind over matter, in a soulhood superior to the body, in God immanent in nature but above and behind nature, and in realms of existence which are invisible and everlasting. Even here and now, he sees, just as the New Testament writers one and all saw, that one may enter on this life of the inner over the outer, and have foretastes of the ever-enduring. "Spirituality!" he says: "This is nothing else than a divineness of soul, a rising above things material, gold and bonds and raiment, and living for the soul in its relation to time and eternity. God is called a spirit because there are characteristics in all material things which separate them from perfection. The word spirit is the ideal for the everlasting. It is an embodiment of love, and of

thought, and of truth, and of life, and hence is felt to be immortal. The spiritual man is, hence, a soul not wedded to dust, but to truth and love and life. To be spiritually minded is life."

These are some of the excellencies to be discovered in the teaching and life of Professor Swing. In these excellencies lie some of the reasons why the community at large put such a high estimate on his services, and why so many men and women were bound to him in bonds of admiration and trust and love.

Why, then, not accept his system and method, and make it the system and method for all? Simply because, holding and uttering whatever he did of truth, there are, as appear in reports of his discourses, and in the popular apprehension of his teaching, omissions of elements which are central to Christianity as a method of redemption, and which enter essentially into the whole scheme of truth which gathers about the cross, and makes it a working force intent on the salvation of all humanity.

The largest fact which it is possible for the mind of man or angel to contemplate is—God. The largest fact of which we can conceive in con-

nection with God is—love. The most obvious and obtrusive fact to be discovered in connection with man is—sin. This sin of man is everywhere apparent, and it takes along with it a train of unutterable vices and miseries and woes. In Jesus the infinite love of God and the inexpressible sin of man are brought face to face and set down at close grips. We have it all in the matchless passage: "For God so loved the world that he gave his only begotten Son, that whosoever believeth on him should not perish, but have everlasting life." Jesus the Christ is there on the cross because man is a sinner and God loves him and wants to save him. But Jesus is there on the cross, not as a wholesome influence merely, but as an expiation. Jesus Christ did not come into the world to condemn men. He did not need to do this. Men were condemned already. They had condemned themselves by their own alienations and transgressions. He came to deliver them from their condemnation and save them. He did this, so he himself tells us, and so the inspired apostles tell us, by atoning for men in a sacrificial and vicarious death. He came to be the ransom of men, their Redeemer,

their High Priest, as well as their teacher and example and brother.

On these two facts, sin and the awful guilt and consequence of sin, and salvation through the death of the Son of God on the cross, stress must be laid. Not in the interest of a system merely is this to be done, but in the interest of the vitality and aggressiveness and saving power of Christianity. Otherwise Christianity has no energy in it to cope with the conditions of the problem which confronts it. For it is not a few refined people alone, a few cultivated and select circles with their philosophical troubles and doubtings, who are to be ministered to and saved; but it is the people who are down at the bottom as well, the people in the alleys and slums and in the midst of the far-away barbarians, full of sin, and ignorant and wicked and vile; and our system of help must be one which will enable us to deal effectually with the raw material of a wayward and disloyal humanity. The problem is to get men, men of all sorts and conditions, men of all races and climes, out of sin into holiness, and then to fire their breasts with the zeal of holiness. In the long run, it will not do to leave out of our

system the features and elements which exactly suit it to this end. We shall not reach the end if we do.

Twenty years ago, Professor Swing himself said, "The impulse [to a good Christian activity] is faith in Christ as the soul's Savior. It has always been the power that has carried the Pauls over the Ægean, or the pioneer Methodist to the wilds of America. It has been the earthquake force that has heaved up from a bitter sea a continent of unfading flowers and perpetual spring. Each heart busy in any pursuit moves by a natural impulse. You know what the love of pleasure does, and you know what is accomplished by what the Latin poet calls 'accursed love of gold.' Beneath all activity lies an impulse, a motive. Under the vast movement called salvation, that movement which to-day gathers the Laplanders to a worship, and makes the Sandwich Islanders join with the angels in sacred song; beneath the movement which to-day is the best glory of all civilization, under this vast renewal of the heart —lies faith in Christ, the impulse of all this profound action. The least trace of infidelity lessens the activity; unbelief brings all to a halt, and

damns the soul, not by arbitrary decree, but by actually arresting the outflow of its life. Unbelief is not an arbitrary, but a natural damnation. Faith in the Infinite Father, faith in Christ the Savior, faith in a life to come, lifts the world up as though the direct arms of God were around it drawing it toward his bosom." These are great words. They were true on the yesterday when they were uttered. They are true to-day. They will be true to-morrow and to-morrow. The vital and aggressive force of Christianity lies in souls redeemed by faith in a living Christ, and in the propulsive energy derived from him.

In that same period of twenty years ago, Professor Swing, in a sermon in which he felt called upon to assert and defend a positiveness in Christianity as against the negation and emptiness of what calls itself "free religion," spoke in this strain: "The 'free religion,' so-called, which denies our idea of prayer, dissuades from hymn and from hope in a future life, does nothing but empty the mind and the heart, and hence can never build up a great life, unless emptiness of soul is one of the foundations of greatness. All the moral greatness of the past is based upon the

assumption of such motives of God and worship and immortality and benevolence and virtue and duty. The great names all grew up out of such soil. These propositions filled the old hearts that made this great world we enjoy with its education, its liberty, its morals, its religion. It is too late, it seems to me, to ask mankind to empty its mind of all these old, grand ideas, and then expect a grandeur of character to spring up from nothingness as a soil, and to grow in a space which has no rainfall, no dew, no sunshine, but which is only a vacuum. To expect a great soul to germinate in a soil of negation, and grow in a vacuum, is to cherish a frail hope; and yet this is the prospect to which what is called 'free religion' is itself hastening and inviting us." Words again which were true on the yesterday on which they were pronounced, and which are true to-day, and which will be true to-morrow and to-morrow. It is a positive faith in a positive Christ, however the statement of it may be phrased, which secures the soul in salvation, and fills the heart with great aspirations, and stirs to unselfish and heroic endeavors to bring the world into reconciliation to God.

But our talk must cease. A conspicuous figure has disappeared from our streets and our circles. One whose words were an inspiration to many minds, and a guide to many feet, and a comfort to many troubled hearts, will utter words on earth no more. A loving and lovable man has gone hence to his reward. He will be missed, amongst large numbers sadly missed and mourned, in our city, and far and wide. When some question of vital moment has been up, and each has been eager to know the opinion of the ripest minds on the matter, it has been one of our first thoughts to turn to the Monday morning papers to see what Professor Swing said on the subject. But this we shall do no more. Like others, here and elsewhere, whose views helped to enlighten and guide the popular mind, he has passed on into the immortal spheres.

In a sermon of his on St. John, Professor Swing makes these words the closing paragraph. Repeating them after him we say our farewell, and bid him joy in the light and glory of the larger world into which he has entered: "In the natural world we perceive that the Creator has prepared a golden bed, into which, every evening, the

sun sinks. * * * But God loves the human heart more than he loves the stars. Hence, the Savior came. St. John points out to us the beautiful horizon where the soul goes down. And when our friends who have loved God die, when a humble child or a Christ-like statesman, when beautiful youth or venerable manhood, bid farewell to earth, and our tears fall upon their dust, we behold best, in John's gospel and dream, the golden couch that receives into its peace these stars sinking down from the sky of this life."

Bishop Samuel Fallows.

He Speaks Feelingly of his Association with the Lamented Preacher.

The death of Professor Swing is a personal loss to thousands of people who were not identified with him in matters of religious opinion. His broad sympathies united him with all classes of his fellow men. His voice was always heard on the side of charity, philanthropy, and reform. He was always in the front rank of advocates, when the interests of the people were concerned. The warm words of cheer and prophetic utterance, when the People's Institute was begun, will not soon be forgotten by those who heard them. His sermons were constructed according to no isometrical rules. They were beautiful, poetical, moral essays, permeated with a spirit of religious devoutness, adorned with the graces of a refined rhetoric, and enriched with wonderful wealth of literary allusion. His satire, though keen, was never malignant. A kindly humor relieved it of all bitterness. From conversations with Professor Swing I believe that he was, in the main, orthodox, in the comprehensive sense of the term. His

passionate love of the doctrine of the freedom of man, and its consequent liberty of individual thought, threw, perhaps, out of its due relation in his teachings, the complementary truth of the sovereignty of God. But the great cardinal tenets of the orthodox faith I feel sure he personally held. But, as I have said, his discourses were elevated essays rather than the usual style of sermons. Doctrinal discussions he could not bear, and did not present. Outside of the pulpit, he was a fine, discriminating critic, and an accomplished litterateur. He was a man of contemplation rather than of action. But, by pen and voice, he aided, with mighty words of well-winnowed wisdom, the men of deeds. He was a Melancthon and not a Luther.

Although occupying, by the force of circumstances, an independent position, he yet craved the sympathy and fellowship which come with a congenial ecclesiastical home. When a course of sermons was being preached by leading divines, in St. Paul's Church, on the distinctive tenets of their various denominations, I requested Professor Swing to preach one on the subject of "Independency." In a very kind manner, but with a great

deal of earnestness, he replied, "I do not believe in independency and, therefore, can not defend it. I am an independent not of my own choosing. I would much prefer to be in harmonious affiliation with others, in a church organization." Whatever doctrinal differences there might be between us, there was no abatement of my love and respect for Professor Swing. The longer I knew him, the deeper and stronger grew my affectionate regard for him. A great and good man has gone from us. Tender and gracious memories will ever be cherished in my heart of his genial presence, inspiring words and uplifting life.

Rev. H. A. Delano.

Simplicity of Religion as Taught by a Great Disciple.

I hesitate not to speak in terms of strongest eulogy of this great disciple. The question to-day of any man is not, did he deny the faith, but did he live the life of God among men? Professor Swing's life interpreted his faith.

As the Pike's Peak of our Rockies rises in lofty and monarch-like grandeur above the range of which it is a part, far above all the inferior and vaunting or vaulting summits, so this man rose among us alone, isolated, silent and majestic, above us all. The ideal of a great future for mankind marched before his mind constantly, a cloud by day and a pillar of fire by night, leading him, as Moses was led, toward the land of promise.

His was a vision of a divine, though invincible, hand, regulating all the vast laws of the universe to splendid harmony, and insuring a divine continuity of history and events, all tending to man's final good. His mind was full of dreams of the things to come, things not yet seen, and, from out

his visions of God, visions of man redeemed from his littleness, he was always making the new heaven and the new earth.

For the prosy and leaden interpretations of a Puritan theology, for a harsh, vindictive and exasperating Calvinism, for the narrowness and bigotry which drew their line through every fair garden and predestinated one half to woe, this man had no taste, no fancy, and no sympathy. And yet those who will read that memorable sermon upon "Paradise Lost" will find the evidence of his belief in a law of penalty and tears and wretchedness for those who willfully run against the edge of thorns binding every flowery path. Against injustice, hardness, cruelty, and crime his face was sternly set, yet, with a heart that always took the offender's place, considered his temptation, and weighed the circumstances. How great, how magnanimous, how tender he was! Like the bird that tarries long and sings sweetly on till captors are very close upon him, this man, knowing he had wings to fly, could afford to be indifferent to all the little agitators who swing their weapons and shout.

He saw God in the Bible and had read and copied his law into that stainless, beautiful life of his, which sunned and shamed us all. But he saw him, too, in suns and storms, in clouds and sunsets, in forest and on lakes, in woodland and in meadows fair, in June days of bloom and beauty, and in autumns rich with haze and mist, aster and golden-rod. He saw him in limping beggar and forlorn mendicant, in the faces of little children, in homes made happy by his love, and in all the order, beauty, grace, and design of the universe. He loved art, not for itself, nor its money value, but for what it expressed to him. He loved poetry, and the songs of all the great poets were upon his lips. Do not forget that while we need men to earnestly contend for faiths, we have the greater need of men whose lives will interpret and unfold their faith. There is war enough, clamor and debate enough. This great, true man has left to us all an example which rebukes the hot contention and the acrid strifes of the hour.

Rev. J. P. Brushingham

Pays an Eloquent Tribute to the Memory of a Great Man.

Strength of character and a love for the beautiful were blended in splendid proportions in the life of him for whom a city mourns to-day. Alas! There is no strength nor beauty in this earthly life, able to resist the stern reaper.

Although the great and good man, who has gone out from among us, was as gentle as a child, he was none the less heroic and manly. Although a "prince and a great man in Israel," he never impressed one as at all conscious of his own greatness. The charm of true greatness lies in the spirit of humility, which says with David Swing: "My Ego is no more than your Ego." I met him frequently among the shelves of rare and ancient volumes, of which he was such a competent and discriminating judge. At such times he seemed pleased to converse concerning the merits of favorite authors with a fellow student whose place was but a humble one compared with his own. There be great preachers and teachers who seem almost to say: " I am

Sir Oracle, and when I ope my mouth let no dog bark." How differently with him,—

> "Whose life was gentle,
> And the elements so mixed in him
> That nature could stand up and say to all the world,
>   'This was a man.'"

I remember a conversation between Professor Swing and several of us younger men in the Methodist ministry, in the course of which he magnanimously sought to explain away his own prominence as compared with that of other men in the same profession.

"For example," he said, "Dr. Hatfield, of the Methodist Episcopal Church, is among the greatest preachers of America."

"Why does he not have as large an audience as yourself, Professor Swing?"

"Oh, he is at work under a different system," was the reply. "Dr. Hatfield has a very large following, but it is distributed throughout the whole country, some in Brooklyn, some in Providence, others in Cincinnati, and in the different cities where he has labored. I have been in Chicago for over twenty years, and have personal friends enough to fill any ordinary place of worship."

He seemed anxious to impress us that his great influence was due to fortunate circumstances, and not to any special ability which inhered in himself.

That last sermon which he preached was so typical of his public ministry, and so filled with prophetic meaning. Its deep significance and rare beauty so impressed me at the time that I clipped it from the printed page and kept it as a treasured legacy, little thinking that it was his last. He saw clearly the great conflict in our present social and industrial life, and besought the clergy of the land to harmonize the contending forces. To him, love was the great gravity principle in the moral universe. To him, there was more power in a single sunbeam of love than in a thousand anvils of strife and hatred. He was the gentle Melancthon, to stand amid the upheavals of these rugged times and always counsel moderation. With that mournful headline in the public press, "Professor Swing is Dead," there came a feeling as if the morning dawn had died away; as if the sweetest zephyrs had ceased to whisper aught but his sad requiem.

His was a unique personality. America has

produced none like him in pulpit or rostrum. His public utterances were original, versatile, broad in spirit, and beautiful in diction. He never repeated himself, yet never copied any one else. All literature was to him a garden of flowers whence he drew the honeyed sweetness of pure, persuasive speech. His sympathies were so broad and tender that even the brute creation found in him a genial and kindly friend.

Too broad and catholic for dogmatism, he could be confined to no pent-up Utica of any one theological system. He was a poet-preacher, who saw all things good and beautiful in God and man. To him

> "There was one faith, one law, one element,
> One far-off divine event,
> Towards which the whole creation tends."

But how shall we speak of him who was wont to speak in accents so tender and pathos so sublime at the open grave, when others died? Not only the family of David Swing, and the Central Church, his throne of power, are bereaved to-day, but all Chicago and the great Northwest suffer loss. Literature and art, poetry, philosophy, and religion, may all bow their heads in grief. A

community can ill afford to lose its great scholars, its noble philanthropists, its patient reformers, its lofty moral teachers.

The great, modest, kindly scholar and friend is not dead. He is even now crowned with the immortality of the good and true. He will live in grateful memory. The truth which he lived and taught will immortalize his name.

From the throne of Central Church there will flow on and on a stream of living truth, "clear as crystal," broad and deep and beautiful.

Rev. T. W. Handford.

The broad and generous charity, the large, hopeful, all-enduring love, that formed the theme of David Swing's ministry, became incarnate in his life. Beautiful and pathetic, eloquent and inspiring as his sermons were, he was the grandest sermon of all. And he, though dead, will be eloquent for many a day. Thousands whose hands he never grasped, whose faces he never knew, will feel sad to the center of their hearts that death has borne away so wise a teacher, so gentle a friend. He has served his day and generation, and has "fallen on sleep," as did that other David of the kingly race. His sun went down at eventide; it went not down in darkness and in storm, but melted in the pure light of heaven. We need not trouble about the future. Prof. Swing will have no successor. Such men can not be succeeded. Beecher, and Spurgeon, and Swing, have done their work. The men are few and far between, who could gracefully wear the mantle of these ascended saints. Other men and other methods will be able to do grand work in the old places. To follow in a procession is one

thing, but to succeed a great man is quite another.

There have been many poets—only one Milton; many preachers—only one Swing. He has gone from us, and yet we can not think that that busy brain has ceased to act, or that that large heart has ceased to love. Milton is not dead. Hampden is not dead. Washington and Lincoln are not dead, nor is David Swing. He has entered the silent land, and we stand by that gate of death that leads to life, silent, and solitary, and sad.

Resolutions Passed by the Fourth Presbyterian Church.

Resolved, That the news of the death of the Rev. David Swing, formerly pastor of this church, has filled us with deep sorrow, and we desire to express to the family and the friends our deepest sympathy in this severe bereavement; and we desire also to record our high appreciation of Professor Swing's services, while a pastor for nearly ten years, to many in this church, and our constant love and respect for him. With feelings of thankfulness we recognize his many services to the community as a whole, and rejoice in the record of labors so manifold and so fruitful. The memory of his life and work will long linger among us. We recognize his great talents, and his life will be an inspiration, as an example of sweet and gentle service, and of untiring devotion to the cause of righteousness. May the comfort and strength his words have often brought to those in sorrow and distress now be the portion of those who see a beloved form laid to his rest, and follow through the unseen portals the immortal spirit that has entered into its eternal home.

Resolved, That the session of the Fourth Presbyterian Church attend the services in a body, and that a copy of these resolutions be sent to the family.

Prof. Swing's Reasons for Withdrawal from the Presbyterian Church.

Letter to the Fourth Presbyterian Church.

My Beloved Congregation: During the past three months our relations have been disturbed, almost daily, by new rumors and new facts, indicating an approaching end of our ties as pastor and people. It has hitherto been impossible for me to address to you any words that might put rumors to rest and cast any light upon the future. Neither you nor I desire to break up associations of long standing—associations peculiarly pleasant, and even sacred. It was human, at least, in us all, to await the command of the ecclesiastical court that presides over such affairs and that is supposed to issue its decrees with sufficient promptness. At last, the court to which this society is amenable has formally expressed its belief, or rather its hope, that, after the close of this year, this church will place itself in a position less irregular—will find a pastor among the Presbyterian clergy in good standing. The session, neither

as a session nor as individuals, has said anything to warrant the hope or conviction expressed by the Presbytery, but has waited the simple movement of the cold church-law.

In this crisis, the session has, in the hope of saving the relations mutually pleasant, urged me to return to the Presbyterian brotherhood; but, as the most precious thing to one who has dared stand up to preach is his capital of truth and his intellectual liberty, the kind wish of the session could not for a moment be entertained. I would therefore announce to-day that, on or before the close of the year, I shall cease preaching to the Fourth Presbyterian Church. It is due to the Presbytery, composed for the most part of my own faithful friends, that I should hasten to confess their authority over this society.

As my heart has always been unequal to speaking above a whisper any words that affected it deeply, this separation will come without any farewell sermon, or any other words that lie near the land of tears. As to the old friendships, some of them will run on under some other roof; none of them will be broken by any act of mine. In this matter of friendship, I hope it will not be

very undignified if I confess here that my mind recalls the song we used to sing in the days of romance and tenderness:

> "Here's a sigh for those who love me;
> A smile for those who hate."

But, thinking of the sacred duties of a minister of Christ, a holier hymn comes to memory:

> "While place we seek or place we shun,
> The soul finds happiness in none;
> But with our God to guide the way,
> 'Tis equal joy to go or stay."

Though I am unable to rise to the sublime height of such words, their spirit will cheer me, and will soften the good-by of

Your devoted friend,
DAVID SWING.

Oct. 31, 1875.

The Reasons for a Central Church.

It is not my purpose to-day to preach a discourse, but to state some of the reasons which led me to begin a public service in this place, and to commence it with great pleasure and with great hope. In the opening up of all new enterprises, of either a secular or religious nature, it is customary for some one to utter inaugural words, that the enterprise may lie before all in its full scope of business, or pleasure, or duty. It seems quite necessary that now, when we are about to enter upon a series of services in such new surroundings, some words should be spoken by way of introduction, words of explanation, and of congratulation, too. Many of you attended the religious services held for a time two years ago in this very house. Many of you left the room then with regrets, and to-day you come back with joy. The reasons for such a return need reviewing.

That there may be some method to my remarks to-day, I shall speak of certain arguments in favor of such a central church as we here found to-day, and shall classify the arguments as material and spiritual.

The material argument is quite large. In an age when all other branches of life study convenience and comfort, religion must imitate the other paths of action and being, and hence will not dare be difficult and inconvenient in her style, when the wicked world, in its method, is studious of public comfort. It is all vain to say that our fathers, in other times and countries, walked five miles to church, in summer's heat or winter's storm. So they walked also in journeying over the world. All things were equally full of toil and vexation. The hotels, where they passed the night, were only barns; the beds on which they slept were hard as the road on which they had walked, and the food on the table was as full of toil and vexation as were the dusty journey and the miserable tavern. Men walked five miles to church, because they knew of no such thing as convenience or comfort. Men exhausted in that day, upon roads and hills and against sun and storm, strength of body and mind which should have been turned along more useful paths.

When the gate was opened to let in the new idea of convenience and comfort, it had to be opened toward religion as well; for when man

has learned that he need not be miserable as to his table, as to his hotel, as to his bed, and as to his home, he will no longer be miserable as to his worship. When a bad idea has become exposed, it is routed everywhere. When Champollion found the clue to the Egyptian stones, he soon read everything in rapid succession. Thus, when man discovered that he need not be miserable in some one thing, he at once sprang to the conclusion that he need not make any part of life more burdensome than fate itself should demand.

There is a tendency in the world to utilize its forces. The modern age will surpass all former times in the quantity of labor it will, in a given time, bring to bear upon a useful task; but it will not waste time and power. It will not walk all day to church and home again, if it can go to church in a few minutes, and in comfort as it goes. It reserves its force for needful ends. Now, when all the places of worship that stood near the center of this great city were torn down and removed, the destroyers of these temples took worship away from the place where all the carriage-ways meet, and again asked a large population to do as our Scottish and Puritan fathers

had done—face the storm and exhaust the day for the kirk. And this central population has declined the invitation. The meeting-house must come to them. It must be located where paths converge—where the public carriages meet. There must be some sanctuary near each multitude.

A second material argument may be found in the peculiar shape of our city. Its business is not spread out for miles along some one street. It is massed into one solid square mile; and hence, in that square mile, there are thousands of business young men, who are quite far removed from the family churches, and who would be quite near to some central church or churches. On account of this peculiar massing of business, the magnificent hotels of this city are located in a most unusual manner. Instead of reaching along for five miles in a straight line, they are in a circle, about a dozen strong, and all within three or four squares of this theater. Owing to recent destruction of dwelling-houses, and to the marvelous beauty and comfort and quiet of these hotels, they are the homes of hundreds, almost thousands, of persons who once lived along the avenues, and who once attended the old churches of the former city.

These statements will give you an outline of the material argument that not only justifies this opening of a new central church, but which entreats us all to enter upon this work with zeal and without delay or misgiving. To have a church to which so many can come so easily, not only from the central portion of the place, but from the three divisions of the city, is an idea that should long ago have touched your hearts and have swept your judgment. It is impossible to postpone this enterprise.

Let us now come to the moral aspects of the case. Here our chief task will be to meet objections; for, in the brief statements already made, I have absolutely given positive reason enough for the existence of this new society.

First, this need not be called an "experiment." It is a service to which most of us come back after a few years' absence. In this very room we sang our hymns and sent up our prayers and examined into the high truths of life for almost two years, and those two years confirmed all I have said about a church accessible to the public. So great a success were those two years, that the best men of the Fourth Church debated

with many of you as to the propriety of holding a central service on the Sunday mornings, debated about some method by which this service here could be continued. They themselves went off to their little church, an inaccessible church, with misgivings as to duty, and for months debated with you and with themselves as to the duty of the future.

Thus we return here, cheered by two years of experience, an experience which even a North Side interest could not readily conceal or erase. The same gentlemen who stand as responsible friends of this movement stood for it two years ago, thus showing that there is nothing of mere impulse or novelty in their conduct, but that their action is based upon the experience of two years, and the reflection of two years more. This would seem sufficient answer to any who may feel that here we are to make an "experiment." It is not so. Here we resume, to-day, a reasonable, most wise union of hearts, that was interrupted by an accident, a beautiful and beloved little accident called the Fourth Church. And now that Professor Patton has removed that accident by his twenty-eight tears shed before the synod, I am

free, not to embark upon an untried sea, but to return "home again from a foreign shore." We know all about this channel and this ship. You heard these hymns before sung in such chorus; you have seen these faces, all happy here, in other days. This is the sober second thought of a thousand persons.

You will please remember, too, that these other two years of worship in this house ended while your minister was still in full communion with the Presbyterian Church. No trial for heresy had ever shown any signs of coming. Hence, into these meetings there entered no sensational element, and they drew their life from no party heat. Hence the return of us all to this place has not in it the least element of a rebuke to Professor Patton, nor of a vindication of me. This service began before any war between that brother and me began, and I believe a central church will go forward, near where we are now, after Professor Patton and I shall have passed away from life and memory. To me, and to all with whom I have conversed, this movement seems to have sprung only from a public need, and contains in it almost no element of the

experimental and sensational. A city of half a million people needs this central society.

Let me now allude to another objection: "You will have no church social life, no prayer-meetings, no church socials, no sewing societies, no fellowship with each other." First, let us deny this gentle charge. Out of this certainly must come, and within a year or two let us hope, a regular church, Independent or Congregational, with its own hall for worship, and with its rooms for all kinds of church life. There are no reasons whatever against the formation and success of a church where all these highways meet. It can easily come, and will soon come. We deny the charge.

But let us make a second answer to the objection. It is these words: The value of a congregation depends upon the number and the righteousness of the people that attend its Sunday morning service. When, out of a thousand or two thousand people in a congregation, some seventy or a hundred gather at a "church social," you must not point me to that scene and call it "church life." Our opinion as to the value of the piety and intelligence of the vast congrega-

tion is such, that, in estimating the moral worth of a church, we should rather look to them of a Sunday in their pews, than to this little playing, feasting group, laughing the happy hours away.

The people who assemble Sunday morning determine the value of the sanctuary. If they are good, righteous citizens, then that two thousand are a noble church, aside from "church socials." And when, out of one thousand persons, twenty ladies meet to sew for the orphans, you must not point us to that scene and call it "church life." Our thought will still run after the one thousand persons not there, and with the feeling that in that one thousand lies the work of the society. The service that blesses the most is the chief service.

And not much should be said about the fellowship and friendship that springs up in the regular house of God. We know all about this. We know that the congregation upon the avenues meet only for the worship of God, and do not stand heart to heart and hand in hand, away from the altars. Each city is full of strangers. We live next door to each other and remain unknowing and unknown. Here, where you will all have

your regular seats, and where some of the stiffness of the more formal churches will be wanting, you will soon reach an acquaintance with your neighbor and a final knowledge of all, not to be found in churches, which would seem to promise more. Hence, while at some not remote day we may have what is called "church life," we must not overrate the market value of that "life" and feel that the church's glory lies in that direction. The grand churches of the seventeenth century, that transformed Christ into a friend and made God to be Love, had no sewing societies and no church festivals. They had religious men in the pulpit and in the pews. This is the aim that should lie before us all, religion at the desk and down in the cushioned seats. All else will be insignificant, if we can reach, at last, intelligence and religion. Thus have I alluded to the objections proposed to you and me. I pass now to advantage and intentions.

In our independent and congregational relations, we, from preacher to people, expect to enjoy freedom of thought. I desire and fully intend to preach the religion of Christ, but in a liberty of thought not accorded me in my former relations.

Congregationalism will afford you and me all the liberty we desire. With that sect there is a concentration upon Christ as a sufficient Savior, and upon the idea of rewards and punishments, that leaves Christianity pure in its principles and power, and leaves the Christian mind free. The denomination that can welcome Storrs and Buddington and Alvin Bartlett and Helmer is liberal enough for all Christian purposes. We do not ask for a church broad enough to permit us to be atheists. In Congregationalism, if at last it should receive us, we shall find liberty enough. Those denominations in which the church property is held by the congregation offer sufficient liberty of opinion. It is where the meeting-house and the lot and the organ belong to a certain creed that thought is enslaved. There pulpit and pew continue to repeat shibboleths because property follows certain formulas of doctrine. Congregational property secures freedom of thought. While property represents dead ideas, men will bow in meekness to the ideas. As Independents or Congregationalists, there lies before us a beautiful prospect of intellectual freedom. As, when Xenophon and his companions after a long wandering in the

mountains of Armenia, lost, starved, home-sick, and harassed by barbarians, at last, from a mountain, beheld the sea, they wept for joy and shouted, "The sea! the sea!" for it was to carry them home; so you and I, coming out of the wilderness where we were lost and starved and sore pressed by barbarians, may well look out toward the wide expanse of liberty and cry out, "The sea! the sea!" It will now carry us all home. The ocean of freedom is broad and deep and beautiful. It washes all civilized shores. All the balmy and fragrant breezes come from its depths. The light of heaven smiles on its face.

This ocean of liberty is the true consolation and inspiration of all who write or speak. He that speaks only by rote, or only to a line marked down by another, can only be a slave. His heart can never be the home of any love or earnestness. I do not speak of this vista of liberty on my own account alone. Not only must a speaker be free, but the audience also loves to feel that they are free minds, and are sitting in a sanctuary where the flag of liberty waves over them. The rigid details of the more iron-like creeds do not oppress the clergy only, but the church membership also..

For the membership of the modern church has risen in intelligence and in the power of its logical faculty, and, as deeply as the clergy, it feels oppressed by the dogmas to which it once subscribed, and from which it knows not just how to escape. Much of the time of the clergy and of the higher order of laymen is now spent in declaring how they do not believe in denouncing it; thus showing with what joy they would hail spiritual freedom, were it placed within their grasp. In that theological war which was waged in this city two years ago, the liberal clergymen did not surpass the laity in the quantity of indignation aroused by such an inquisition held over words and sentences. Clergymen, from their theological studies, often endure, or forgive, or even enjoy, a certain amount of theological skirmishing and conflict. They look sometimes upon such trials as matters of course. But the laymen, trained to the useful in religion, and thinking more of Christ than they do of theologians, often feel very deeply the private and public wrong done by such arraignments for heresy. Their cheeks burn with shame that ministers should degrade their calling, and that, in a skeptical age, Christianity should be so exposed to new criticism and new contempt.

Not alone, then, am I in the power to appreciate a church where the discord of a "trial" can not come, but you all equally rejoice that here freedom of opinion pours around you its health-giving and joy-bringing atmosphere. We all desire to escape a repetition of certain foolish processes brought by hasty men.

Our age, in its Christian department, is attempting to find broader grounds in doctrine, upon which a larger multitude may stand in a sweeter peace. That there are a hundred sects, and that these war with each other must result from some defect in the mind or in the sentiments of the heart. Such discord can not but come from either ignorance or selfishness. There must be some one religion in which men might meet; for God is one, and heaven is one, and virtue is one, and vice is one. Our age is attempting to find the ideas that separate men and the other ideas that bring them together. It wishes to destroy the former, and crown the latter. It is seeking a higher unity of thought, that there may be a deeper unity of sentiment and love. The Calvinist and the Arminian, the Baptist and the Episcopalian, and even the Catholics under the lead

of Hyacinthe and Dollinger, are seeking this wider ground of faith and love. As rapidly as this noble truth is found, the ideas that have separated hearts and have torn the church to pieces will be cast out and despised, and toward the better central truth the public will turn with a new affection.

In assembling here to-day, we come only in the spirit of the Christian age, seeking the higher truth that will bind more nearer together and bring more of peace and goodness to society. We all come, not to contradict and complain, but to affirm all the precious truths of the Gospel, and to love them the more because of our perfect freedom. Not as an enemy do we appear on the horizon, but as the fast and firm friends of all the churches of whatever name. I know the spirit of this audience. Ten years have mingled us much together, in public and private, and I feel free to say that I know your hearts; and, knowing them, confess with joy that our combined desire is to hold, not an unhappy, negative religion, but one full of positive devotion to Jesus Christ, and to all the precious interests of humanity.

We come, not as iconoclasts, but as lovers of man. We do not desire to be a rude force, like lightning or a storm, but to be a gentler influence, like sunshine and dew, under which the gentlest plant may grow and reach its own peculiar blossoming. If we shall wish to deny certain doctrines, once believed, it will be that Christ may not be injured by the inventions of men. If we shall ignore or slight other ideas, it will be that they may not hide from us that Way, Truth and Life, in whose presence is noonday, in whose absence is night. Setting forth each day from Christ, as the radiating point of our system, we desire to apply his life to human life, his pardon to human sin, his hope to human hearts. Believing that Christianity underlies, not only a heaven beyond the grave, but all good homes and cities and empires here, we all wish from Sunday to Sunday to seek out these adaptations with our intellect, that we may obey them with our soul.

And, besides the words of Christianity, there remains its spirit, something above delineation in language. Those who assemble here desire, not only to deal in the morals and theology of Christ, but to live in the midst of that divine

charity that enveloped our Lord in all hours. Toward even Pilate and all the adverse throng, Christ was full of tenderness. From Christ comes the lesson that ill-will, anger, self-worship, are only painful blemishes upon the soul, and that, until man can deal in perfect kindness with those who differ with him in thought, he is yet far down in the depths of barbarism. One of our public men, who had lived a long and serene public life, confessed, lately, that in early manhood he had felt that he could not afford to get angry at a fellow, for anger was such a disgrace to the soul.

There is a spirit of Jesus Christ more Godlike than even His words; a spirit which all may feel, but which none can express,—just as one may feel in his bosom the beauty of a day in June, but can never embody the heart-beat in language. But such a spirit there is. It will sit down and talk with the skeptical scientist as Jesus talked with the woman at the well or with the ruler at nightfall. The wider the difference of opinion, the more eager this spirit of Christ to show us benevolence. It leaves the ninety and nine in the fold of truth, and goes forth with

a smile and a benediction toward the one infidel or atheist or skeptic who may seem to be wandering in the mazes of entangled thought. To this doctrine and spirit of Christ, we, the Central Church, would subscribe anew, this day. We would renew the vows of former years. We ask all the great circle of churches around to extend us their good will. We omit no one, not even the Catholics. We shall love to offer them all the help of our right hand and our heart's best wishes and best love.

The Duty of the Pulpit in the Hour of Social Unrest.

David Swing's Last Sermon.

While men slept the enemy sowed tares among the wheat.—Matt. xiii. 25.

It would be a happiness to all of us, could we meet to-day having in our hands branches from the woods or shells from the shore where we may have recently attempted to find pleasure and rest; but the events of the last few months, and the gloom of the future, have stolen from prairie and seacoast their long-found charm.

The trees and the waters have for many weeks past sighed over the infirmities of our country.

To find the images of greatness, we have been compelled to look into the past. When President Cleveland intervened, and, perhaps, saved this city from being plundered and burned, some men feared to thank him for such a quick intervention. July must deal very gently with criminals who are to vote in November.

Not since 1861, has the sky been as dark as it is to-day. We have unconsciously built up within

this generation two black passions—the one, the feeling that money is the only thing worth living for, and the other, that work must hate capital. Thus the level of all society is lowered—the moneyed class by its worship of gold, the other class by its life of hate. While wealth has inflamed its possessors and worshipers, there has lived and talked an army of angry orators, whose purpose has been to make the men who work in the vineyard hate the men who pay them at nightfall. In such circumstances, the vineyard will soon be, first, a battle field, and then, a desert.

It would seem that all the Christian clergy, Catholic and Protestant, and all the ethical teachers should, this autumn, enter into a new friendship with these two discordant classes, and preach to both alike the gospel of a high humanity. The churches and pulpits of all grades possess a vast influence. They do not hold any "key to the situation," or any "balance of power"; they can not open and close the gates of the earthly heaven and hell for America; but they possess an enormous moral force—a power that should no longer be exhausted upon little theological issues and practices. All the intellectual and spiritual

resources of the pulpit should be exhausted in the effort to advance human character. Society needs speedy and large additions to both its righteousness and its common sense.

What saved the country from a great calamity last July, was the fact that the school-house, the church, and the press, of the last fifty years had quietly created an intelligence large enough to stand between the people and their ruin. When the new kind of autocrat ordered all the railway wheels between the two oceans to stop, and had sat down to enjoy the silence of locomotives and iron rails, there were so many noble and educated men in the railway service that the voice of the autocrat was the only noise that died out. It was not President Cleveland alone that came between us and a great calamity. He was aided by the high common sense of a large majority of the railway employes. The railway union of working men was not formed for a career of mingled cruelty and nonsense, but that men might help each other in honorable ways and in hours of great wrong and need. The union was not formed in order that railway men might become beggars, at a time when their work

was bringing almost a barrel of flour a day for each family. With wages at two dollars a day and wheat at half a dollar a bushel, the strike and trouble of July were not only unreasonable but malicious.

Nearly all clergymen stand close to the people. They are reared in the philosophy that gives bread to the hungry. The gospel of Christ is one of infinite sympathy. Men who from choice enter the ministry of the Judean religion are never so happy as when they see the laborer sit down under a good roof to a table spread with abundant food. In the life of the average clergyman, a large part of his thought and public utterance, and actual labor and sympathy, is given to what is called the common people. The upper classes need little. There is nothing in the millionaire that appeals to the heart. The rich are so self-adequate that they may draw admiration and esteem, but not sympathy. The heart of the pulpit is freely given to the middle and lower classes. In all time, the common people have attracted to themselves the most of both philosophy and poetry, but the attention and the affection, they won in the former times seem weak,

compared with the love that has been flung to them in this passing century. Under the influence of this sympathetic philosophy, wages have been advanced, humane laws have been passed, the facts of health and disease have been studied, and new action has come with new light; and when into such an age of both inquiry and action there is projected such a scene as that of last July, the spectacle does not belong to reason or humanity, but only to despotic ignorance and ill will.

Labor may, and even must, organize, but the laborers must organize as just and law-abiding men, country-loving men, and not as bandits. The depressing memory of last July is not to be found in the fact that labor was organized, or wholly in the fact that it "struck." The strike was, indeed, perfectly destitute of common sense, but the chief disgrace of the hour lay in the willingness of free men to obey a central despot and join in such acts of wrong and violence as would have disgraced savages. Benevolence is humiliated that it must feed and clothe men who will break the skull or kick to insensibility the brother who wishes to earn bread for his hungry family.

It was discovered last July that some of the labor unions employ fighting men to go to and fro to hunt up and knock down those who do not join in the folly—those who are satisfied with their wages or who must work. Not every workman is a trained pugilist. So men are hired to spend the day or the week in pounding men who are noble and industrious. The cry "I am an American" does not avail as much in Chicago as the words "I am a Roman" availed Paul in Jerusalem. When Paul said he was a Roman, the mob fell back; but when Mr. Cleveland said, "These pounded men are Americans," it was thought by some that he was not the proper person to make the remark. And yet, our pulpits have, for fifty years, been trying to make Christians, and our schools and printing presses have been trying to endow these Christians with sense.

Quite a number of clergymen have banded together to preach the gospel of personal righteousness; that Christianity is Christ in human life, Christ in society, Christ in money, and Christ in work. We preachers must all come to that definition of the church. This height of thought will make all dizzy for a time; but the quality of

our old Christianity will not meet the demands of a republic. A despotism may be sustained by Catholics or Protestants, but a republic must be sustained by men.

Labor guilds are as old as work and capital; but one kind of labor guild is new, and let us all pray that it shall not live to become old. In the darkness of the fourteenth century, the young workingman looked happily forward to the day when he could be admitted into the guild of his craft. His mother and sisters looked after his habits, that his character might be above reproach. The approach to the initiation day was much like a youth's approach to his first communion. New clothes, a feast, new conduct, new inspiration, new hopes came with the hour that placed this new name upon the noble roll. But this was in the dark ages. In the close of the nineteenth century, when the heavens and earth are ablaze with the light of Christ, when love for man is written everywhere in letters of gold, when congresses of religion meet to teach us that all men are brethren, then the men who join a guild shake a bludgeon at their brother and are advised by a reckless king to buy a gun. Some

men call this phenomenon a commercial disturbance. It is nothing of the kind. In the South Sea Islands it is barbarism; among the carnivorous animals it is called ferocity; in our civilized land it is infamy.

It seems evident that Christianity asks laborers to be organized into societies. If a church may be organized that Christians may help each other and confer with each other about all things that pertain to the church, why may not carpenters and railway men form a union that many minds and many hearts may find what is best for the toilers in their field? The word "Church" means a gathering of people, but if the exigencies of religion may demand an assembly, so may the exigencies of a trade. But none of these assemblages can sustain any relations whatever to violence or any kind of interference with the liberty or rights of man. For a vast group of railway men to sign away their personal liberty and permit some one man to order them around as though slaves, is a spectacle pitiful to look upon; but to band together for interference with the rights of man is, not a mental weakness, but a crime.

It is a great task for a labor guild to study and fully learn what are the facts and the needs of itself. Before men quit their employers, they should all know the reason of the move. After men have been idle for a winter and have come to regular work and regular pay, if they hasten to strike, their reason ought to be so large that the whole world can see it. But we do things differently in enlightened America. Our men hasten to throw down tools and their wages, and, at last, when starving, they ask some committee to make a microscopical search for the reason of the distress. And, before this reason is known, eminent men express themselves as in full sympathy with it. All the railway wheels in America were ordered to stop out of sympathy with a reason which a committee was looking for with a microscope. The railways were giving work to four millions of people. This work was all "called off" by a man with some telegraphic blanks, and the poor families supported by the Northwestern lost two hundred thousand dollars, the workmen of the Illinois Central one hundred and sixty-four thousand dollars, of the Milwaukee and St. Paul one hundred and seventy-five thou-

sand dollars, and thus on to the millions—all which loss was ordered from sympathy with men who were getting six hundred dollars a year.

Labor unions will waste their work by the millions of dollars' worth, and will soil their name and ruin the sympathy of literature, art and religion, as long as they trust their cause to hotheaded, ignorant, illogical men. Labor should have for its chieftains our Franklins or our John Stuart Mills. These should be its guide. If our land possesses no such minds, then are we on the eve of untold misfortune. When labor shall have Franklins for its walking delegates, it will enter upon a new career. Capital will confer with it, congresses of workingmen will meet, and men will find the wages of each toiler and of each new period, but nothing can be done by a foolish despot with a club. Yes, something can be done— the Republic can be hopelessly ruined through a ruined manhood.

The wages and whole welfare of the laboring man have been much advanced in twenty-five years, but the gun and club have taken no part in this progress. Conference, thought, reason, benevolence, have accomplished the blessed task,

and they will do much more when they are invited to help our race. Moral power makes laws. It shames the guilty. It dissolves adamant. It founded the Christian Church. It has civilized whole races; it has emancipated the mind; it has freed slaves.

It may easily be remembered that a London man a few years ago unveiled the wrongs inflicted upon poor young girls. This injustice did not need to be examined by a microscope. The heart of London became aflame with indignation. The Archbishop of Canterbury, and the Archbishop of Westminster, Cardinal Manning, the Bishop of London, Sir William Harcourt, and Sir Robert Cross, flung their minds and hearts into the cause, and the parliament passed a new law for a longer and diviner protection of girls.

To many labor unions all talk of moral power carries the weight of only nonsense. The moral influence theory is indeed defective, but it is the only one within human reach. If a dozen men should resolve that they have rights to seats in a street car, their theory seems good; but, on getting into one of these vehicles, if they find the seats all taken, unless they can club those persons out

of those seats, the theory of those dozen unionists is very defective. When a man resolves that he ought to sit down and then stands up, his resolution is defective. But what makes it defective? The rights of the man who is sitting down. So when a set of men resolve that they will work only for four dollars a day, they hold an imperfect platform, because of the rights of the men who will work for three dollars. Should a clergyman resign his pulpit because his people will not pay him six thousand dollars a year, his theory is incomplete indeed, unless he can kill the preachers who will come for five thousand dollars. But he must go to and fro with his imperfect theory. It is spoiled by the rights of other preachers. Thus, against all labor unions not strictly moral, the laws of the human race rise up. The rights of mankind oppose them. All society is founded upon the rights of man— not of the man who works for three dollars a day, but of the man also who works for one dollar or for any sum whatever. Any force in a labor union means anarchy. A guild, without violence, may be imperfect, but, with violence, it is infamous.

Where would our city and perhaps our nation have been in this September, had not the laborers in the town of Pullman and in the whole land been for the most part law-abiding? The churches may confess the rashness of the strike, but we must forgive the mistakes of those who respected the rights of mankind and the laws of the land. Many toilers were so patient and law-abiding as to give promise of being worthy citizens of a great country. What all those workmen need is a leadership worthy of their cause or their flag.

The flag of labor is a perfectly glorious one— too grand to be carried by a fanatic or a simpleton or a criminal. Capital is nothing until labor takes hold of it. A bag will hold money, but a bag can not transform that money into an iron road, a bridge, a train of cars, an engine. An armful of bonds did not fling the bridge over the arm of the sea at Edinburgh; the bonds of England did not join the Mediterranean to the Red Sea; gold did not erect St. Peter's at Rome; nor did it lift up any of the sublime or beautiful things in any art. Money came along and attempted to buy the canvases of Angelo, but it did not paint

them. The millions of people who came here last summer did not come to see the millions of money, but to see what labor had done with money, and they saw a great spectacle. What domes! What arches! What "Courts of Honor!" What canals! What statues! What machines! What pictures! What jewels! What thought! What taste! What love! And yet the whole scene was the matchless emblazonry of labor. As God manifests himself in the external objects of earth and in the millions of stars, thus man speaks by his works, and in our world labor sits enthroned. Capital is a storehouse of seeds; labor is their field, their soil, their rain, and their summer-time. Over a potency so vast and godlike, only Wisdom herself should preside. If our age has any great men— men whose hearts are warm and pure, and whose minds are large as the world,—it should ask them to preside over the tasks and wages of the laborer. Anarchy, crime, and folly should be asked to stand back. Those three demons may be called to the front when our laborers are seeking for poverty and disgrace.

You have all heard of the hostility of capital to labor. But there is no special truth in the

phrase. Labor is just as hostile to labor. The whole truth is this: Man is not anxious to spend his money. There is a saying that "the fool and his money are soon parted," but we have not reached the maxim that labor loves to make presents to labor. Did you ever know a blacksmith who was happy to pay large bills to the plumber? Are the carpenters anxious to have their tailors advance the price of a suit of clothes? Are the "walking delegates" for the plasterers anxious to pay the farmer a dollar for wheat? If reports be true, there are laboring men in the West who are so hostile to the labor of their brothers that they are going to buy most all needful things in the shops of England.

Thus labor is as great an enemy of labor as it is of capital. The hostility between labor and money is a mischievous fiction, gotten up by dreamers and professional grumblers, who wish to ride into office or fame by parading a love for the multitude. This false love ought soon to end its destructive career. Last June and July it cost the workingmen many millions of dollars. Had some walking delegates of Christianity told these men that labor and capital are eternal friends—

that labor is the language of money, the body it assumes, the life it lives,—our summer would have been full of industry and honor. How could Krupp hate the men who are doing his will in massive iron? How could Field hate the men who were laying his cable in the ocean? The church must help stamp all our industrial falsehoods into the dust, and must wave over all men the flag of brotherhood.

So rapidly has friendship grown between capital and labor, that a law is now before the British parliament looking to a compensation to each laborer or his family for injuries the workingman may have received in the execution of his task. When passed, this law will each year give ten millions of dollars to the working class of the three islands. This law is not coming from the "club" or "gun," but from the Christianity of England.

This new humane philosophy has counted all the toilers who have been injured in their toil. It saw fifty-seven men killed while building the Forth bridge, and 130 die among the wheels and machines used in digging the Manchester canal. This new kindness has studied longer and found

that of each ten thousand men employed on the railways, fourteen are killed in a year and eighty badly crippled. In the long past there was no love that counted these dead or injured men. A dead laborer was as a dead horse or a dead dog. The riots and destruction and barbarity of last July set back all this new friendship, and made brotherly love despair of the present and future. The evil one hath done this. Endless abuse, endless complaint, endless violence, openly taught anarchy, have succeeded in making work the enemy of money. You can recall the Bible story of the person who came at night and sowed tares among the springing wheat.

The fact that the United States army had to hasten hither to save life and property can not all be charged upon the immigrants in our land. We have of late years been producing a group of Americans who care nothing for right or wrong, and who have become the masters of all the forms of abuse and discontent. It is evident that the influx of anarchists ought to cease, but we must not forget the crop our nation is growing out of its own soil. All the cities seem uniting to make law ridiculous. The alien who will sell

his vote for a few shillings is not so low as the American who will prefer these votes to principles. The immigrant may act through the absence of patriotism for his new land, but the American acts through total depravity.

The foreigners are generally manipulated by political confidence men, who are home-made.

The general theme of this morning is too large for the narrow limits of an essay, but it is possible for us to feel that our great Christian organism ought to be applied, from these dark days onward, to the making of the Christlike character. The church, Catholic and Protestant, has lived for all other causes; let it, at last, live for a high intelligence and for individual righteousness. Literature and science and the public press will help the church. All these wide-open and anxious eyes must perceive clearly that our national and personal happiness must come from the study and obedience of that kind of ethics which became so brilliant in Palestine. Our Jewish friends need not call it Christian, and our rationalized minds need not call it divine. What is desirable and essential is, that its spirit shall sweep over us. Called by any name, it is

a perfect salvation for our country and for each soul. The time and money the church has given to a metaphysical inquiry and teaching have been a total loss. In the great college courses, there are studies in classic language, and in high mathematics, that strengthen the intellect; but no such virtue has ever been found to flow from the theological studies of the church. For hundreds of years the mind has found in these enigmas its slow doctrine. There, thousands, even millions, of thinkers have found their grave. There, the colossal mind of even a Pascal grew confused and weak. There, great men have lost their blessed earth while they were fighting over the incomprehensible. God did not give man this globe that it might be made a desert or a battlefield, but that it might be made the great home of great men.

As often as creeds and dogmas have detached the mind from humanity, literature and art and science have rushed in to save the precious things of society. But these agencies have done this only by carrying, in prose and verse and science, the laws of love, duty and justice, by delineating man as a brother of all men and as a subject in

the mighty kingdom of law and love. In an age and in a republic marked by an amazing effort to turn all things, all days, all life, into gold, our pulpits must make a new effort to reveal and create man the spiritual being, man temperate, man studious, man a lover of justice, man the brother, man Christlike. The same science that is seeking and finding the sources of wealth, and that is filling the young mind with longings to become rich, can find and teach all the worth of man as a spiritual being, and can compel a great nation and a great manhood to spring up from the philosophy of the soul.

To reach a result so new and so great, the pulpit must select new themes. It must cull them from the field where the mob raves, from the shops where men labor, from the poverty in which many die, from the office where wealth counts its millions. Even so beclouded a pagan as Virgil sang that when the mob is throwing stones and firebrands, and is receiving weapons from its fury, if wisdom will only become visible and speak to it, it will listen, and at last obey. We have the mob; it is high time for a divine wisdom to speak to it.

Our planet not only rolls on in the embrace of the laws of gravitation, of light and heat, vegetable and animal life, and the strange encompassment of the electric ether, but it flies onward amid spiritual laws far more wonderful—laws of labor and rest, laws of mental and moral progress, laws of perfect justice and of universal love. Oh, that God, by his almighty power, may hold back our Nation from destruction for a few more perilous years, that it may learn where lie the paths, in which, as brothers just and loving, all may walk to the most of excellence and the most of happiness.

The Redemption of a City.

David Swing's Unfinished Sermon.

Who redeemeth thy life from destruction.—Psalm ciii. 4.

The theological form of redemption is no longer clearly understood. The term passed through many centuries without having its import much questioned. All the Christian myriads assumed that there was a heavy account standing against each living soul and that Christ had come to redeem those who were lying in jail under this debt. He had paid off the old claim and stood forth in the light of a kind redeemer. At last came the Calvinists to teach that this floating debt was paid for only a part of the debtors. The Arminians taught that arrangements had been made by which all debtors could arrange to have their old account erased. In the long meanwhile, the import of the word "redemption" was a commercial meaning.

Mr. Gladstone has recently written an essay against Anna Besant's memories of her early theology. It would seem that Anna Besant does injustice to the intellect and faith of the modern

churches at large; but there are many congregations in England and our land to whose membership her delineation of a doctrine would sound like the purest truth, while that of Mr. Gladstone would come under the old terrible phrase of "philosophy falsely so called." The ideas of the statesman are almost those of the new school of Presbyterians.

The word redemption sprang up when men first began to fight and take prisoners on land and sea. To kill these prisoners was not always the best manner in which to dispose of them. Perhaps rich families would pay much money or many camels or kids for their release. From such a source the word soon passed to a spiritual meaning, and we hear Job saying: "I know that my Redeemer liveth; he will at last appear and buy me back from my cruel captors." We hear the psalm singing of the kind God who buys us away from destruction. Thus, step by step, came the thought and sentiment that named Christ the Redeemer.

As the word is older than the formal theology of the church, it may be thought of as one of the great general terms of all languages. We

are all captives. In the great war of man's life, some armed ignorance or vice has taken us prisoners, and we are all waiting for some redeemer to come. It is not only on account of heaven the captives are waiting. Earth enters into all their longings. They wish to be brought back and set free in these continents and years. Having no money of their own, they hope for help from their friends, and they recall the dream of Isaiah, when men would be redeemed without money or without price. The wealth of the world would be offered to each poor heart. In the galleries of Europe there is often seen a beautiful picture of a Magdalen, reading. She had been redeemed. When some unseen hand drew back for St. John the curtain of heaven, he saw in one happy field one hundred and forty-four thousand of the redeemed. They had once been prisoners, but the quality of our world had made them, like the captives of Zechariah, "prisoners of hope." Earth has no hopeless islands or continents. It may be all swept over by the winds and melody of redemption. Christ did not create all this work of rescue, but, bringing a large part of it, he expressed the whole fact. As

one summer-time does not contain all the magical working of the sun, but only illustrates millions of past and coming years, so Christ did not bring all of redemption to our world, but rather did he teach us that all the human host has marched or may march through an atmosphere beautifully tinted with redeeming grace. It is not all the grace of God; much of it is the grace of man. It comes from God, indeed, but it comes through humanity.

Our age is moved deeply by the study of ideals in art. Each generation is amazed at its own progress. In the great Field Columbian Museum, one can see the history of many an idea; the boat-idea, beginning at three logs bound together with a piece of bark, and passing on toward the ocean palace; the transportation-idea, beginning with a strap on a man's forehead, passing on, through the panniers on a goat or a donkey, and reaching to the modern express train; the sculpture-idea, moving from some stone or earthen or wooden outlines onward toward the angelic forms that seem about to live and speak. There you will see the wooden eagle that marked the grave of some Indian. And what a creature

it is! Nothing but the infinite kindness of civilization could persuade us to call it a bird of any known species. And yet perhaps the Indian, when dying, was happy that such a wooden bird was to stand on his grave and keep his memory green.

Into our age, so full of new and grand conceptions in art, there must come the marching ideals of human life. Man is moving through a redemptive world. All lips should sing each day the song of the old harpist, "Who redeemeth thy life from destruction." What our age needs is a rapid advance of the ideals of life. A Catholic priest who has spent thirty years in the temperance cause said, last week, that the saloon is the greatest enemy that Rome has left in the world; that the criticisms we Protestants make of Rome's dogmas were harmless, compared with the ruin of mind and soul wrought by the saloon and its defenders. No one will deny the truth of the priest's complaint, and all are glad to mark the new effort of the Romanists to set up new ideas. Protestants should not, can not, hate a Catholic; but all good citizens must cherish little regard for any one who has not yet gotton beyond the saloon idea.

Such are not churchmen—they are saloonmen. They have not been touched by the new redemption of the new age. When they die, they ought to sleep under that wooden eagle of the museum, because the bird and the man stand equally far away from any known shape of terrestrial beauty. May great success come to the Civic Federation, which is attempting to redeem this city from the grasp of those men, in office and out of office, who, being Romanists, disgrace Rome's altar, or, being Protestants, disgrace all humanity! Nothing is so beautiful as the face of the Redeemer; but each man and woman who leads toward a higher life is a redeemer of our race. Christ was a fountain of redemption, but humanity at large composes the great flood. Each noble soul, each good book, each great picture, each piece of high music, is a redeemer, and when the soul, young, or mature, has once started toward its salvation, then, each field, each forest, becomes a page in its divine book, and each bird-song, a revival hymn, sweet as those of the old Methodists.

For many centuries, the Christian estimate of man's life was inadequate. Solemnity was never a full justification of the human family.

Solemnity is neither a virtue nor a vice. One can not live for it. Weeping can not possibly be a human goal. God would not create a world that it might weep. Nor is self-denial an explanation of rational life on this globe. We admire the self-denial of a poor mother who toils hard, and eats and sleeps little, that her children may the better live, but we all regret that that poor mother could not have enjoyed ten times as much sunshine as fell upon her heart. Christ was the man of sorrows, but not because self-denial is the reason of being. Times may become so dark and oppressive that the salvation of the many can come only through the sufferings of the few, but the universe was not made for the general display of dark and oppressive times. Self-denial is not, therefore, the ultimate ideal of man. Self-denial assumes the misfortunes of other people, but the "other people" must finally rise above those misfortunes, and thus end the empire of self-abnegation. Self-denial must follow us through infancy; but what is to be with us and stay with us after we have become men?

Nothing, therefore, will explain the human race, except the many-sided greatness and happi-

ness of each individual. The former Christian times all came short of finding adequate aims of society. The three years of Jesus were not a perfect picture of human life. They were a sublime picture of man, as caught in a storm, and as saving ship and crew, but in the uncounted years of that Son of God there is no crown of thorns. He wept for one night in a gloomy garden, but in the matchless sweep of his existence there are no tears. Thus we perceive that the existence of man is to be explained only by the greatness and completeness of his ideals. It is not enough for a man that he is a good judge of pictures, for it may be that he drinks twenty glasses of beer in a day, and pays the family servant girl only two dollars a week. How strange it is that a Catholic will belong to both a church and a saloon! The human ideas must grow more numerous and more adequate, that they may make a complete manhood and womanhood.

The redeeming process must go forward until we are wholly free. It was once enough for a man if he were a Presbyterian or a Catholic; but such a goal is no longer adequate. This

kind of person must now add to his name a new group of virtues. He must be intelligent, temperate, just, kind, lofty. The human beauties have grown more rapidly than the beauties of art have advanced.

It is seen how music has run forward from the old monotony of the Hebrews and Greeks to the wonderful compositions of the Italians and Germans. The modern soul would almost die under the old music. It would not be high enough, nor low enough, nor wide enough, nor sweet enough. But morals have advanced by the same path, and yet this city, encompassed and inspired by ideals many and great, permits itself to be governed by the abandoned classes. It is as though the orator, Daniel Webster, had asked some African ape to speak in his stead; it is as though Jenny Lind had asked some steam foghorn to sing her part. When, from the splendor of this city, from its high people, from its intelligent and sunny homes, from its churches, from its immortal summer of 1893, one passes to the centralized government, the heart cries out: Alas, Jenny Lind, why did you suppose that a fog-horn could take your place and sing for us that mighty

song, "I Know that My Redeemer Liveth." In the midst of the discord it is difficult to believe that a redeemer lives.

It was hoped by many, before Mr. Stead published his book on Chicago, that it would contain some full and fair estimate of the virtues and vices of the new and large city. But the volume was not what was needed. It was full of all kinds of trifling and injustice. It made sport of men who founded institutes and universities, and made no important distinction between a business man and a swindler. The book was written most recklessly. But it revealed one fact, the great need of a treatise whose theme shall be this one city. It ought to be written by a calm and just mind—some Dryasdust, perhaps, whom no fact could escape. It would need no literary decoration. Its facts would be all the paint it could bear. We need a perfect picture of our mental and spiritual shape. In this long tempest, some bearing must be taken of the valuable ship. If the people could know all the facts in the case, they would fly to the ballot box as to their only refuge, and would make every election day a great day of redemption. Why should such a

city, so situated, so vast, so intelligent, go to the simple for its philosophy and tax gamblers for the spread of such midnight darkness? Money would come from noble people, could it only come for good purposes.

The redemption of such a city is a great work. They who gird themselves for such a task, and who toil to the end, will reach more laurels than can be worn by one forehead. The new era calls them and will inspire them and the future will reward them.

The ills of a city will not all vanish when it shall become well governed. A most perfect and most honest government will not bring a perfect salvation; for intemperance and idleness and extravagance will remain, and those two great forces called labor and capital will still be here. They are both one, only capital is larger than labor. When a man's labor is worth six hundred dollars a year, he is worth several thousand dollars. It would take quite a sum invested at six per cent. to equal such a man. Capital is condensed labor—labor crowded into a package of bills or gold, like the air crowded into a Westinghouse cylinder. The living laborer sets free the

condensed labor and makes it assume the form of some external object. Both are one, only capital is the larger. They will draw nearer to each other as the world advances in intellect and goodness.

In this widening of human ideals a large part of the community has outgrown the law of demand and supply. The Rossis and Ricardos, who stated that law so clearly a hundred years ago, were not thinking of the welfare of the workingman, but only the causes of a price. The study and the law were cold blooded. A workingman received fifty cents a day or less, because the need was not great and the workingmen were numerous. In our age there is a vast multitude of employers who pay something to a man because he is a human being. An element undreamed of by the last century enters into the wages of to-day. Mr. Childs did not regard the law of demand and supply. His heart made some new laws, and he paid as much to the human being as he did to the trade of the man. He could have secured labor at a low market price, but he hated the calculations of the last century, and paid men what pleased his own

benevolence. Few of you make any effort to secure help at the lowest rates. The human being—man, woman or boy—steps in and draws a few additional pennies. The sweat shops are places where love has not yet come. There, the law of demand and supply works in all its old-time barbarity.

In our largest mercantile house there are clerks who receive twenty thousand dollars a year. In one of our music houses we can find the same kind of fact. Great salaries are following labor's flag, but it is vain to say that those salaries come from demand and supply, for we know that these fortunate clerks could be procured at a much lower rate. Wages are being modified by the sentiment of human brotherhood. It must not be raised as an objection that this sentiment is not universal. Perhaps the man who raises the objection has not yet become perfectly redeemed himself. We should all be conscious of the slowness with which perfection spreads over the mortal heart.

When the town of Pullman was projected, two or more members of its small but rich syndicate opposed the construction of such a beautiful vil-

lage. They said, "beauty of streets, of houses, library, theatre, market-place, church, lakes, and fountains will yield no interest on the investment. Plain, cheap huts will do as well." But the higher ideal carried, and three million dollars were thus flung away. Some of the founders remembered the sweat shops of the world, and some remembered also the black slaves who had received from capital neither a home nor wages. There may be defects in the Pullman idea, but, viewed from a hundred gambling dens and five thousand saloons, it looks well. Seen from our city hall, it looks like a group of palm trees waving over a spring in the desert. While traveling through hell, Dante was cheered when, looking through pitchy clouds, he saw a star.

We are not to assume that the town of Pullman has reached its greatest excellence. It is injured by the unrest of the Nation. Perhaps many of our greatest employers will, like Mr. Brassey, of England, decline to accept of us profits beyond five per cent. We must all hope much from the gradual progress of brotherly love. * * *

Here the Professor's last manuscript ended.

www.ingramcontent.com/pod-product-compliance
Lightning Source LLC
Chambersburg PA
CBHW022103290426
44112CB00008B/538

David Swing

A memorial volume

Ten sermons, selected and prepared for publication by himself